I0764156

Le Marchant

Major-General Le Marchant
Killed at Salamanca 22nd of July 1812 Aged 47

Le Marchant
Wellington's Scientific Cavalry General

Denis Le Marchant

With a Short Biography by
John William Cole

Le Marchant
Wellington's Scientific Cavalry General
by Denis Le Marchant
With a Short Biography by John William Cole

First published under the title
Memoirs of the Late Major-Genl. Le Marchant

Leonaur is an imprint of Oakpast Ltd

ISBN: 978-1-78282-297-4 (hardcover)
ISBN: 978-1-78282-298-1 (softcover)

http://www.leonaur.com

Publisher's Notes

The views expressed in this book are not necessarily those of the publisher.

Contents

Preface to Original Edition

This *Memoir* of the life of General Le Marchant is intended for private circulation among his friends. Conscious that his father's career was cut off before he had attained a position sufficiently conspicuous to make the details of his life an object of interest to the public, the author's sole object in the present work has been to place on record some memorial of the services of an officer who bore a high character in his profession, and whose memory is still affectionately venerated by many of his companions in arms.

In the course of this narrative the author, although confining himself as closely as possible to the life and services of General Le Marchant, has been obliged to introduce several facts of a more general nature, and which it is hoped may not be without interest to the military historian. These he has considered it his duty to verify with the most scrupulous care, in proof of which he could appeal to communications with which he has been favoured by various officers of distinction, did he not fear lest by associating their names with a work of this description he should confer on it a character of pretension to which it does not aspire.

L'Hyvreuse.

CHAPTER 1

Major-General Le Marchant

Major-General John Gaspard Le Marchant was one of the few remaining descendants of a Norman family,[1] which is believed to have settled in Guernsey in the reign of King John.[2]

His lineal ancestor, Peter Le Marchant, was unquestionably the person of most consideration in the island in the reign of Edward the First, being not only Bailiff, or chief civil magistrate, but Lieutenant-governor, or King's representative. These offices were conferred upon him by Otho de Grandison, (see note following), the secretary and favourite of that monarch and for many years the Lord of the Channel Isles, a nobleman whom he served with more zeal than judgment; for it is reported that Edward the First having imposed a small duty on ships frequenting the port of Guernsey, towards the expense of erecting a pier, the Lieutenant-governor, much to the indignation of the islanders, applied the receipts of the duty to his patron's use.[3] Other acts of maladministration are also imputed to him, for which the heirs of Otho de Grandison were called to account in the reign of Edward the Third.

---

1. There is a tradition that the first of the name known in the island was the cadet of a noble family, whose *château* stood in the neighbourhood of Cherbourg at the beginning of the last century. The name has long been common in Normandy. It appears, from a book printed at Paris in 17—, intituled, "*Preuves de la Genealogie de la noble Famille de Le Mar-chant de Saligny*," &c. that one branch of the family was ennobled in the fifteenth century, whilst an elder branch had been ennobled some time previously. Their alliances are enumerated in this treatise, and embrace some of the most illustrious houses in France.

2. Several copies exist of an Act of the Chief Pleas of Guernsey, providing for the erection of a bridge in the Vale parish, dated the 4th of October 1204, recorded in the usual form by several Jurats or magistrates, of whom James Le Marchant is one.

3. Berry's and Duncan's *Histories of Guernsey*. The latter is a work replete with information on the island.

******

Note:—Otho de Grandison was one of the most distinguished men of his day in England. He accompanied Edward the First, when Prince of Wales, to the Holy Land, and was rewarded soon after the King's accession by large grants of land in England and Ireland, and the Lordship of the Channel Islands. He took a part in the conquest of Wales. In the 17th Edward I. he was sent as Embassador to Rome, and he was subsequently employed to negociate a treaty with France. Indeed, he appears to have been actively concerned in all the transactions, military and diplomatic, of this reign. He is supposed to have died in about the twelfth year of Edward the Second, when he left his brother, William de Grandison, his heir. This nobleman, who was a retainer of Edmund Duke of Gloster, transmitted the property to three sons, Peter, John and Otto.

The first and last were soldiers; John was Bishop of Exeter.—(*Dugdales Baronage*, 17.) They had large domains in Kent, Somerset, and Hereford, and it is remarkable that many individuals bearing the name of Le Marchant appear to have been at this period owners of lands on or in the neighbourhood of the Grandison estates. One of them was member for Wells.—(*Palgrave's Parliamentary Writs*.) A Robert Le Marchant also held lands in Devon at the time that John de Grandison was Bishop of Exeter; whose son, Roger Le Marchant, has been handed down to posterity as twice assisting the Sheriff of Devon in an illegal arrest. From these circumstances, and the similarity of Christian names in the two families, it is not unlikely that some connection, perhaps of Norman blood, existed between the Le Marchants and the Grandisons, and that the Le Marchants above mentioned were emigrants from Guernsey.

A Robert Le Marchant certainly sold his lands in Guernsey in the reign of Edward the First, and is supposed to have left the island, for there is no further trace of him there. The Le Marchants were considerable proprietors of land in England during the reign of the three Edwards; but, in the time of Richard the Second, they fell into obscurity or became extinct, even the name having disappeared.—(*Testa, de Nevill, Temp. Hen. III. Edw. I. Rottulorum Originalium. Temp. Hen. III. &c. Placita de quo warranto, Temp. Edw. I, II, III.*)

******

John, the eldest son of Peter Le Marchant, redeemed the character of the family. He succeeded his father as Bailiff, and it was in his time that Guernsey was captured by the French. He sacrificed his property rather than give up his allegiance; and, having taken refuge in Jersey, he so distinguished himself there as to obtain a certificate, which is still extant, wherein the bailiff and *jurats* of the island acknowledge his great services in defending their castles against several attacks made by the enemy, stating, that without his assistance the island would probably have been subdued.[4] He eventually recovered his rank and estates in Guernsey, where he died at an advanced age.

The prosperity enjoyed by the family at this remote period continued undiminished for many generations. Notwithstanding the equal division of property under the Guernsey law of inheritance, the Le Marchants were, up to late years, among the chief landed proprietors of the island. They also filled the highest posts in it, and appear as taking a leading part on all occasions when the public peace was disturbed. [5] Drouet Le Marchant was captain of the citadel of St. Peter's, under the celebrated Earl of Warwick, during the wars of York and Lancaster. James Le Marchant, a Jurat of the Court in the time of the Commonwealth, had the boldness to remain in Guernsey that he might promote the royal cause, after the surrender of the island, and he acted so openly that proceedings were instituted against him by the special order of the Long Parliament, and it was with difficulty that he effected a precipitate retreat to France.

He found an asylum at Flamonville in Normandy, the seat of his kinsman the Marquis de Brouk, where he remained until the Restoration; and I feel a pride in stating, that the friendship thus cemented continues between his descendants and those of his noble host. Equal devotedness to the Stuarts was not shown by all the members of the family. The Rev. Thomas Le Marchant had been ordained and presented to the livings of St. Thomas and the Vale under the Protectorate, and it being therefore requisite at the Restoration that he should be reordained, in order that he might retain his preferment, he could not brook the idea of acknowledging his ordination to be invalid, and indignantly resigned his livings.[6]

---

4. Duncan's *History of Guernsey.*

5. The grant of the coat-of-arms to the family in the reign of William the Third, specially records their gallantry in the wars with the French.

6. This excellent man, after taking his degrees at Cambridge, passed some years at the academy at Caen, where he enjoyed the friendship, (continued next page),

The spirit and energy thus displayed by various individuals of the family, in a limited sphere, might have led us to expect that some of them would have left their native island in order to push their fortunes in England; but, upon a strict inquiry, it cannot be ascertained that from the time of Edward the Second a single instance occurs of their having done so. These indigenous habits, however, were characteristic of the gentry in Guernsey, and may be easily traced to local circumstances. This little state was a solitary survivor of the feudal colonies of the middle ages. Annexed to England as far back as the Conquest, its inhabitants were enthusiastically attached to the religion and government of England, whilst, by a singular anomaly, they continued to use the language and laws of their Norman ancestors.

The dangerous sea by which they were surrounded, caused their communication, both with England and France, to be irregular and uncertain; and being equally neglected by the two countries, they formed a distinct community, whose institutions and pursuits, and consequently manners, were peculiarly their own. The government was virtually administered by less than a dozen families, the baronial proprietors of the soil, who possessed almost exclusively the wealth of the island. From them were elected the *jurats*, or magistrates of the Royal Court, by which all causes, criminal and civil, were tried; and they had the entire control of the states of the island and of the municipal councils. Their services were gratuitous, and a rigorous enforcement of the distinctions of rank, which marked their feudal origin, was the sole badge of this harmless despotism.

No aristocracy ever exercised power more mildly, or was more willingly obeyed. The rents of their estates were not paid in money, but in the produce of the land; and this circumstance, as well as the frequent sittings of the manorial courts, in which the lord or his seneschal presided, brought the landlords into frequent communication with their tenants, and was in most cases productive of mutual esteem and attachment. The peasantry lived in comfort, and the aristocracy knew no luxuries. Expensive establishments there were none,—and, till very recently, even the richest households had seldom more than two or three domestics, and those females, the labour of the men being reserved for the gardens, in the cultivation of which their masters

---

of the learned Bochart and Huet. They corresponded with him on his return to Guernsey, and many of these letters were preserved until a fire at Grandesmaison's. Mr. Le Marchant was the author of a Treatise on the Laws and Institutions of the island, which is still highly esteemed.

took great pride.

Shooting and fishing were to be had in abundance, without creating any differences between the higher and lower classes. The simplicity of this mode of life,—its amusements, and the various duties attached to it, endeared it to the gentry in Guernsey,—an unwillingness to exchange importance at home for insignificance abroad, might also, perhaps, have strengthened these feelings. Altogether the ties which united them to their native island were so strong as to remain unbroken for several centuries, and this is more remarkable, as many of them had been educated at Oxford and Cambridge, and having afterwards travelled on the Continent, were far more refined in their tastes than the English country-gentlemen of their day. Indeed, the few travellers whom accident or curiosity brought to Guernsey, were surprised to find on this wild and sequestered spot individuals with accomplishments and information such as were then rarely seen except in the great capitals of Europe.

John Le Marchant (the father of the subject of these memoirs) was one of the first Guernsey-men that held a commission in the army. He was the second son of Thomas Le Marchant,[7] of Le Marchant Manor, Lieutenant-Bailiff of the island. His parents had not designed him for any profession, but the natural ardour of his disposition, excited by the sight of the 7th Dragoons passing through Oxford during his residence there as a student of Pembroke College, prompted him forthwith to purchase a cornetcy in that regiment. He served the three last campaigns of the Seven Years' war in the army of Prince Ferdinand of Brunswick, under the immediate command of the Marquis of Granby, with as much reputation as an active, intrepid, and intelligent subaltern usually acquires.

On the declaration of peace, he retired on half-pay, and married Mary, the eldest daughter of Count Hirzel de St. Gratien, (see note fol-

7. Mr. Le Marchant belonged to the branch of the family settled at l'Hyvreuse, a seat near St. Peter's, the gateway of which forms the vignette of the first page of this work. It was a very extensive property. The house was pulled down in the middle of the last century, upon the death of Mr. William Le Marchant, who left an infant family in great pecuniary embarrassments, and the estate sold. Part of the pleasure-ground was purchased by the States of the island and converted into a public walk. The gateway was only demolished a few years ago, for the purpose of widening the high road. This branch of the family became extinct not long since by the premature death of Alfred Le Marchant, LL.B. and F.R.S. which was a heavy loss to the island. The manor of Le Marchant, mentioned in the text, is a part of the town of St. Peter's, once possessed and inhabited exclusively by the family.

lowing), Marechal-de-camp of the Swiss Guards in the French service, a nobleman of Picardy, whose sister[8] had become the second wife of his father, Mr. Thomas Le Marchant. The family was nearly connected with Count d'Olon, [9] a former lieutenant-governor of Guernsey, and had consequently for several years occasionally visited the island. The young lady eventually became a considerable heiress, and her fortune enabled her husband to reside more in England than was common with the Guernseymen of that time. He was a person of a highly cultivated mind, and lived much in the best society of the day.

******

Note:—St. Gratien's is the name of a hamlet near Amiens, adjoining the estate of the family. The father of the count was colonel of a regiment in the Dutch service, under William the Third. He was killed at Tournay. The family were Protestants. It is a remarkable circumstance, that in a skirmish near Warburgh, the corps to which Lieutenant Le Marchant belonged was opposed to a Swiss regiment, commanded by the Count de St. Gratien, the brother of his future wife. The Swiss were defeated, and the count fell into the hands of the English. Lieutenant Le Marchant obtained an audience of Prince Ferdinand, and applied for his release. The Prince, after listening to his statement with great kindness, handsomely answered, "I should most readily have complied with your wishes, but it is no longer in my power. The count has been exchanged at the personal intercession of Marshal Contades, and is now restored to his friends." The count afterwards became a distinguished officer in the French service, and stood high in the opinion and favour of Louis XVIII. He emigrated to Russia in 1792,

8. This lady had lived for some time and was highly esteemed at the court of Berlin, whither she accompanied her relative the Count de Bourgay, a French Protestant, who had attained the rank of a General in the British service, and enjoyed the confidence of George the Second. The object of the Count's mission to that court was to negotiate a marriage between the Prince of Wales and the daughter of Frederick the First, since well known as the Margravine of Bareith. The princess has left an amusing account of the negotiation in her memoirs. It was an unfortunate business, for the negotiation failed, and the envoy was drowned in crossing the Elbe on his return home. The Queen of Prussia offered to keep Miss St. Gratien as her maid of honour, and to provide for her, but she preferred returning to Guernsey.

9. The Count D'Olon was a French Protestant, who had served with distinction under William the Third. He was the secretary and intimate friend of Rouvigny Earl of Galway, by whose side he fought at the unfortunate Battle of Almanza.

where he received a high command, and having accompanied Suwarrow into Italy, shared the glory and reverses of his chief. He died at an advanced age at Anspach, about the close of the last century.

★★★★★★

John Gaspard Le Marchant, the eldest son of this marriage, was named Gaspard, after the celebrated Admiral de Coligni, a collateral ancestor of his mother. He was placed at an early age at a school at Bath, kept by Dr. Morgan, where he passed several years. He had little to recollect of this part of his life, except the distinction he acquired by a successful fight with a boy of very superior strength, the tyrant and terror of the school, in which only one schoolfellow had the courage to stand by him,—that schoolfellow was the late Sir Sidney Smith. After he left the school his preceptor used to say, that of all the dunces he had ever known Le Marchant and his friend Smith were the greatest. It is due, however, to Dr. Morgan, who was a respectable scholar, to add, that General Le Marchant always acknowledged that the fault lay more in the pupil than the school. His father brought him home almost in despair, when he suddenly, to the extreme surprise of his family, devoted himself closely to study, and, with the assistance of his father's butler, who had been an American loyalist and was a very well educated man, he in some degree repaired his former neglect, and, what was still more important, contracted habits of industry and application that remained to him through life.

The inclination he showed for the army was so strong that his father placed him, by way of trial, when scarcely sixteen, in a regiment of the York Militia, which happened to be commanded by a friend of the family. The result was by no means encouraging, for before long be took offence at some expressions addressed to him by his colonel and sent him a challenge. Fortunately the colonel was a sensible, kind-hearted man, who did not consider it beneath him to reason with an inferior officer. The cause of offence was satisfactorily explained, and no unpleasant consequences followed beyond a lecture. A similar affair, in which he was about the same time engaged with a country gentleman from whom he had received some provocation, went further, as it was stopped only by the interference of the police. These, however, were the only instances to my knowledge of his being concerned in duels. No one hated them more than himself.

At the age of eighteen he was appointed to an ensigncy in the

Royals. He joined the regiment at Dublin, in the year 1783. Few persons ever entered a profession under less favourable auspices. All his connections lay in a quarter too remote to serve him; indeed, he could scarcely boast of an acquaintance out of Guernsey. A foreign name, and an insignificant fortune, were almost insurmountable obstacles to success, at a time that beardless colonels and grey-headed subalterns too plainly demonstrated the ordinary channels of preferment. Many minds would have sunk under these difficulties. It was not so with this young soldier; Nature had armed him too well. His keen and searching eye, his expansive forehead, his commanding deportment, his tall, manly, and muscular form, denoted even to superficial observers, talent, spirit, and strength, equal to no ordinary undertakings. Notwithstanding his subordinate rank, and entire want of any other than personal recommendations, he soon gained admission into the highest society in Dublin; and among those with whom he formed an acquaintance, which afterwards ripened into intimate friendship, was the Lord-Lieutenant, the Marquis of Buckingham, one of the most respectable noblemen of the day.

★★★★★★

Note:—Dublin was never more interesting than during this year. It was crowded with the Protestant volunteers from every part of Ireland, whose enthusiasm excited alarming apprehensions in the government. These were increased by the outrages which were frequently committed. Several soldiers in the Royals were at different times missed, whilst on the night-guard. They were supposed to have deserted, until the bodies of some of them were found in the Liffy. An order then issued, that there should be double sentries, and that no loitering about the guard-room should be allowed. Shortly after, as a young officer of the light company was crossing Carlisle-bridge about midnight, he suddenly felt himself grasped round the middle, and raised almost over the parapet: he made a desperate effort to cling round the assassin, and thus saved himself from falling, but the wretch nearly succeeded in stabbing him to the heart before he could recover himself. A struggle followed, in which the officer gained the superiority for a moment, extricated his hand, drew his sword, and plunged it into the body of his adversary. As the Royals lost no more men, it is probable that the previous murders were by one individual.

******

In the year 1784, the Royals received orders to embark for Gibraltar; but Ensign Le Marchant was nearly prevented accompanying them. The night previous to the embarkation, he was prevailed upon by an officer of rank to accompany him to a gambling-house, where his inexperience and credulity soon inflicted on him a loss of 200*l*. A person present advanced the money on his bond; but how was it to be repaid ? He was musing on the necessity of quitting the army, for staying behind the regiment was quite incompatible with retaining his commission, when the paymaster generously offered to advance the required sum, on the single condition of his never touching a card again. The debt was discharged, and the condition most faithfully observed.

Gibraltar has always been a tedious quarter; and there is nothing but the society of the military to render it tolerable. This resource was not open to the young ensign. Afraid to disclose a gambling debt to his father, and bound in honour to lose no time in reimbursing his benevolent creditor, he was obliged to use every possible expedient to save from his pay. He withdrew, therefore, from the mess, and lived in total seclusion. Conduct so different from what he had before pursued, brought upon him the dislike of his brother officers. Insinuations were whispered of his penuriousness; and as he disdained to exculpate himself, in the absence of his friend the paymaster, they were fully believed, and he gradually sunk into general disrepute. His high-mindedness, however, was well rewarded, for he devoted all his leisure hours, thus sufficiently numerous, to the cultivation of his talents for music and drawing; and the sketches he then made of Gibraltar and the coast of Barbary, became, at no distant period, chiefly instrumental in promoting his first and most important advancement in the world.

After persevering in this course of life for nearly three years, he was attacked by the yellow fever, from which he with difficulty recovered. On his convalescence, he was sent on the sick list to England. During his stay at home, he engaged himself to a young lady in Guernsey, of great beauty, the eldest daughter of John Carey, Esq. one of the *jurats*, or magistrates of the island. It was an imprudent step for both parties, as neither of them was of age; and upon its coming to the knowledge of his father, he was immediately remanded to Gibraltar. His second residence there proved more agreeable than the first. The paymaster had arrived in his absence, and the suspicions of his brother officers having been most effectually disproved, their resentment had changed into respect: their kindness, however, did not reconcile him to his situation. He had now passed four years in the regiment, and was still a junior Ensign, without any immediate prospect of promotion. In the hope of better fortune in the cavalry, he purchased a cornetcy in the Inniskilling Dragoons, which he shortly after joined in England.

The Inniskillings did not possess in those days the high character for discipline that they now deservedly enjoy. In fact, when the young cornet joined, he found the officers at such variance with the commanding officer, Lord Heathfield, that they were not upon speaking terms. He declined taking any part in these disputes, and his prudence did not pass unnoticed by Lord Heathfield, for his Lordship gave him the command of the guard of honour employed to escort the King from Dorchester to Weymouth. The king, surprised at seeing the junior cornet in a post so superior to his rank, made inquiries, which led to his Majesty's promising to promote Cornet Le Marchant on the first opportunity. He might, however, have been overlooked had he not just at this time happened to make the acquaintance, and quickly to gain the regard, of Sir George Yonge,[10] the Secretary at War, who was staying at Weymouth during the Parliamentary recess.

Some months afterwards, Sir George went himself to the king to recommend Cornet Le Marchant for a vacant lieutenancy in the Bays; and although there were many applicants for it, and among the most pressing the Marquis of Townshend, the king was firm, and Cornet Le Marchant was promoted. This was not all his good fortune. His drawings at Gibraltar had been shown at court by Sir George Yonge, and admired; they procured him frequent invitations to the royal circle; his merit became known, and he acquired the king's personal esteem and protection, which, those who know the characters of the master and the servant, need not be told, were never withdrawn from him.

Sir George Yonge, still anxious to advance the fortunes of his young friend, now procured him leave of absence for two years to travel upon the Continent. He had passed a winter at Strasburg, when the expectation of a war with Russia caused him to be recalled; not, however, before he had perfected his knowledge of the French lan-

10. Sir George Yonge, Bart. K.B. was the son of Sir William Yonge, the eloquent and well-known supporter of Sir Robert Walpole. He had many of his father's parts as well as failings. After filling various high offices of state, with the reputation of considerable knowledge and capacity for business, he went into retirement and died without issue. His latter years were embittered by the failure of a speculation into which he had entered in the neighbourhood of Tiverton, which borough he long represented in Parliament.

guage; and the elegance with which he both spoke and wrote it, were subsequently of essential service to him. On his return to England, he joined his regiment in Cornwall, and whilst at Truro, narrowly escaped a fate as dreadful as any that could be encountered in the field. He retired to rest one night much fatigued by his military duties, and, as may be supposed, slept soundly. On rising late the next morning, and looking out of the window, he perceived the street full of tables, chairs, and other articles of furniture, scattered about in great disorder; he immediately rang the bell to inquire into the cause, when he learned that there had been a serious fire during the night, which had consumed several rooms in the house: the different inmates had taken precipitate flight on the alarm being given, and in the confusion he had been entirely forgotten.

His promotion was now as rapid as he could desire, for in less than three years after his entrance into the Bays he purchased his troop. During this interval he was united to the object of his youthful attachment. His wife was worthy of his constancy, and marriage realised all the domestic happiness he had anticipated. Unfortunately it was soon to be interrupted, as a few months after the birth of his eldest son, in the spring of 1793, he received orders to join the Allied army on the Continent.

At the end of May, Captain Le Marchant landed at Ostend, with the squadron under his command. Several regiments of cavalry were already in the town, and their state was not calculated to encourage a soldier of ordinary observation. The officers, in general, were wholly ignorant of their duty. A long peace had generated habitual indifference to military discipline, and any attempt to enforce it on the part of the commanding officer, was met by open insubordination. The messes were mostly dissolved. The privates and their horses were equally neglected, and the mutual confidence, that now so justly prevails between the different ranks of the service, was yet to be earned. Nothing but a spirit of uncommon energy was capable of bringing such a chaos into order, and this was not exactly the characteristic of the general in command. His mild and amiable disposition was so averse to any act of severity, that excesses were daily committed with impunity.[11]

11. This officer afterwards had the misfortune to incur the displeasure of the Duke of York, by a misunderstanding of his orders at Villiers en Couche. But all imputations on his courage were removed by his brilliant success and honourable death at the Battle of Cateau. The charge of the heavy brigade under his command on that day was a bold design boldly executed.

His difficulties were increased by the intelligence that a large body of the enemy had been seen in the neighbourhood, and he thereupon, with an unnecessary diffidence of his own talents, called a council of war, at which he invited Captain Le Marchant to be present, which the latter wisely declined. Before the council had adopted any means of defence, the invaders were ascertained to be the Dutch allies. A few days after there was a fresh alarm, of which Captain Le Marchant observes in a letter:

> The detachment of Light Dragoons posted in the front of our line, about six miles from the town, met a detachment of Dutch troops on their march from Furnes to Ypres, took them for French, and were so dreadfully frightened that they galloped away like madmen. They rode their horses so hard, that several died the same evening, and others were seriously injured.

Such was the army with which the Duke of York, a youthful and inexperienced commander, took the field to oppose an enemy whose numerical superiority was directed by a succession of veteran leaders of established military reputation and skill. The unfortunate issue of these campaigns cannot be held, by any impartial observer, to diminish the credit that so deservedly attaches to the administration of his Royal Highness as commander-in-chief.

Captain Le Marchant was not blind to the opportunities thus offered for individual distinction. The subsequent occasional extracts from a journal he composed for the amusement of his wife and family, will afford a more faithful narrative of this part of his life than could be presented in any other form.

> Ostend, June 7, 1783. I am almost every day busy in examining the country. Some days since I discovered a weak post that was not guarded, by which our outposts might have been cut off. It was rectified immediately.

Lord Herbert[12] having arrived from England to take the command of the Bays, that regiment joined the main body of the Allies in the last week of June. The Duke of York was then employed, with a large portion of the infantry, before Valenciennes; the cavalry were encamped within a short distance to cover the besiegers. The Austrian Count Hohenzollern, who commanded the camp, did not suffer his troops to lie idle. On the 30th of June he undertook a *coup de main*

12. Afterwards General the Earl of Pembroke, K.G. and Governor of Guernsey.

against the French camp at Cassel, consisting of 30,000 men. Captain Le Marchant's activity had already been noticed by the general, and his squadron was selected to accompany the expedition.[13] The design was completely successful, and it was accomplished by the Austrian and British cavalry alone; for the Prussian infantry, satisfied with surprising the enemy, did not follow up their advantages. The cavalry being ordered to advance, pursued the French infantry into the standing corn, where they rallied. A general charge then took place, in which Captain Le Marchant commanded the right. The French gave way and fled in great confusion, and sixty of them fell by the sabre.

On the same evening the following order was issued by Count Hohenzollern:—

> I beg the officer commanding the British cavalry in the absence of Lord Herbert, to express my thanks, in my name, to Captain Le Marchant, and to all his brigade, for the precision with which he executed my instructions at the engagement at Cassel this morning, and to assure all the corps, that I esteem myself both happy and honoured to have had him to command troops that showed as much spirit as intrepidity. I thank also, equally, the officers attached to my person for their bravery and discipline.
>
> Hohenzollern.
>
> Camp at Cysoing, June 30, 1793.
>
> *(Je prie Monsieur le Capitaine Commandant de la cavalerie Anglaise, en l'absence de Milord Herbert, de témoigner en mon nom à le Capitaine Le Marchant, et à tout son brigade, combien je lui ai de réconnoissance de la précision avec laquelle il a rempli mes intentions à l'affaire de Casselle ce matin, et d'assurer toute la troupe que je me conte héureux et me fais l'honneur d'avoir en lui de commander une cavallerie qui a montré d'autant d'ardeur que de bravoure. Je remercie également les officiere qui étoient à cote de moi, de leur bravoure et de la bonne ordre qu'ils ont eues.*
>
> *Hohenzollern.*
>
> *Du Camp de Cysoing, June 30, 1793.)*

13. The troops were ordered to begin their march before sunrise. Captain Le Marchant visited the men in the night to see whether their accoutrements were in proper condition. He was surprised to find them all lying on their faces. On inquiring the reason, he was informed that they had just dressed their queues for the morrow, and they were afraid of lying in any other position lest it should be necessary to dress them again. On such points was discipline thrown away.

This skirmish being the first engagement Captain Le Marchant had witnessed, I cannot help transcribing the interesting reflections he made upon it in a letter to his wife.

> I am just returned from a scene that, on cool reflection, makes my soul shrink within me; but it is one of the horrors of war.—What gave me most pain was to see that the Austrians gave no quarter. Poor devils on their knees, merely begging for mercy, were cut down. My own people, thank God! were as merciful as possible; and, I think, destroyed none in the pursuit, except such as would not give themselves up. Dives's (his junior captain) party had taken five men alive, but leaving them for an instant in pursuit of others, some Austrians came up and butchered them. I made a complaint to Hohenzollern, who supposed his men might have seen some of their comrades receive similar treatment from the enemy during the engagement. He seemed to be very sorry for it.
>
> My people behaved remarkably well in the face of the enemy, that is, for young troops. They have an implicit confidence in me, so that I hope in time we shall be esteemed by our friends the Austrians, who are, at present, as superior to us as we are to the train-bands in the city.

The Prince of Hohenzollern, in addition to the above public testimony of his approbation of Captain Le Marchant's conduct, named him particularly in a report transmitted to the Duke of York. It was, therefore, not a little to his disappointment, that, a few days after this engagement, the command of the forces at Cysoing was transferred to the Prussian General Knobledorf, an officer whose want of military talent was not redeemed by many private virtues. He soon taught the unfortunate Flemings the loss they bad suffered by the removal of the Prince of Hohenzollern.

His frequent appropriation of the property of both friend and foe indiscriminately to his own use, combined with his indifference to the licentiousness of the soldiery, richly entitled him to the appellation bestowed on a well-known French general, of *le Père de Maraud*. No object was too insignificant to escape his attention; and instances of his rapacity repeatedly occurred, so glaring, as to excite alternately the ridicule and indignation even of his own officers. One of them showed Captain Le Marchant a note, which he had received from the general's *aide-de-camp*, in the following words:—

My friend,

The general wishes to see you tomorrow, to speak to you on the subject of your post. Come at ten o'clock.

I am, &c.

Aide-de-camp to General-in-Chief Knobledorf.

P.S. You will do well to bring a nice calf with you.

All this time the duties of the cavalry were very severe. In one of his letters, Captain Le Marchant writes:—

July 1793. I have just returned from having been two nights on duty, without daring to sleep a wink, for our posts are within a few hundred yards of the enemy, and one unguarded moment might be fatal.

July 10. The heat has become intolerable: it is much worse than at Gibraltar. I have sent my cart this morning into a wood belonging to the National Assembly, and it has returned with some fine young trees, sufficient to shade my tent, being fixed in rows around it, and also enough to shade my troop of horses. You see, we in some respects admit of the doctrine of the National Assembly—Liberty is a convenient system to those who have nothing to lose.

In the beginning of August, Captain Le Marchant was appointed Major of the brigade commanded by the Honourable General Harcourt, (later Field-Marshal the Earl of Harcourt), consisting of the Horse Guards Blue, the Second Dragoon Guards, and the Inniskillings. As he was entirely unknown to that general, except by character, the appointment was particularly agreeable to him. The day after he entered upon the duties of his office, he witnessed the engagement at Lincelles; a name which the Guards still bear on their standards, unobliterated by their more recent trophies of the Peninsula and Waterloo.

The Allies passed August in marches and countermarches, more fatiguing in their execution than important in their results. At the close of the month they established themselves at Wilder, where Captain Le Marchant resumes his journal.

26th August, Camp at Wilder. We have moved from our encampment facing Bergues, which was said to have been chosen in the hope of our taking the town. We summoned the garrison to surrender, but I conclude the answer was not a pleasant one, as it never was made known.

Our present position is divided from the enemy by the Yser, a river much smaller than we could wish, but wide enough to increase the difficulties of an attack. We are ranged along its banks, with our right on Crochte and our left on Wilder. Cassel being in our front and Bergues in our rear we are placed between two fires; and the country is so extremely well-wooded, that our cavalry, in which the strength of our army lies, cannot at present be employed to advantage.

We are taking, however, every possible pains to clear the country, by cutting away the timber and hedges, so that the peasants will hardly know their homes again, when they return. I say, when they return, because not a soul of the original inhabitants is to be seen. They all join the soldiery in opposing our progress; and conscious that if they are taken in arms they will be put to death, they always fly, abandoning their homes and property to us. Whole villages, therefore, are seen utterly deserted, except by a few poor creatures, whom extreme old age or illness have incapacitated to make their escape. I rode this morning through the village of Ekellsbeck, which is only a short mile from our camp. I found all the doors and windows of the houses wide open, and all the implements used in the different branches of trade lying as if the different artisans had gone to dinner, and were to return in an hour.

The houses looked as if they were inhabited; the household furniture was not in the least disorder, and every thing in its ordinary place, so that you might tell the employments and habits of the inhabitants at once. It was a melancholy sight: the only consolation is, that the inhabitants have absented themselves from a consciousness of having done their utmost to oppose us. It is incredible how strongly the lower classes here, are attached to revolutionary principles; and no wonder, since the revolution is held out to them as ensuring wealth and power to all that support it. I have not seen a young healthy man in any village we have gone through since I left Austrian Flanders; all either join the army in the field, or are occupied in completing the fortifications in the French garrisons. The women and very old men conduct the farms; and a miserable set they are.

Sept. 6. Yesterday part of our little army marched out in three columns to attack the French, who were advancing their posts very near to ours. Their advances having generally proved preludes to an attack, we determined for once, to be beforehand with them. They were driven from all their posts, and retired precipitately to Cassel. We took eighty prisoners. What they had killed, we know not. On our side, General Fabry, one of our most distinguished officers, who commanded our advance was wounded: a Captain of Hanoverians, and three subalterns, besides a hundred and forty privates, were also wounded.

We were unfortunate in the business, as the plan laid down could not be followed up. Two out of our three attacking columns did not come up in time to support the centre column, which, of course, sustained the whole brunt of the business, and thus met with the loss above mentioned. Though our object in driving the enemy back was attained, it cost us far too dear to be a matter of exultation. If General Fabry dies, which, I fear, is almost certain, his loss will be irreparable.

Between seven and eight o'clock, (on the 6th of September,) I was writing a letter, when I heard a discharge of small-arms. I went immediately to the general, and we had not time to mount our horses, before all our advanced posts were attacked. I thought so ill of our position and means of defence, that I instantly directed my servants to remove my baggage to the rear. Lord Herbert laughed at my prudence, and bet me five guineas that his own baggage would be safe tomorrow. In an hour our whole line, which from right to left was not less than four miles, was engaged.

Our front thus occupied, the French were not satisfied, but they made a sortie from Bergues on our rear. For seven hours they kept up an un-intermitted, wonderfully hot, and intense fire. At three o'clock they pushed hard to turn our right flank (where we were) and we were so pressed as to dismount the Inniskillings to act as infantry. Our resistance checked their impetuosity, and towards four o'clock they began to retire, and their fire gradually subsided, till at six in the evening it entirely ceased.

Such were the operations of our right. Our centre, commanded by Sir William Erskine,[14] supported a severe cannonade from eight o'clock till sunset, but maintained its ground; whilst our rear repulsed the sortie made upon it from Bergues.

We met with a very different fortune on our left. On that point

14. Sir William Erskine highly distinguished himself in the Seven Years' War.

the French were successful, and drove us back upon Respond; and as there was some danger of their cutting off our retreat to that place, we began our march during the night, leaving most of our wounded behind us.

My adventures during the night were of the most unpleasant description. It was my duty to keep up the communication between our right and left columns, and I had passed and repassed frequently without accident, until at last I lost sight of the troops, and from the darkness could not find them again. It rained and lightened as if it was doubtful whether I was to perish by water or fire. The country was quite strange to me, so I bent my course through the worst of cross-country roads, by a guess of the situation of Respond on the map. I knew my risk of falling into the enemy's hands if I verged too much either to the right or left, and the probability of becoming a prisoner added to my anxiety.

At last, I overtook some baggage-waggons, which were so overloaded with the miserable incumbrances of soldiers' families, that the horses were incapable of proceeding; and there they were, certain of being taken at break of day by the enemy. I hoped, by finding them, I had got into the proper route, and I went on with some satisfaction, until I met other troops, which proved to be Hanoverian infantry, the officers of which assured me that no cavalry had gone past them, and that they had themselves lost their route, and did not know which way to proceed. Having heard that the line of march was through Respond, I tried to find out the great road leading to it, when two of the emperor's Light Cavalry came galloping like the devil towards me, and said they had been into Respond, where they were unexpectedly challenged by French sentries, and that the French must have taken the place since the morning.

What was now to be done? A consultation was held between our party, which, if I have not mentioned it before, consisted of the Austrians, Arden, and myself. They were for going back to the troops whom we left, not knowing where they were. I was much against it, as it would make us follow the great *pavée*, that has Bergues on one side and Respond on the other; and I expected that in the morning the enemy would, from both sides, issue out in strength and cut off all stragglers; therefore, I proposed to push forward for Hondschoote, and risk the chance of finding it; but we should be safe in being on the other side of that *pavée*, and when the morning arrived we should discover our road and push for it.

It fortunately turned out that my advice prevailed, and more luckily than could be expected, we found the right road, and reached the town at two in the morning. In less than two hours we were joined by the cavalry, from whom we learned that there had been, during the night, a smart action at Respond, and that the French took it from us. Marshal Freitag, in utter ignorance of what had passed, marched at the head of his regiment to the gates, where he received and returned the challenge of the sentinel, and then entered the town. In the course of a few minutes he was wounded and taken.

Prince Adolphus, (the Duke of Cambridge), fell into the same trap; but fortunately, as they were conducting him to confinement, the party was attacked, and in the bustle he crept off his horse into a ditch, and got back to his friends, with a slight wound on his shoulder and the side of his head. Our fugitives soon joined the main body, and we now, in our turn, attacked Respond, and took it, and found the marshal; so that we recovered our great man in the most astonishing manner possible. All this happened within a few hours, in the dead of night, when, at times, I could not see my horse's head.

The greatest part of our troops arrived here early in the morning, (the 7th,) and we learned that our killed and wounded had been very considerable. One regiment, out of thirty-six officers, has but eight remaining; one company of Austrians has, out of eighty men, only one officer and thirty remaining. We collected these debris of our original force, and took up an encampment. In the evening, the enemy again attacked us, and we had some hard fighting, without gaining any advantage; but we kept our ground.

On the morning of the 8th, the action recommenced, and at two o'clock we were forced to give way, and retire to a post on the banks of the Yser, where some infantry, of various nations, with the Hessian and Hanoverian cavalry, were concentrated, under the command of General Harcourt. We made the best arrangement of them we could, in the expectation of an immediate attack. I cannot express how shamefully our Hessian Allies conducted themselves during the short period of twenty-four hours that they were with us. They showed a degree of unwillingness and cowardly apprehension that clearly proved they would not have defended the post an instant; they even withdrew their men from the battery where we had placed them, and slunk away to their horses; and nothing but the general's threats to report them to their commander-in-chief would have brought them back. We were in this agreeable position, and in this good company, when we learned, what we had too great reason to expect, that almost all our baggage, ammunition, &c. had fallen into the enemy's hands. Poor Lord Herbert is among the sufferers. My prudence has saved me.

On the 9th we abandoned our post, and marched to Furnes, where we joined the Duke of York, on his retreat from Dunkirk. His Royal Highness had been informed of the preparations of the French to attack us in great force by one corps from Lille, and another from Dunkirk. A combined movement like this upon our left and front would have been irresistible: so the duke determined to fight them separately, and we accordingly received orders to march immediately to Ypres, which had already fallen into the hands of the troops from Lille. Our men were in sad condition from their previous hardships and losses; indeed, in one regiment, not even the officers could muster a change of linen among them.

However, we began our march, and after proceeding some miles, an orderly-dragoon came from the duke to stop us. General Harcourt dispatched me to learn the cause of the delay, and it was with no small degree of pleasure that I heard from the duke, that General Beaulieu had arrived at Ypres before us, and obliged the French to retire. The duke was overjoyed, for the attack would have been desperate, and at best, must have been attended with dreadful loss.

During the 10th and 11th, we were kept by false alarms in constant expectation of an attack from the enemy. On the 12th, I accompanied General Harcourt to Dixmude, to secure that post. On our route, I met an Hanoverian officer, whom I had posted, at the beginning of the battle, at a bridge at Ekelsbech. I asked him how he was, &c. 'Why,' says he, 'you see me here, together with Spicer, (pointing to his companion;) we are, with twelve sergeants and forty men, the only remains of my regiment, which, upon the morning of the 6th, consisted of six hundred men! Poor fellows! they were brave men, and God be with them.'

At Dixmude I slept undressed between sheets for the first time these two months:—would you believe it? I did not sleep sound. Perhaps I did not enjoy myself the less in musing on my novel situation. In fact, during these same two months I have not even taken off my clothes or boots, except to change them. Often fatigued to death, so much so as to fall asleep on my horse. A little bit of dry bread that has been lying in the bottom of my great coat, was as carefully divided between the general and his staff, as would have been the richest dainty between epicures at home. It would appear unaccountable to you, how persons accompanied by the number of servants and horses that we all are, can be in want of the comforts, much less of the necessaries, of life. The fact is this: attacks are generally made by the enemy at moments least expected, when we hurry on our horses, and think of nothing but our immediate responsibility as officers; we take our posts, and the army changes its position half a dozen times before our servants can find us out again. All they can do, is to stick to some column, and trust to chance for a rencontre.

Our capture of Menin, at the close of October, was the last event of importance in this campaign. The different armies had been so incessantly engaged, and had suffered such severe losses from the various accidents of war, as to be wholly unequal to any serious undertaking, and it appeared the common wish of friend and foe to consume the few remaining weeks of the season in desultory movements of detached corps, without trying the chance of a general engagement.

The Austrians, under Count Walmoden, to whose corps I was attached, fixed themselves at Cysoing at the end of September, on the very spot from which we had started to begin the campaign, and we could hardly stop to take breath, before the French appeared, and we had some smart skirmishes with them, in which we were invariably successful. We were, however, too weak to maintain our post, and therefore fell upon Tournay, where we remained only a few days before we received an order to return.

The enemy gave us all possible opposition. We were occupied almost the whole day in driving them out of the woods along our route. It was here that Crawfurd [15] took a light squadron of our regiment, and together with Hay,[16] overtook a regiment of French infantry, which immediately formed a hollow square, and kept up a very brisk fire. Crawfurd perceived their object was to gain a village on the plain, at no great distance, where they would be safe from the attack of cavalry. He passed them at the distance of 150 yards, then wheeling round his squadron between them and the village, he charged with such impetuosity, that although the fellows stood and fired to the last moment, the old Bays rode through their ranks and committed a terrible carnage; not one of them escaped. Our loss was inconsiderable.

In November we were again established at Tournay; and the French having ceased to attack us, we were as quiet as in an English country town. No one can have profited by this suspension of hostilities more than myself. I have been busily engaged in making drawings of all articles in the military equipages of our Allies that differ from ours, such as saddles, accoutrements, arms, &c. I have also paid particular observation to the mode of training the Austrian cavalry to the use of the sabre, in which their superiority over us is incredible.[17]

To our great surprise, a young boy, with a national private's coat and a knapsack on his back, as a French deserter, inquired yesterday at the general's quarters for Count Harcourt (the general's *aide-de-camp*); and who should he prove but a younger brother of the count, who, having been enrolled under the con-

---

15. Colonel Crawfurd, afterwards a General and G.C.B.; one of the most distinguished officers of his day. He was attached to the Austrian army under the Archduke Charles, where his daring exploits created no little astonishment. Few men have borne such close resemblance in person and conduct, to the youthful heroes of ancient Greece, or the chivalrous favourites of the Italian poets. He had the misfortune to be dreadfully wounded, and taken prisoner at the Battle of Wurtzbourgh; and Napoleon paid an honourable tribute to his merit by permitting him, during the early part of the late war, to travel in France for his health, but it never recovered sufficiently to admit of his resuming active service. He married the Dowager Duchess of Newcastle, and died, a few years since, no less respected than beloved. His gallant brother, Major-General Robert Crawfurd, fell at Ciudad Rodrigo.

16. Later Lieutenant-General Hay, the Lieutenant-Governor of Edinburgh Castle. He frequently distinguished himself in the partial engagements of cavalry in these campaigns.

17. Captain Le Marchant also employed himself in military drawing; and his plans of the different positions of the army gained him great credit.

scription, had taken the first opportunity of coming over to us. He is quite a child, and has been brought up with the greatest care and indulgence. He says he was put on the advanced post, and it being foggy, he stole off and got into a wood, that he hid himself there during the day, and at night directed his march by the stars. He found his way to Orches, an Austrian post twelve miles from hence, where he heard of his brother, and immediately came to make himself known.

He informs us that his father is confined in one of the common gaols in Paris, with an old nurse who had been brought up in their family, but who, in her dotage, had been regardless of her expressions, for which she had been hurried into confinement, whilst his father's only crime was being a suspicious person. The rest of the family are under confinement (*en arrestation*) in their own houses.

Captain Le Marchant was thus engaged, when he received intelligence of the sudden and dangerous illness of his father, who expressed an earnest wish to see him before he died. Leave of absence was most difficult to be obtained, but the friendship of General Harcourt having overcome all obstacles, he proceeded to England, though with faint expectations of finding his father alive; and his fears proved too well founded, for as he approached his home, after a most hurried and fatiguing journey, he met the funeral procession at the door.—He stayed no longer with his family than was indispensably necessary for the arrangement of his affairs, and on the first week in February had rejoined the army, which was then in quarters at Ghent. His journal shall relate his subsequent proceedings.

I arrived at Ghent on the 7th of Feb. 1794. I was billeted in an excellent house, the owner of which was the Baron de Levendeghem, one of the most opulent nobles as well as the greatest misers in the city. His wife and himself were both frightfully deformed, and yet their children, especially two daughters, were remarkably handsome. The baron played off the anxious host upon me, and his daily invitations would, if accepted, have left me very little time to myself

At last, I suspected that this extreme civility originated in his desire to make a Catholic of me; and he candidly avowed it to be so, but added, that the affection his wife and himself bore towards me, made them wretched at the idea of my inevitable perdition in the next world. I tried to remove his apprehensions, and pressed him so hard on the weak points of his own faith, that his attack was soon changed into a defence. Like most theological disputants, we ended where we began; though, I believe, the old man never quite despaired of my conversion. The other nobles were less austere in their pursuits. They were most civil to the English officers, and gave frequent public entertainments on their account. Balls and plays were likewise very common, as was indeed every other mode of gaiety.

Early in March, we marched to the camp at Hulst, near Coutray, where a large force of all nations was assembled. From thence we soon moved to Valenciennes, and took up a position in front of that town, on the side of Quesnoy.

April 15.—I passed this day in company with some of the great men in the army, the Prince of Cobourg, General Mack, and others. The prince is a thin old man, with a countenance not very expressive. Mack is a man of forty, extremely like the Abbé MacCarty: he has some complaint in the head that keeps him in constant pain. In consequence, he wears a black *caul* over his skull, sewed round the bottom with thick black hair, which gives him a very grotesque appearance. He lies all day on his bed, writing with a pencil his instructions for the movements of the army: when an action takes place, he is lifted from his bed to his horse. It is singular, that with these habits, he is a passionate admirer of the sex. He is accompanied everywhere by a female attendant. I have made a sketch of his face, which is thought to be very like him.[18]

6th March. Our force, consisting of about 15,000, is now encamped at Marquair, a village between Tournay and Cysoing, the scene of our unfortunate operations last year. I am attached to Sir Robert Laurie's brigade, as brigade-major.

On the 16th of April, the whole combined army was drawn up on the lines above Solesmes, near Cateau, where the emperor and our duke passed through the ranks of the finest troops that ever took the field. We rested all that night upon our arms, and on the next morning at daybreak the different columns marched to a general attack of all the French posts.

18. This sketch is in my possession, and has been pronounced by competent judges to be a very striking likeness.

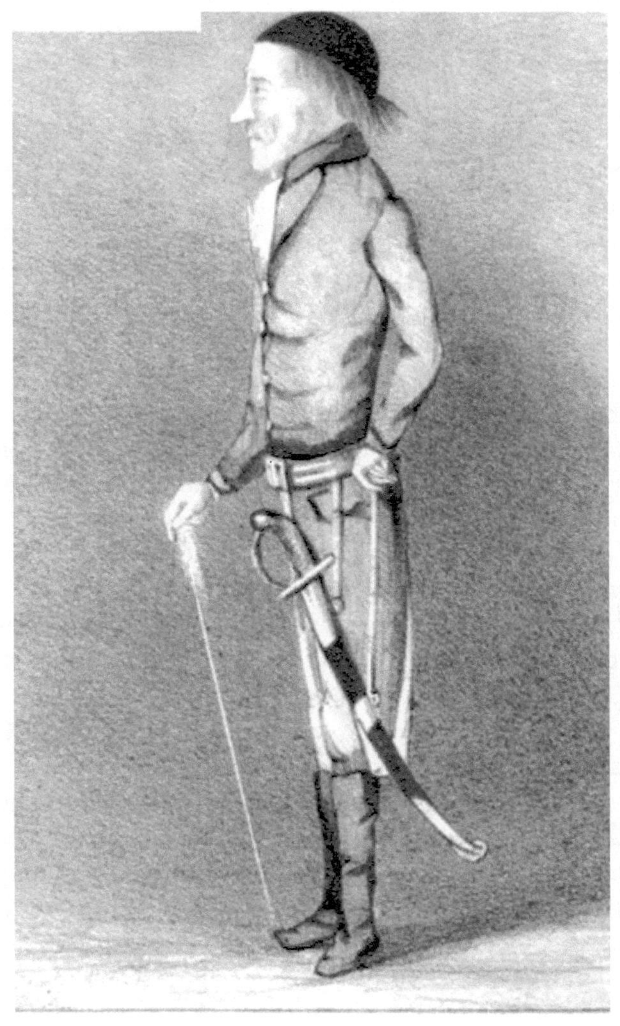

General Mack
Drawn by General Le Marchant

We were blessed with fine weather, and our troops were in high health and spirits. I was in the column commanded by the duke in person: we soon got into fire, which lasted incessantly until four in the afternoon, when the enemy abandoned the redoubt which we were approaching to storm, and left us masters of the field. Our loss was inconsiderable. At night we had the satisfaction to learn that all the different columns of the Allies had been equally successful.

The Dutch were entrusted with the surrounding of Landrecy. They fought with unusual gallantry, and accomplished their object.

On the 21st of April, the enemy attacked us at daybreak, with the design to recover their posts. The action lasted till night, with the same advantage to us. They retired to Guise, leaving five cannon and a large number of their people in our hands. Their loss in killed was very severe.

On the 22nd of April, the enemy advanced upon us,[19] at six in the morning, in three columns, of twenty thousand men each. Our posts along Blaudain, Pontasain, &c. were all engaged at once, and a continual roar of musketry and cannon was kept up till nine at night, such as the oldest officers of the Allied army declare never to have heard on any former occasion. We lost and recovered our posts several times, and every inch of ground was most obstinately contested on both sides. Unfortunately, the country was well wooded, and not adapted to cavalry, in which our strength chiefly lay.

The French force appeared to be inexhaustible; whilst their attacks became more and more vigorous; at length, as the night was drawing on, they got round our right flank and penetrated within a mile and a half of Tournay. The fate of the day was evidently turning against us, when General Fox, with only 600 men, marched down to Frozennes, gave the enemy one discharge of musketry, and rushed into the village with fixed bayonets. The struggle lasted half-an-hour, and cost us 280 men. It decided the fate of the day, which, we must own, hung on a

19. "The French on this day drove back the advanced-posts of the Prince of Cobourg, and flushed with this success, they advanced on a large body of Austrians, but these, supported by Sir Robert Laurie's brigade of British cavalry, resisted them successfully, and forced them to retire in great disorder." (*Annual Register* for 1794.) The brigade here mentioned was that of which Captain Le Marchant was the major.

straw.

The boldness with which this measure was executed intimidated the enemy to such a degree, that they took the alarm, and from that moment their fire slackened, and their ranks fell into confusion. We immediately advanced, and they soon gave way on all sides. At ten o'clock we were again masters of almost all our posts, and the remainder were quietly evacuated the next morning. Our loss is estimated at between 4000 and 5000 men. The enemy must have suffered still more.

April 26th.—Cateau. I am safe. The British cavalry has taken this day thirty-four pieces of cannon.

The affair was most glorious to us, for none of the infantry turned out of the camp, nor did they fire a shot; all, therefore, fell by the sabre. Small troops of our cavalry charged whole regiments; and the whole was effected with so little noise, that you would hardly have imagined it to be a general action. We lost General Mansel, and a few officers; and, I am sorry to add, a good many men, owing to the baseness of a French regiment, who laid down their arms, and begged for quarter: it was given them, and our cavalry (the Blues) passed on to charge some other corps, when the scoundrels took up their arms and fired on the Blues, who, by that time, had their backs turned to them. But they were punished as they deserved, every one with death.

My brigade was the only one that did not charge, the enemy not having given us an opportunity, in the position in which we were. We were merely exposed to a cannonade.

May 26th.—Tournay. The last mail went off just after the action of the 22nd, during which I had been fourteen hours constantly on horseback, so that I was too fatigued to be capable of any farther exertions; I, however, wrote to you to say I was safe, and I trust my letter will have reached you with the usual punctuality. Although this is the 25th, I am not yet recovered: I am always sleepy and stiff, proceeding, doubtless, from cold and exercise united; but I eat and drink well, and have good nights, so that if we have the fortune to be allowed a few days' rest, I shall be myself again. But when we consider that in less than five weeks I have been in seven general actions, independent of the alerts and alarms that offer, without turning out to be any thing, it must be allowed the campaign is tolerably fatiguing. It will not continue so brisk, be assured; and my firm belief is, that the Allies will seize the first favourable moment of coming to an accommodation with the French Government.

When we set out in the present campaign, we thought that we had left Flanders so well protected by its fortified towns, that it would have been unnecessary to leave an army stationed in the Low Countries; and of course we calculated on being sufficiently powerful to force the enemy, wherever we might meet them, particularly in the country that we proposed to make the seat of war, which was about Cambray and Maubeuge: and it was with this view we provided ourselves with such an immense body of cavalry. Unfortunately for us, we marched upon Landrecy, and opened the campaign before our towns in Flanders, which had been dismantled by Joseph the Second, were completed in their fortifications; and what was the consequence?

Whilst we were carrying on our operations against Landrecy, the enemy marched an army of sixty thousand men into Flanders; carried Courtray and Menin, and obliged us to shift our theatre of war from their country into our own, which, among other disadvantages, is so well wooded that our cavalry (the strength of the Allied army) is rendered utterly useless. The effect of this will be, that the Allies must be occupied for some time in driving the enemy from Flanders; and when that has been accomplished, our fortifications will have been destroyed. Of course, to defend the country from invasion, a large army must be stationed in it for the rest of the campaign, which will weaken us to that degree that we shall be little able to push to future conquests; besides, we no longer possess the superiority over the enemy which we had in an open country.

The battle of the 22nd was a trial of strength, and it has taught us, that in an enclosed country they are almost equal to disciplined soldiers, and if they are capable of bringing the *whole* of the combined army to so near an issue on our own ground, and within a mile of our camp, what are we to expect if we have to detach part of this army for the protection of Flanders? Is it to be imagined that they will now allow us to change the seat of war, whilst they are masters of a force, which it is impossible for us to oppose by equal numbers and take what precautions we may, our position is too extensive for us to avoid some part of it being left unprotected, and open to the attacks which they will infallibly make, the instant we commence offensive operations?

Whatever reinforcements we have, the enemy will receive threefold, and I am therefore confident the game is up, and we are incapable of making a successful war.[20] I suspect our leaders are not more sanguine than I am, but nothing transpires. I have never known secrets kept before, they generally get out by bits.

The journal, from which the above extracts are taken, terminates somewhat abruptly about the period of the Battle of Cateau, on the promotion of Sir Robert Laurie to the command of the British cavalry, when the brigade, of which Captain Le Marchant was the major, devolved to general afterwards Sir David Dundas, K. B., one of the few surviving veterans formed in the school of Prince Ferdinand of Brunswick during the Seven Years' War.[21] His proficiency in the more important branches of military knowledge had been already proved by his writings, and any officer might be considered fortunate in having the opportunity to receive the instruction, which he gave to his personal staff, both by precept and example. A deportment somewhat austere, and habits perhaps unnecessarily frugal, as they were better suited to a Roman camp than to a luxurious age, induced superficial observers to detract from the reputation, to which he was most justly entitled, by his profound tactical skill, upright and impartial conduct, and silent unostentatious generosity.

Under such excellent auspices, Captain Le Marchant served the campaign of 1794, high in the esteem of his general, and profiting by the impressive lessons in the art of war, which the scenes before, him furnished to an almost unprecedented extent, by the repeated battles and complicated movements of so many armies[22] within so limited

20. I need not observe of these speculations, that they are wholly opposed to what was the current opinion of that day.

21. The general has inserted in the earlier editions of his *Regulations*, some excellent comments on the principal actions of this war, of which he was so well qualified to be the historian; and it is to be deeply regretted that his modesty should have induced him to leave the task to his friend and patron General Roy, as the sudden and premature death of that distinguished scholar and soldier deprived the world of a work which would have been invaluable, if the merit of it had corresponded with the learning and abilities of the author

22. The conflicting armies in Flanders were computed at four hundred thousand men.

a compass. When the Allies were preparing to enter winter-quarters, he was promoted, at the recommendation of General Harcourt, to a majority (by purchase) in the 16th Light Dragoons, and at the same time received orders to join that regiment in England.

Having quitted the theatre of war, he hastened to rejoin his wife and family in Guernsey. His voyage was not without danger, for as the merchant-vessel in which he had embarked approached the island, she was hailed by a king's cutter, and required to heave-to, and this injunction not being obeyed with the alacrity expected on such occasions, the cutter ran alongside and fired, when one of the bullets actually went through Major Le Marchant's hat, and grazed his head. The accident, however, was soon forgotten, as in an hour afterwards he was restored to the domestic happiness, to which he had been so long a stranger.

From Guernsey he immediately removed with his wife and family to Weymouth, where his regiment was in attendance on His Majesty; and he thus exchanged the hardships and privations of an active campaign for the gaiety and luxury of a brilliant court:—a transition strikingly illustrative of the variety of military life. He, indeed, little expected, after an interval so long as seven years, to be recollected by the king; but he was agreeably mistaken; for His Majesty received him in the most gracious manner, and honoured him by repeated marks of kindness both in public and private—a distinction that led to his intimacy with the most influential persons of the day; and it is not a little to his credit, that, regardless of his personal interest, he made no other use of this advantage than to benefit his profession, by procuring attention to the plans, which he subsequently brought forward for its improvement.

Weymouth was destined to be a fortunate residence to him. Here he first became known to the king, and here also he made the first step towards establishing his reputation with the public, by his successful efforts to introduce the sword exercise. The idea of it was originally suggested to his mind during his campaigns in Flanders, by the many instances of discomfiture which our dragoons experienced in single combat with the enemy.[23] Full of the importance of providing a remedy for so serious an evil, he put himself under the tuition of a sergeant

23. It was not in single combat alone that our dragoons showed their awkwardness as swordsmen. Major Le Marchant was informed by the surgeons, that many of the wounds, which the men received in the field, could have been inflicted by no other swords than their own. One of his acquaintances, a captain of dragoons, wounded himself in the foot seriously during the confusion of a *mêlée*. The horses were perhaps the principal victims, as they were often gashed about the head and neck by their riders.

in the Austrian cavalry, from whom he learned the little that was then practised in that service; and not finding his views much forwarded by this assistance, he sought every opportunity of consulting with all individuals among the different armies, who were distinguished for their practical skill in the use of the sword.

The immense body of cavalry in the field, and the diversity of the nations of which it was composed, materially aided his researches. No sooner, however, did he set about the formation of a Code of Instruction from what he had thus gathered abroad, than he saw how impossible it was to reconcile such unconnected materials, and he was obliged to begin by creating a system of exercise, combining attack and defence, upon principles almost entirely his own. Having effected this to his own satisfaction and that of a few military friends who were interested in his studies, he proceeded to perfect himself in the *practice* of the exercise, which he soon learned to execute with no inconsiderable degree of skill and gracefulness. His next step was to instruct two active intelligent privates of the 16th Dragoons, and their proficiency answered his most sanguine expectations. With their assistance, and the approbation of his commanding officer, a detachment of twenty selected men and a few officers was formed with equal success.

At this stage of his proceedings, he endeavoured to procure the co-operation of other regiments in an experiment so calculated to be useful, but without effect, partly from the opposition which generally attends the introduction of an additional article of discipline, and partly from the influence of the *old* officers, whose ages and inaptitude for such an exercise naturally excited a disrelish for such an exhibition.[24] It therefore became necessary to resort to a higher source of authority; and he accordingly submitted to the consideration of the Duke of York, the Code of Instruction under which he proposed to train the whole British Cavalry in the use of the sword; and after due personal inquiry from His Royal Highness, and the report of a Committee of General Officers in its favour, the proposed code received unqualified approbation, and was *established under Royal authority among the permanent regulations of the cavalry.*

24. I think it unnecessary to cite more than a single instance, as all prejudice of this description has long since disappeared from the service. "I shall be very glad to see what you have to recommend on the subject of the sword exercise, because I am always glad to learn. *I am sorry Major—— is not likely to listen to your proposals of training his people;* and I trust I need not express how glad I should be to have you.—2nd Dec. 1795."—Letter from Earl Pembroke to Major Le Marchant.

Orders were then issued to Major Le Marchant to begin his course of instruction with all possible dispatch, and on his suggestion[25] detachments from every regiment of Regular and Fencible Cavalry in Great Britain, consisting of an officer and twenty men, were assembled at different periods, at four distinct stations, where, in the course of six months, he completed their instruction in the practices and evolutions of the new exercise—an instance of zeal and devotion to the service, on the part of an individual, which has few parallels. By these detachments, the instruction was conveyed to their respective corps, and such was its popularity among the men, that before a year had elapsed, the system had become part of the regular exercise and daily practice of the whole of the British cavalry.[26]

The increased attention necessarily paid by the men to the use of the sword, was soon found to inspire them with proportional confidence in their personal dexterity, whilst it led at the same time to the most successful course of instruction in horsemanship that has yet been adopted, as without skill in the management of the horse, no proficiency could be attained in the use of the sword.

But a triumphant test of the merit of the invention was afforded by the late war, during the course of which, Major Le Marchant had frequent opportunities of observing, that our dragoons evinced as marked a superiority in single combat with the enemy, as they had experienced defeats during his first campaign in the Netherlands.[27] His system has survived him, and having continued in full vigour for

25. The affinity which this mode of communicating instruction bears to the system since practised, as well by Dr. Bell, as in the Ecole Normale, at Paris, is sufficiently obvious. It is no more than justice to Major Le Marchant to observe that his suggestion was entirely original.

26. The instruction was not confined to the Regular and Fencible Cavalry, it was extended to the Yeomanry; and Major Le Marchant's attention to the discipline of those corps gained him the friendship of many distinguished persons, whose zeal for the defence of their country had brought them into temporary service.

27. The following extract from an account of the Battle of Vittoria, relates an incident of frequent occurrence—"When within a short distance of the river, four of the French Light-horse advanced on the main road to look-out, and were overtaken by an equal number of our dragoons, when they wheeled about and attempted to make off without effect They were assailed on the near side, when three instantly fell from their saddles covered with sabre wounds, and their affrighted horses galloped at random."—*United Service Journal*, No. 10.

28. It was practised during *the whole of the war*, and for many years after, without the least alteration, but it has *recently* undergone various modifications, probably improvements, as no system is likely to be perfect on its first introduction.

thirty years,[28] it may well be deemed to have been instrumental to the glory of the British arms during that period.

Major Le Marchant's *Treatise on the Sword Exercise* was printed by authority of the adjutant-general in the year 1797, and many thousand copies of it have since been sold for the benefit of the service, as he refused any pecuniary remuneration. His labours received a more honourable recompense by his promotion, in the spring of 1797. to a lieutenant-colonelcy, without purchase, in Hompesch's Hussars. He went to court soon after to thank His Majesty for this favour; and as he waited in the presence-chamber, an officer of rank came up and told him that he was not in his proper uniform, his name having appeared in the *Gazette* the day before, as Lieutenant-Colonel of the 29th Dragoons, (a regiment very preferable to Hompesch's). Before he could recover from the surprise which this unexpected intelligence had given him, he found himself before the king, who after asking him how he could be so little of a *martinette* as to appear at court in a wrong dress, added with his usual good-humour, "I dare say many persons will claim the merit of your promotion; now I wish you to know that whatever merit there is in it rests entirely between you and me, for no one else is concerned in it."

The king, indeed, was fully qualified to appreciate his services, having known him from the period of his entering the cavalry, and having watched the progress of the Sword Exercise from its very commencement, uniformly predicting its success, when many officers of note, were equally confident of its failure.

Upon the publication of the *Treatise on the Exercise*, His Majesty used to recommend it with much warmth to the officers who frequented the Court, and probably was better acquainted with its contents than most of them.

These were not the only marks of favour that Lieutenant-Colonel Le Marchant received from the Royal Family. His Royal Highness the Prince of Wales condescended to be instructed by him in the Exercise, and presented him with a richly mounted sword in token of his approbation.

The attention he had paid to the use of the sword, naturally brought its construction more particularly under his observation, and thus opened a fresh field to his ingenuity. The swords then in use in the British cavalry were of various descriptions, scarcely two regiments having the same pattern; but one of the most popular was a wide, long, and heavy blade, mounted with a cumbrous fantastic handle. The campaigns in Flanders threw them all into general disrepute. The blades were so brittle, that they often were broken by the slightest blow; whilst, at other times, they would shiver in the hand, from the metal in the blade and handle not being properly balanced.

But their greatest defect was their weight, for they were too heavy even for the strongest men to wield; so that the sword not having the poise which is absolutely necessary for carrying the edge correctly, it frequently turned in the hand, and inflicted a contusion rather than a wound.

It appeared to Lieutenant-Colonel Le Marchant that the weapon might be much improved by divesting it of all that was superfluous in the handle, by altering the proportions of the blade; by shortening it, and, above all, by proportioning its weight, to the strength of the lowest standard of dragoons then admitted into the Service. The scale of proportions he followed the most closely was that of Andrea Ferrara, and he did so not from a blind admiration of a name, but because single combat being the system of war when that celebrated cutler flourished, it was likely that the construction of the sword would receive greater attention at that period, than under the modern system of tactics.

Impressed by these considerations he visited the principal sword manufactories at Birmingham and Sheffield, and having witnessed the necessary experiments and consulted the persons best versed in the different processes of working steel, he departed fully satisfied of the advantages that would arise from his proposed alterations. In 1797, he submitted to His Royal Highness the Commander-in-Chief, "*A plan for constructing and mounting in a different manner the Swords of the Cavalry*,"[29] which was approved, and afterwards directed to be observed as a regulation throughout the service. He was at the same commanded by His Majesty to adapt his pattern to men of the standard of the Horse-guards Blue, and having done so, the sword was adopted by that corps under His Majesty's special direction.

As an acknowledgment of the utility of the suggestion, he received a letter of thanks from the Master-General of the Ordnance, accompanied with a present of a sword, on the blade of which was an inscription recording the occasion of the gift. Mr. Osborne, the first sword-cutler in Birmingham, if not in Europe, paid him a similar compliment.

29. From this "Plan," which enters into great detail upon the construction of swords, I have extracted the preceding statement.

It may not be a superfluous remark, that this sword continues to be used at the present day, (1841), with very little alteration, [30] and that it has been introduced into many of the continental armies.

Gratified as Lieutenant-Colonel Le Marchant must have been by these honourable distinctions, he yet did not appreciate their value, as he would have done under other circumstances. They were bestowed on him at a moment, when every good man, especially a husband and a father, was thinking of his country, much more than of himself. England was then supposed to be in the most perilous position that any nation ever survived. Our campaigns in the Netherlands had come to a disastrous termination. The French arms had triumphed, not only there, but in Austria, Prussia, and Italy, and the complete destruction of our continental allies seemed almost inevitable. The mutiny of the Nore suspended our dominion of the seas, whilst it invited an attack upon our shores, which we were ill-prepared to oppose, for the violence of conflicting factions had sadly damped that patriotic spirit which of old had been looked to as our most effectual defence. It was doubtful which was the most dangerous, our avowed enemies abroad, or our more insidious enemies at home, but between them both, we had a most melancholy prospect. The two following letters will show that this picture is no exaggeration.

Lieutenant-Colonel Le Marchant to Mrs. Le Marchant at Guernsey.

Newcastle, March 7,1797.

> You will see by the papers in what a prosperous state we are. The funds at 49¾ and are expected to be lower. Some of the principal banks in this part of the country have stopped payment, and all credit has sunk along with them. Not a guinea is to be seen anywhere; nothing but paper. It is expected that Mr. Pitt will go out; yet what will that produce? If peace, it must be such as will eventually ruin the country, and by a perseverance in the war, what is to be hoped for? You can have no idea of the dejection of the public mind: and I cannot help so far

30. "The swords adopted at the suggestions of Major-General Le Marchant were considered very great improvements upon those in use before, and they differ but little from those of the present regulation, our sabre being somewhat less curved to render it more handy for the thrust, which is found to be more deadly and certain. The principle which guided Major-General Le Marchant in the selection of his sword has never since been departed from."— Letter to the author from Lieutenant-Colonel —— late of —— Dragoons.

participating in it, as to regret that we did not make some small investment last year in the American funds. It would have been a resource for our children.

People here are as much afraid of invasion, as you can be in Guernsey.

I do not expect to be above six weeks longer in England, as my party will be conveyed from hence to Bath on coaches, in order to save time, as our presence in Ireland, (to teach the sword exercise) General Dundas tells me, is much wanted.

Earl Pembroke to Lieutenant-Colonel Le Marchant.

Arlington-street, April 24,1797.

Could you, from where you are, send sufficient directions for a private yeoman's sword to be mounted for Lord Spencer. You will not forget the sword you are to have mounted for your old Commanding officer, who is not yet to be put upon the shelf. The measure of removing him and his fellows from regimental situations being suspended, if not totally dropped. Sad work at Sheerness; sad work in Ireland, I fear; sad work in the Tyrol. The Lord protect us, for it seems we cannot, or will not, protect ourselves. And so believe me your melancholy old brother officer.

Pembroke.

When men of sense and firmness could regard public affairs with the gloomy feelings expressed in these letters, no one can wonder that the government was under the deepest alarm, or that it had recourse to measures, the policy of which it is now more easy to criticise than to controvert. Among other precautions, it was deemed expedient to prevent the dispersion of those friends of the Crown whose assistance might be most valuable in such an emergency, and this led to Colonel Le Marchant's receiving a distinction which he never ceased to prize as the highest honour that could have been conferred upon him. Upon his calling at the Horse-guards, preparatory to his departure for Ireland, for the purpose of forming the cavalry on that establishment in the sword exercise, he was told by Sir William Fawcett, the adjutant general, that he must find some officer[31] to supply his place on that

31. His brother-in-law, Lieutenant Carey, of the 16th Light Dragoons, who had been his assistant in instructing the cavalry in Great Britain, was the officer selected for that service. He afterwards served as Deputy Barrack-Master General in this country, and has since been Military Secretary, both in India and Ireland, to the Commander-in-Chief; and then a Major-General.

service, as it was the king's special command that he should on no account quit this country during the present critical state of affairs.

Being thus left without employment, as his regiment was stationed in the West Indies, he established himself in London, that he might be at hand should his service be required. Here he prepared, and submitted to the commander-in-chief, "a plan for preventing peculation in the foraging of the Cavalry,"[32] which was approved by His Royal Highness, and carried into effect. He also composed a work entitled *The Duty of Officers of Cavalry on the Outpost*, the substance of which, he had collected whilst serving with the outposts of the Prussian Cavalry in Flanders. General Dundas, by whom it was revised, pronounced it to be the best treatise on the subject he had ever seen, and it was directed by the Duke of York to be printed, under the authority of the adjutant-general. Through some accident, however, it never went to the press, and no trace of it can be found among the papers of its author.

These occupations did not prevent his frequent attendance at court, and he was called therein the month of June, to thank the king for appointing him to the junior Lieutenant-Colonelcy of the 7th regiment of Light Dragoons, on which occasion His Majesty kindly said to him, "I will not have you go to a bad climate, and I am glad to have had an opportunity of removing you." He afterwards learned, that he owed this appointment solely to the king.[33]

He joined the 7th Light Dragoons in the autumn of 1797, and in consequence of the absence of his senior officer, Lord Paget, whose appointment was almost as recent as his own, he found himself in the command of the regiment. Having obtained his Lordship's permission, he commenced a thorough reform of the regimental discipline

32. The foraging of the cavalry was formerly a most fruitful source of fraud. I recollect hearing the subject of this biographical sketch say that, when he entered the Iniskillings, scarcely a horse was fit for service, although the government was at great expense to keep up an efficient establishment. The allowance for the subsistence of the horses, was paid to the captain of the troop, and all he had to do, was to make his horses look tolerably well at the monthly inspection by some of the district staff. A liberal supply of water to the poor animals on the appointed day, gave them a temporary comeliness sufficient to secure their commander from any unpleasant observations. It is, however, but justice to add, that this lax and most unguarded system was generally productive of more advantage to the quartermaster, than to the captain of the troop. The evil has long since been corrected, and nothing can be better conducted than the present mode of supplying the cavalry with forage, as the fine condition of the horses sufficiently testifies.

33. His letter to the Duke of York on quitting the Military College.

which had been previously much neglected. Every department was rigorously investigated, and whatever abuses came to light, were swept away with an unsparing hand. The interior economy of the corps was put on an entirely new footing, and under such judicious regulations, that neither officers nor men could neglect the proper discharge of their respective duties.

Perhaps he exacted somewhat more than could be expected from individuals who had long been accustomed to a laxer rule, and he may have allowed too short a time for old prejudices to die away, and wholesome habits to spring up in their room. His strictness certainly bordered on severity, but it was never wasted upon trifles; no man was less of a *martinette.* He directed his attention exclusively to what he considered indispensable to the improvement of the corps, and he carried his interference no farther; whilst he invariably maintained an urbanity of manner, and a high, honourable, and gentlemanly conduct, which, combined with moral qualities, that no one could dispute, insured him the attachment of many, and the respect of all. So far from using the privileges of his rank as an exemption from personal labour, he gave an example to those beneath him, of the most unqualified devotedness to the task be had undertaken.

He compiled from his own papers, as well as from printed works not in general circulation, a code of instructions for the officers under his command on the different heads of regimental duty. It omitted nothing essential in the practice of the riding-school, or in the manoeuvre of the field; and it was written in a clear and forcible style, particularly adapted to the purpose for which it was intended. Three or four days in the week he regularly assembled in his room all such officers as were desirous of learning, and explained to them the principles of Field Movements; besides which, he was unwearied in superintending the drills and perfecting the practice of the evolutions, though he never encroached on the province of his officers so as to lead them to forget their own responsibility; for no one could be more alive to the importance of their acquiring that confidence in themselves, which is the most valuable attribute of military rank.

All this could not be effected without great fatigue both to officers and men, though to none so much as to himself. His iron frame and constitutional energy made him view it very lightly, but the men, accustomed to lighter work, and not having the same motives for extraordinary exertion, became discontented, and rejoiced not a little on the arrival of Lord Paget to assume the command. His Lordship had scarcely appeared on the parade, when he was greeted with loud cheers from the ranks. He immediately checked his horse, and addressing the men in terms of dignified rebuke, expressed his entire approbation of Lieutenant-Colonel Le Marchant's conduct whilst in command, and observed, that they were proving the necessity of the strictest discipline, by an act of insubordination, which he considered as a personal insult to himself.

Those who have heard his Lordship, either in the senate or in the field, may easily imagine the effect which this sensible and soldier-like reproof produced. I shall only add, that the intimacy with which he honoured Lieutenant-Colonel Le Marchant, ended only with the life of the latter.

Lord Paget's opinion afterwards received ample confirmation from General Dundas, the colonel of the regiment, whose zeal for the advancement of all military knowledge led him to go down expressly to inspect the corps. He declared publicly, "that he was quite delighted with what he saw," and strongly recommended Lieutenant-Colonel Le Marchant to lose no time in preparing his code of instructions for the press, expressing his confidence, that it required only a little revision to render it highly beneficial to the service. With this advice, the lieutenant colonel so far complied as to commence the revision of his code, but he was soon diverted from the task by designs which be considered of greater importance; and, the only part of it that ever came before the public, is to be found in a work which he presented to the commander-in-chief, entitled, *An Elucidation of several parts of His Majesty's Regulations for the formation and movements of Cavalry*, which was published in 1797, by His Majesty's directions, and has since passed through five very large impressions. It consists merely of extracts from the larger treatise of General Dundas, with illustrations and examples suited to the immediate instruction of officers on entering into the Cavalry Service.

His indefatigable assiduity, working as he said, from six in the morning till twelve at night, enabled him, about the same time, to produce another work, under the head of *Instructions for the movements and discipline of Provisional Cavalry*, a popular and useful manual which his accustomed disinterestedness rendered as little profitable to himself, as his other publications.

CHAPTER 2

The Establishment of the Royal Military College

Lieutenant-Colonel Le Marchant had now established his reputation as one of the most able regimental officers in the army: but not satisfied with that distinction, his ambition aimed at something more, and he had the sagacity to perceive how much lay within the reach of enterprise and talent. The experience of his campaigns in Flanders, and of his service at home, as well as the difficulties he had encountered both in introducing the sword exercise and in his other efforts to improve the discipline of the cavalry, all combined to convince him that the real drawback to any essential reform of the service, arose from the officers, and not from the men; so that, until the former were adequately instructed, the character of our armies could never be permanently raised.

Such, indeed, was the opinion of the most distinguished generals of the day, many of whom had directed their attention to the instruction of the officers under their immediate command with considerable success. But their exertions were only productive of a temporary and limited effect; a few instances of personal merit had little influence on the service at large, and a body of intelligent officers was not to be created, except by the establishment of some uniform system of instruction, embracing the principles and practice of warfare in all its branches, and which should be accessible to officers of every grade and arm.

This was so obvious, that various ingenious plans for the general diffusion of military knowledge had from time to time been received and partially approved by the government, but these had subsequently fallen to the ground, partly from the imperfections they presented upon closer examination, but principally, perhaps, from considerations of a political nature. Any interference on the part of government with the education of the higher ranks of the army was regarded with extreme jealousy by the public, as a step towards withdrawing the officer from civil society, and making him the creature of the crown. This feeling, unfortunately, checked the support of the responsible military authorities, and the sanguine spirits that had contemplated the rapid regeneration of the army through systematic instruction, now turned their last, hopes on the dearly bought lessons in the field which our active participation in the war promised to afford.

To minds of an ordinary stamp, these obstacles appeared insuperable, and it required all the enthusiasm that belonged to the subject of this *Memoir* to attempt, at a moment so apparently inauspicious, the correction of evils coeval with our military annals, and growing, as it were, out of the spirit of our free institutions. He probably would never have come forward, had not long and deep reflection, accompanied by a confidential intercourse with many of the greatest tacticians of the day, supplied him with better materials for the task he meditated, than had been possessed by most of his predecessors in the same track.

His first essay was *A Plan for establishing Regimental Schools for Officers throughout the service*, which he had in some degree carried into effect whilst in command of the 7th Light Dragoons; but observation soon convinced him, that although a commanding officer might be a perfect master of his regimental duties, he might yet want the knowledge and experience necessary to instruct those under his command in the more complicated and difficult science of actual war. This project was therefore abandoned as altogether inadequate to the end in view; but not until he had worked out the details with a care that marked no inconsiderable sacrifice of time and labour.

Other plans followed, and shared the same fate. These disappointments, however, to a mind so ardent in the pursuit of its object, only led to increased exertions, and he was insensibly approaching the end of his labours, when he thought himself still far distant from the goal. Ruminating on the subject of his speculations, as he was travelling alone in the autumn of 1798, he became firmly persuaded that nothing short of a *national establishment, on a scale far more extensive than had yet been proposed*, would be found to yield any solid or adequate advantage to the state. He no sooner arrived at the inn where his carriage stopped, than he committed his ideas to paper; and he was often heard to say, that as he wrote he felt the most perfect confidence in the success of his undertaking. He did not leave the inn before he had sketched out, at no inconsiderable length, the leading principles on which he intended to proceed, and it is a singular circumstance, that he had no occasion to deviate from them afterwards. He now resumed his labours with increased vigour, and the development of his plan afforded him additional encouragement In a letter to his wife, dated the 13th of December, 1798, he says:

> My plan goes on agreeably to my most sanguine wishes, and I have no doubt it will succeed, though there is much more to arrange than I expected. My mind furnishes me, as I go on, with so many new ideas, that I see the impossibility of its embracing a complete system at once; it can alone be led on progressively. Lord Paget will relieve me in about three weeks, by which time my work will be in sufficient forwardness to be shown to the duke. I need not tell you that I am indefatigable; and I am sure I ought to be so, for my plan is so extensive that it is a most laborious undertaking; at the same time it will be as good a test of my talent for my profession as I can wish for.

His work being sufficiently matured, he submitted it to the Duke of York, in January 1799. His Royal Highness, after reading it attentively, expressed his general approbation of the design, but added his fears, that the difficulties of carrying it into effect could not be overcome: that the Duke of Richmond had some years before proposed a national military institution, and ministers had been very favourable to it; but when the subject came to be more discussed, so many objections were started by public men, as well to the principle as to the expense of the measure, that His Grace proceeded no farther in it. His Royal Highness added:

> I have no wish to discourage you, yet I can hardly recommend you to sacrifice your time and talents to a project which seems so very unlikely to succeed. Nothing can be done as long as people think on the subject as they do now, and I despair of your removing their prejudices, for prejudices they are, unless you can absolutely demonstrate them to be groundless. This cannot be done in a moment, and it will require stronger arguments than those you have laid before me. If you will revise your plan, and accompany it with all the details necessary for satisfying the public, it shall have my warm support.

Nothing, perhaps, could portray more strongly the confidence which Lieutenant-Colonel Le Marchant reposed in his own powers, or could redound more to his credit, than his determined perseverance in his plan, after receiving so discouraging an answer. To learn from His Royal Highness the unfavourable state of the public feeling on the subject, and his own apprehension that it could not be brought round to sounder views, would alone seem sufficiently appalling to have justified the immediate abandonment of his scheme; but when, coupled with this disheartening avowal, he was told that a nobleman of the Duke of Richmond's distinguished talents and powerful influence—a cabinet minister at the time—had been unable to stem the tide of public opinion, and had been forced to relinquish a favourite object of his ambition; it is impossible to withhold our admiration of the comparatively obscure individual, who, in despite of these formidable obstacles, could accomplish such an undertaking with the almost unanimous approval as well of his own profession as of the public at large.

Lieut.-Colonel Le Marchant left the duke with an assurance that he would soon render the measure worthy of the public support; and he kept his word. In three months from that time, he presented His Royal Highness with an elaborate statement of his views, comprising all the financial estimates necessary to a clear elucidation of the expense attending his proposed plan. The income and expenditure of the establishment in all its branches were calculated with mercantile minuteness, and the result certainly showed the possibility of conducting it at little or no charge to the government.

Whilst he was employed in drawing up this statement, he had frequent interviews with the duke, as well as with His Royal Highness's private secretary, and the adjutant and quartermaster-generals. These able and experienced officers kindly afforded him the assistance of their valuable advice, founded on their knowledge of his Royal Highness's sentiments. The precise points on which objections rested being thus ascertained, he no longer worked in the dark, nor wasted his strength in useless speculations. He went to the core of the matter at once, and brought together such a mass of fact and argument in support of his views, as gradually gained the duke's entire acquiescence. His Royal Highnesses decision might have been the more readily adopted, from the circumstance, that General Jarry, a French tactician of the highest eminence, was at the time an exile in this country, and ready to turn his talents to the best account.

On the invitation of His Royal Highness, that veteran willingly undertook to instruct our officers in the art of war, with Lieutenant-Colonel Le Marchant as his coadjutor. In furtherance of this object, government sanctioned a temporary establishment for military instruction, on a limited scale, at High Wycombe, in Bucks; and thus, under the auspices of King George III., was laid the foundation of what has since become the Royal Military College. It opened on the 4th of May, 1799, under the direction of the above-mentioned officers, without the aid of professors.

The first stone of the edifice being now laid, Colonel Le Marchant foresaw its completion at no distant period. It is true, that but a small portion of his plan was adopted, and that small as it was, his reputation would suffer as much by its failure, as if the whole had been fairly tried. The principle of it, however, was publicly recognised, and this once appreciated, he was confident the rest must necessarily follow. And so it proved. The experience of a few months sufficed to demonstrate the utility of the establishment, and the necessity of its extension. The lectures of General Jarry were greatly admired—by all who could understand them—but being confined to the higher branches of the military art, and delivered in a foreign language, they were quite lost on the generality of officers, who knew little of their profession beyond the mere routine of regimental duty. A preparatory course of instruction was indispensable; and government were reduced to the alternative of appointing the requisite professors, or breaking up the establishment.

This crisis did not find Lieutenant-Colonel Le Marchant unprepared. Sensible, from the first, that it was by public opinion alone his plan must stand or fall, he had circulated upon the opening of the Institution, a concise sketch of his design, amongst those persons whose interest or advice was likely to afford him any assistance. The time was now arrived to judge of the impression produced by the work; and as it may not be without some interest for those who choose to trace the fortunes of its author, I have ventured to reprint it almost entire: the only parts I have omitted being the preface and the appendix.[1]

1. The Duke of York, with the same view, sometime afterwards, caused to be printed and circulated a very well written paper by General Jarry, entitled, "*Explanatory Remarks on the Utility and Nature of the Military Instructions which are given at High Wycombe, by order of his Royal Highness the Duke of York.*" It relates exclusively to General Jarry's Lectures, and is no mean monument of his professional knowledge. The general was also the author of a *Treatise on the Duties of Light Infantry*, which I have heard highly commended by competent judges, especially by the late General the Hon. William Stewart, K.B., who was considered one of the best Light Infantry officers of his day.

Outlines of a Plan for a Regular Course of Military Education.

The different periods of life at which persons enter into the British service, render it impossible that everyone should be alike capable of pursuing a regular course of education. It becomes necessary, therefore, to adapt the system of instruction to the particular circumstances which characterize. the British army, without regard to the mode of military education observed by other nations, or the regular course of study usually pursued for the attainment of science.

It is proposed then, to found a Military College, to be conducted under the direction of officers of approved ability; over which establishment the commander in chief should preside as chancellor.

The immediate object of this institution would be, "to instruct the mass of the service in the degree of science requisite to subordinate stations; and to afford the means of a perfect education to those, who, aspiring to rank and responsibility, apply early to the study of their profession."

To effect these purposes, the instruction must be arranged and conducted under separate courses of study, forming three distinct departments of the college, each appropriated to the views under which individuals may enter into the service as officers; at the same time extending the plan of education to the ranks, by the instruction of soldiers' sons, who may eventually become intelligent non-commissioned officers, and be made capable of filling with credit even staff situations in the several corps of the army.

The first of the three departments to be for the instruction of youth in the several branches of science, after having finished their classical studies.

The second for cadets of the army, and soldiers' sons; who will be formed to the practical duties of the service.

The third is intended for the improvement of the staff of the army.[2]

First Department.

For the Instruction of Youth.

This department would constitute the junior course, and be calculated for the instruction of those who are from early life intended for the military profession; and who, by becoming students in this depart-

2. The object of instruction attached to this department, is anticipated by the arrangements made for an academy in Buckinghamshire.

ment, may be well grounded in science, previous to their attaining that age which entitles them to hold commissions.

The principal points of instruction to which their attention would be directed, consist in the study of Moral and Natural Philosophy; Logic; the several branches of Mathematics; Geography; History; and a knowledge of the German and French languages: to which may be added, if deemed expedient, Dancing, Fencing, and Riding.

Quarterly examinations to be held for the several degrees, when those students who adopt the service, will eventually remove from the first to the second department of the college.

The students to be admitted from the age of thirteen to fifteen,[3] and with the approbation of the resident governor. They are to be boarded, and educated in the several branches of science; the particulars of which will be hereafter detailed in the Regulations of the Department, and this at a fixed allowance of seventy pounds annually for each student, free of all other charges whatsoever.[4]

The number of pupils admitted to this department must be limited, at the same time that the benefit of the Institution should be confined as much as possible to the instruction of officers' sons, and those who may be intended for the service; but as the acquirements treated of enter into a finished education, equally whether men are designed for military or civil stations, the regulations of the department should not operate to the exclusion of those whose rank and circumstances entitle them to aspire to elevated stations.

The master to be appointed by the chancellor, and in consideration of the privileges attached to the Institution, to subject himself to the control of the governors of the college, and to the rules and regulations prescribed for the department.

Second Department.

For the Cadets of the Army, and Soldiers' Sons.

Cadets.

This first branch of the department is calculated to inform the body of the army, by instructing those who enter the service without

3. In order to obviate the disadvantages that would arise in the loss of rank to those who become students at fifteen, it will be requisite to allow students to lodge their money for vacancies at sixteen, and their rank to bear date from that period without interruption to their studies.

4. The sum allowed to the master for each student, is calculated upon the ground that the college be exempted from the payment of taxes, in like manner with the Military Establishment at Woolwich.

being, by previous education, qualified to become officers.

With this view, every person, before a commission is granted him, must be required to enter as a cadet, in order that he may attain a competent knowledge of the service; and by passing an examination in that probationary state, prove himself equal to the duties of a subaltern officer.

The cadets will do duty with a legion, consisting of four companies, formed from two hundred soldiers' sons, recruited without bounty, who are to be educated on the establishment in the practical duties of that service to which their natural genius may lead them.

The course of instruction attached to this department would be elementary in point of science; whilst its practice would be directed to every situation comprised in regimental arrangement, whether of cavalry or infantry.

The cadets of both services would be taught plain geometry and trigonometry; to make sketches of an outpost or country when sent on patrol; to draw the different manoeuvres treated of in His Majesty's regulations, writing therefrom the words of command appropriated to every rank that directs the execution of each movement; and, as far as time and circumstances might admit, employ such means to confirm them in a knowledge of the theory, as would insure their becoming correct and intelligent officers in practice.

Such cadets as were intended for the cavalry, would be instructed in horsemanship and the use of the sword. They would be attached to that division of the legion which is mounted and formed to the cavalry service; thereby become acquainted with the treatment of horses, and the interior economy of a regiment in quarters, as well as with its movements in the field. Their drills would be conducted indiscriminately together with the legion, in order to unite practice with theory, which is indispensably necessary to a perfect knowledge of a military system.

Upon the same principle, the cadets destined for the infantry will be attached to companies, and receive instructions in the several branches of duty which relate to that particular service.

In order to obtain admission to the college, as cadet, every person should first be approved of by the commanding officer of a regiment, as successor to a vacant commission (and if by purchase, the purchase-money should be lodged with the regimental agent, by whom application would be made to the chancellor for an order of admission). Cadets, intended for the cavalry service, to remain six months at the college; and those designed for the infantry, to continue three months;[5] during which time the paymaster should draw on their respective agents monthly; for the former, at the rate of four shillings per day, and two shillings and fourpence for the latter, being for the purpose of defraying the expenses of the department.

Each cavalry cadet to take with him his charger, in order to be broke at the riding-school, and enable him to attend his military exercise, for which forage and stable will be allowed.

Accommodation for the cadets to be provided in the college, and messes to be established on reasonable terms; the same attendance to be allowed as is usual at the Universities, as no servants should be admitted to this establishment.

The cadets to pass two examinations for their degree; which having taken, they should be entitled to hold commissions in the several corps for which they were intended. Notice of their having received such degree to be officially transmitted by the board to the chancellor, and their commissions made out, antedated to the period at which they entered the college.

Legion.

The establishment of the legion will be a very necessary branch of this department of the college, and an institution not less munificent than beneficial to the service; it would be formed according to the rules and regulations established for the army, with the additional advantage of being taught reading, writing, and arithmetic, and will insure to the service a constant succession of persons qualified to become non-commissioned officers, or even to supply staff situations in corps; whilst it will contribute essentially to the improvement of the cadets, by affording them the means of exemplifying what they have at first acquired in theory.

Three years' residence at the college will enable the legion to become soldiers, and of a proper age for service; in consequence, a draft of one-third may be made annually into regiments of the line, free of expense.

The legion to be recruited from soldiers' sons, not under the age of thirteen, and not exceeding fifteen years old. These, however, should be recommended by commanding officers of regiments to the resident governor; after which, and having passed the board, they should be attested (without bounty) and admitted on the foundation of the college. These boys are to be considered as effective soldiers, and kept

5. In time of peace their residence would be for a longer period.

on the establishment of their respective regiments, in the proportion of two boys to each corps.

Seventy boys only to be received in the first year of the institution, alike number in the second year, and sixty in the third year; at the commencement of the fourth year, sixty-five to be discharged from the college, and returned to the several regiments from which they were sent; this draft will be made every year, and the legion recruited to its usual establishment.

The legion to be divided into four companies, to whom officers and non-commissioned officers should be appointed from the line.

The horses required to mount one company of the legion, to be recruited from foresters, at twelve guineas each, measuring from thirteen to fourteen hands, and tails not docked.

Twenty horses to be received the first year, and the number to be completed in the second year to fifty-eight.

No distinction to be made in the pay between the mounted and dismounted companies, but the general pay to be fourteen-pence per day. This allowance would be found fully adequate to the expense of clothing and subsistence.

The whole of this department would be conducted under the immediate direction of officers of the line, as a Military Establishment, founded on the basis of His Majesty's regulations, having in view the future uniformity of practice throughout every rank and situation in the British Army.

Third Department.

For Improvement of the Staff.

This department is intended only for officers of experience in the duties of regimental service, who possess a competent knowledge of the several branches of science pursued in the junior departments of the college.

The immediate purpose of this institution is, to lead progressively from minutiae to a knowledge of military operations, upon those principles which direct the great scale of war, and thereby to expand the genius, that responsibility may not precede information; for though no reluctance is felt in acknowledging inexperience while in subordinate stations, yet, having once arrived at rank, enquiry after information too naturally ceases, from a dread of ridicule, or the galling imputation of incapacity.

The instruction appropriated to this third department of the college will be calculated to qualify officers to become *aide-de-camps*, and fill other staff appointments[6] with the ability due to their high importance. It will explain the nature of the country, and form the eye to that perfect knowledge of ground, which is necessary to a judicious choice of position, and to the conduct of offensive and defensive war.

It will point out the modes of attack and defence, appropriated to local situation, with the several duties inseparable from an advanced corps, co-operating with the movements of an army.

It will minutely detail the sections that compose an army, and specify the proportion that troops of each branch of service should bear to each other.

It will enumerate the different departments of any army, comprised under the heads of Civil and Military Staff; enter into the particular duties of each, their relative powers, and their connection with the general conduct of the army, as well in what relates to the interior system, as to its service in the field; the principle upon which movements are conducted, and the general motives that determine the choice of position for an army, both in the field and in cantonments.

It will treat of the great principle which should regulate command, and the policy requisite to high authority, in order to maintain discipline, inspire energy in the troops, and insure a perfect co-operation in every branch of the service. It will point out generally the resources of an army, in the various means of procuring supplies of forage and provisions; the power of influencing the good disposition and support of the natural inhabitants of a country that may be the theatre of war; through whose means intelligence of the enemy can be obtained, with the several other aids so indispensable to the operations of active service.

Finally, it will show the proper administration of finance, in regulating the expenditure by the receipt, and checking the accounts of the several departments.

Officers, who have been less than four years in the army, will not be considered eligible to enter on this course of military study.

Apartments to be provided in the college, where each officer will be allowed forage for two horses, and accommodation for one servant.

---

6. In the Austrian service, the knowledge necessary to staff officers is properly considered of such high importance as to have given rise to an establishment for the express purpose of instructing men of ability and qualifying them for commands. They are incorporated under the denomination of the *Etat-Major*, and are employed on all services that require intelligence and ability.

Every necessary convenience, with the means of messing, will be attached to the establishment, subject, however, to the rules of the Institution.

Application to the chancellor for admission, is to be made through the commanding officers of corps.

No person under the rank of a field officer will be adequate to conduct this department, as the instruction he will be required to give can only result from great ability and much experience.

The college being divided into three departments, it is not requisite to the system of instruction that the whole plan should be adopted at the same time: any part may be separately established, and the plan afterwards completed, as circumstances may render advisable.

The detail of rules and regulations for the college, the immediate course of instruction proposed, together with the examinations to be made in every branch of science appropriated to the several departments, are omitted, it being the immediate object to submit for consideration the outlines of a plan, which may be readily completed, if found deserving farther notice.

Heads of the College.

Chancellor and Commander-in-Chief.
Governor.
Lieutenant Governor.
Superintendant.

The Governor is not to be under the rank of Major General, and will be required to take an active concern in the conduct of the institution.

The Lieutenant Governor and Superintendent are not to be under the rank of Field Officer. They are to reside at the College, and one of them invariably be present.

In the absence of the Chancellor, the *Senior Officer* is to be invested with the entire control over every department, in all matters that relate to the good order and strict adherence to the established rules and regulations. And no alterations or amendments are to be made but by order of the Chancellor.

A Board will sit at stated periods to examine the junior departments for their several degrees, and transact such business as may be under their immediate cognisance.[7]

---

7. The remainder of the work is devoted to the estimate of the income and expenditure of the college.

******

The work being once in circulation, he awaited the public decision upon its merit with the deepest anxiety. He considered his fortunes as a soldier to be set upon the die, and he was not the man to regard them lightly. His suspense was rendered still more harassing, by an additional cause of solicitude. In order to prosecute his plans most effectually, he had previously placed his wife, to whom he was most tenderly attached, with her friends in Guernsey, where she had now continued for two years, a period quite long enough to exhaust her patience, and she had began to urge him so warmly to abandon his projects and return to domestic life, that he found it very difficult to resist her entreaties. One of the letters he addressed to her on the subject is so characteristic of him, that I have ventured to insert it.

> Since my last letter, I have distributed about thirty copies of my proposed plan, and I am happy to say, that no objections are made to it as a system, whilst the amendments that have been proposed, will enable me to render it more perfect, should government determine upon founding a system of general instruction for the army. Everyone in and out of office, allows the necessity of the measure, and as far as it is possible to judge, I have more reason than ever to count on its success; but time must be allowed for opinion to circulate and people in power to make up their minds.
>
> The duke told ——that he approved of my prospectus, and should take it immediately to the king, and I find the leading generals canvassing it with an interest that is very encouraging to me; I cannot, however, say when any thing will be known, though I trust my next letter will report further and material progress.
>
> I feel most sensibly the length of our separation, and you cannot regret more deeply than I do the necessity of its continuance. My chief wish, my most anxious desire, has always been to make you happy; and this has proved most fortunate for both of us, as I fear that without the ties which bind me to you and our children, I might have been content to live like too many around me, indifferent to the present and regardless of the future. I have worked hard to bring myself forward in the line of my profession: I have attracted public notice, and I trust good opinion: I have got into that connexion, which is the first in

the country, and bids fair to establish whatever I may have the ability to bring forward for the public good.

But the progress of an individual who depends on his talents, and not his birth and interest, must necessarily be slow and attended by innumerable difficulties. I am of this description; and considering the circumstances under which I started, we must admit, that I have had more success than I had reason to expect, and after the perseverance with which I have pursued my object,—when it may be said to be within my grasp,—I am sure you will join with me in submitting to the arrangements which the exigencies of the moment require.

The present period of public affairs is big with great events, and it is at such a moment alone, that an opening is given to men of enterprise, and, therefore, not to be sacrificed to domestic considerations. Peace is the period for indulgence; war for professional exertions. One year more must determine the good or evil of the present political struggle; and since we have done so much as to sacrifice two years of happiness to my pursuits, I think it would be folly for me now to desist and give up all thoughts of the distinction that I have laboured so long to attain. Some men, and those of high rank, leave their homes and comforts to seek their fortunes in the East; others hazard all in the West; surely the same reasons that justify these privations, ought to exonerate me from the imputation of any want of judgment, whilst I pursue the more safe career of home service. I ask you but to wait a little longer, and I think you will see, upon reflection, that I do not ask too much.

The confidence he expressed in the preceding letter was amply realised. Letters soon flowed in from all quarters, expressing the highest approbation of his plan, but unfortunately so few have been preserved that I can only find two of them, and those of rather a late date, worthy of being presented to the reader.

Lord Auckland to Lieutenant-Colonel Le Marchant.

I have received your letter of the 7th, together with its enclosure, and there is not a single remark or opinion, either in the one or the other, to which I do not give my entire assent; for certainly it is not necessary to possess military science in order to comprehend the utility and great importance of forming young officers in the manner, and with the views which your papers so justly describe; and the circumstances of the times in which we live, strongly impress the necessity of such an institution for the British Empire.

I shall be exceedingly happy, when I go to town for the season, to have the advantage and pleasure of seeing you, and of conversing with you, whenever you may find it convenient. I return the well-written paper of General Jarry, who speaks most feelingly to me of the advantage which he has derived from your friendship and co-operation. I am, with great truth and esteem,

Your faithful, humble servant,

Dec. 11,1795. (Signed) Auckland.

Colonel Crawfurd (afterwards General Sir Charles Crawfurd, G.C.B.) to Lieutenant-Colonel Le Marchant.

My anxiety for the success of this Establishment is equal to my conviction of its infinite utility and importance. The advantages of it to the military service of this empire are incalculable. As we stand at present, when an army goes upon service, we are so destitute of officers qualified to form the quartermaster-general's department, and an efficient corps of *aides-de-camp*, and our officers in general have so little knowledge of the most essential parts of their profession, that we are obliged to have recourse to foreigners for assistance, or our operations are constantly liable to failure in their execution. The getting officers from the allies, that you may be acting with for the most confidential situations in your army, is subject to very serious political objections, as well as highly disgraceful and injurious to the service from the jealousies and dissensions which it naturally excites.

It is, to a certain degree, resigning yourself into the hands of your allies, and it brings much too near you their cabals and intrigues, the mischievous consequences of which we have sufficiently experienced. But if your army is conducted in all its branches by your own officers, you have it entirely in your own hands, and of course are not subject to the inconvenience just stated. That we might have as good a quartermaster-general's department, and as good a staff in every respect, as other nations, I am quite convinced. The projected institution, if ably conducted, would insure this essential object, and though some officers would, of course, attain greater perfection than others, yet a general instruction would be diffused through the army, which could not fail to work an essential improvement in it.

In short, I have seen so much both in peace and war with those armies which are reckoned the best in Europe, that I am sure I do not speak at random when I assert that our army is susceptible of being made at least equal, (and in my opinion,) superior to any other in the world. This is certainly no trifling consideration, for, upon the excellence of your armies, and the method in which they are conducted, depends very much your success in war; and, consequently, the glory and prosperity of the empire.

The success of the French in the present war is a striking proof of what the superior talents and science of officers may effect. Their armies, though labouring under great disadvantages, in many essential points of interior discipline and arrangement, have *generally* been victorious from the superior excellence of their officers. The vulgar idea of their having been often conducted by men of no knowledge or experience in the profession, is perfectly erroneous. Go back to the commencement of the war, and you will find a most able military committee established, whose first care was to select from the engineers, artillery, and staff, of the old army, (few of those emigrated,) numbers of excellent officers, men of very extensive science and great abilities, of whom they composed quartermaster-general's departments, corps of *aides-de-camp* and other staff officers, for all their armies.

Where the commanding generals were incapable of directing the operations, those officers assisted; for instance, when political considerations induced the government to place civil persons at the head of their armies, or military persons in whose abilities, science, and experience, they had no confidence—this system has invariably prevailed. In the course of the war, you have certainly seen some of their commanders-in-chief shine by their own light; but those who did so, were consummate generals.

In short, I think that instead of the experience of this war having diminished the importance of military instruction (as some people adverting to the armies of France have pretended), it has served to place its absolute necessity, and the eminent advantages that may be derived from it, in a more conspicuous light than

> any other war that is recorded in history. No more, I think, need be said to prove how indispensably the projected establishment is to insure the success of your military operations, with which the honour and prosperity of the Empire are so immediately combined. I have examined with attention your printed outline of a plan for the Military College, and I think it is in general well arranged. But in order to make it of the utmost possible immediate utility, it ought to be upon a more extensive scale. The departments ought not to be limited in number, and every step should be taken that can induce officers already in the service to resort to this seminary for instruction.

There was one letter addressed to him on this occasion which must have pleased him more than all the rest; it was from the Duke of Richmond. That high-minded nobleman praised his design in the strongest terms, and wished him the success that his abilities and perseverance deserved.

These suffrages to the merit of his plan were well-timed. The Duke of York being now secure of the support of some of the most distinguished political characters in the country, came forward actively as the avowed patron of the institution, and authorised Lieutenant-Colonel Le Marchant to choose the necessary professors—a trust he most conscientiously discharged. His first appointment was that of Mr. Isaac Dalby, (see note next page), to the mathematical chair, and the situation could not have been filled by an abler or a better man. One of the first practical mathematicians in England, the new professor was a perfect master of all those branches of science that were applicable to military operations. He excelled also in his mode of conveying instruction.

His language, though familiar, was remarkably perspicuous and precise, and he possessed a boundless store of illustrations, collected in a long and busy life, which had been passed in the indefatigable pursuit of science. His simple manners and benevolent disposition, beautifully harmonizing with the philosophical independence of his character, gave him an influence over his pupils, which their age and military habits made it difficult to obtain. Two other gentlemen were appointed to act as his colleagues, who were also very intelligent persons, and fully justified the preference they received, which does not appear to have been lightly given; for Lieutenant-Colonel Le Marchant says, in a letter to his wife:

Lord Moira has been with me several times to recommend one of his *protégées*; but I shall not think of him if I can find any one better qualified for the situation: whatever patronage I may hold, shall be for the benefit of men of ability. There is no room in the college for even a single drone.

******

Note:—Mr. Isaac Dalby, F.R.S. was born in a remote part of Cornwall. His parents were too poor to defray the expenses of a village-school, and he learnt to read and write in the tin mine where he passed his childhood. Some accident led him to seek his fortune in London. He made friends of a few individuals of great talent in his own class, one of whom, a shoe-maker, had the credit of being the author of the finest parts of Mickle's *Lusiad*, another was the celebrated Mr. Crabbe; and a third was that self-taught genius Mr. Thomas Simpson, the geometrician; but he lived most with mathematical instrument makers, many of whom were profound mathematicians; and by their assistance he cultivated a natural taste which he had for science, until he acquired considerable proficiency in it.

The mathematical club, held at this time in Spitalfields, by persons little above the degree of artisans, and to which *no gentleman* was, under any pretence, admissible, discussed questions that would have puzzled Royal Societies. Mr. Dalby was a distinguished member of this learned though humble body, and he would probably have not been known out of it, had not Mr. Wales, master of Christ's Hospital, the astronomer to the expedition under Captain Cook, taken him by the hand, and drawn his merit from obscurity. He contributed several papers on scientific subjects to the Royal Society, and was elected a fellow in the most flattering manner.

He was afterwards chosen by General Roy, to assist in the Trigonometrical Survey, which, after the death of the general, he continued in conjunction with Colonel Mudge, The account he published (in two volumes) of this laborious undertaking is a most valuable work, and it has been brought within the reach of the unlearned reader by Professor Playfair's popular and most elegant critique upon it, in the tenth number of the Edinburgh Review. Upon his appointment to the Mathematical chair at Wycombe, he published *A course of Mathematics for the Student of the Royal Military College*, in two volumes, which has gone through several editions, and he was a frequent contributor to the periodical publications on scientific subjects.

This excellent man passed the last sixteen years of his life at Wycombe, in the enjoyment of an income more than adequate to his wants, and of society that was fully sensible of his worth. He was an interesting specimen, perhaps one of the last, of the English philosophers of the old school. There was not a particle of refinement about him, and yet there was nothing coarse, or vulgar. What is termed strong sound sense was his great characteristic, and combined with his extensive knowledge of science, and a peculiar force of expression, it made him a delightful companion. I recollect a striking instance of his self-command. He was once attacked by an inflammation of the bowels, which the physicians at last pronounced to have come to a mortification. He received the intelligence with perfect calmness, and desired Colonel Le Marchant to be sent for, who found him employed, in reconciling his wife and daughter to his approaching dissolution. The poor women not acquiescing so cheerfully as he expected in his reasoning, he appealed to the colonel, whether the arguments he had used were not perfectly unanswerable. Contrary to all expectation, he recovered, and lived to deplore the loss of his patron, whose son cannot withhold this feeble but honest record of his merit.

★★★★★★

He was proceeding in his selection of the professors of fortification and military drawing in its various branches, when the Queen's Dragoon Guards, the regiment he then commanded, received orders for immediate embarkation on foreign service. His disappointment at this unexpected interruption was materially softened by the unsolicited permission accorded to him by the Government, to name some officer to hold his place in his absence, and he accordingly fixed on his friend the late Major Brock, of the 16th Light Dragoons, and then joined his regiment, which was one of the finest in the service, with the most sanguine expectations of distinguishing himself. He wrote to his wife, "I am determined to rise to the head of my profession; nothing but death shall stop me," and the following letter, which he received upon his departure, was not calculated to damp his confidence.

The Adjutant-General to Lieutenant-Colonel Le Marchant.

8th August, 1799.

I could have much wished, for the benefit of our young establishment at High Wycombe, that your services had not been required in the field this year, and, indeed, for the benefit of the service at large, I wish you could have been spared till the plan you have suggested and arranged, for a complete System of Military Education, (so essentially necessary, and, unfortunately, so long neglected in this country,) had been in such a state of forwardness as to have enabled those, who have the honour and reputation of the service much at heart, to have looked forward to its establishment and completion with confidence. Strange that we should expend such immense sums in the coarser materials and neglect those finer springs, which are to give life and motion to the whole piece of mechanism, and without which the machine can never arrive at that degree of perfection, which the excellence of its composition might promise. *Adieu!*—I wish you every possible success.

The expedition of which he was to form a part not taking place, he was released in the course of a few months from his regimental duties, and allowed to return to High Wycombe, where he found every thing precisely as he had left it, government having made no appointments after his departure; some of the most important departments were still left without instructors, no regular system of instruction could yet be attempted, and the fate of the institution seemed almost as doubtful as before. He saw that all depended on his own personal exertions, and it may be anticipated that he did not spare them. He hastened to London, and renewed his solicitations at the Horse Guards with fresh earnestness; but the duke could render him no farther assistance. His Royal Highness had strongly recommended his plan to the ministers, under whose consideration it had now been lying for some months, and they alone could carry it into effect. His Royal Highness also felt a laudable unwillingness to add to their embarrassments by any augmentation of the army estimates already of an unprecedented amount.

He now felt more forcibly than ever the difficulties of his situation. Hitherto he had been dealing with men of his own profession, whose pursuits naturally disposed them to regard his plan with a favourable eye; whilst their general knowledge of the subject in question greatly facilitated all his communications with them. These advantages abandoned him on his entrance into the Treasury, where he had to tread upon entirely new ground. The official gentlemen to whom he was now referred being strangers to him, naturally denied him the confidence he enjoyed at the Horse Guards, though they treated him with marked respect, as soon as they learnt an offer he had made to lend his services until the proposed institution should be fully established, and then retire without any other recompense than the honour of having thus contributed to so important a measure. Still they forced him to prove his case step by step, a process that frequently involved him in contests somewhat foreign to his ostensible vocation.

He was, however, by no means ill-adapted to succeed either in controversy or negotiation. The fallacies that are used with so much success against ordinary minds, were in general wasted on him. It was a maxim with him, to keep his mind steadily fixed upon his own views of the matter in question, and to be intent on pressing them as clearly and strongly as he could, without suffering his attention to be diverted from them by an over anxiety to answer the arguments of his opponent. This made him on all occasions a formidable disputant; and I have heard persons who lived much in his society at this period, observe, that the tact and skill with which he contrived to produce a favourable impression of his plan at the Treasury, would have done honour to an experienced diplomatist. It would be ungrateful to omit that he was far from being abandoned by his friends in such an emergency. Some of the noblemen, whose Yeomanry corps he had instructed in the sword-exercise, came forward strenuously to his support, and their influence was sure to be felt in any quarter where it was directed.

But his most effectual aid was derived from the Honourable John Villiers and Mr. Huskisson. These gentlemen were no sooner satisfied of the merit of his plan, than they adopted it as warmly as if it had been their own. Their familiarity with official business enabled them to point out the most proper course for him to pursue, and they spared no pains, in facilitating his progress through the magic circle that invariably surrounds the leading members of the administration. His memorials were thus prepared in the form best suited to the persons to whom they were addressed; and what was more important, they were sure to receive due consideration. But this was not all; the confidence so deservedly reposed by Mr. Pitt in these gentlemen, gave them opportunities which they never neglected, of directing his attention to the subject far more effectually than could have happened, had it come before him in the ordinary-routine of business, and the good effect of their exertions was soon visible. The following correspondence is sufficient to show how much the public are indebted to Mr. Huskisson for his disinterested zeal on the occasion,

Letter from Mr. Huskisson to Lieutenant-Colonel Le Marchant.

Downing-street, 2nd November, 1799.

You will receive your papers at the same time with this; I could not get at them sooner. I am glad to see you adhere to this subject with your usual perseverance, as I am convinced it will prove most beneficial to the public. The ministers are so completely satisfied that it will, that whatever delays you may experience with them, from the pressure of other national concerns, you may rest assured of their ultimately giving it every necessary support and protection, either from their own authority, or by application to Parliament, as may appear most proper. I hope none of your papers will be found missing, but I have not had time to ascertain that point.

Lieutenant-Colonel Le Marchant to Mrs. Le Marchant.

December 5,1799

Yesterday I received a letter from Mr. Huskisson, saying that Mr. Secretary Dundas wished to see me this morning, to hear the details of my plan from my own mouth. I sat up all-night to prepare myself for the interview, and at one o'clock I knocked at the great man's door, much pleased at the opportunity of telling my own tale. Well! we met, and I was half an hour with him; during which, I detailed my views of the Institution, and the necessity of making it a national establishment. He gave me a patient and uninterrupted hearing, and I very fortunately felt no hesitation or difficulty in relating what I had to say. I proposed, among other things, that the East India Company should pay 5000*l.* a-year towards the establishment; to which he assented, and told me, that as soon as I was prepared with my detail, he would lay it before the Chairman of the Board of Control; he added, that there was no doubt we were in want of this Military Institution, and he hoped what General Jarry had proposed did not interfere with my arrangements.

I told him, that on the contrary, we were acting together, and it was to be considered as a beginning of a more extensive system of instruction. He asked me what arrangements the duke was disposed to make: I told him that His Royal Highness waited my further detail: in the meantime, masters were providing, and every thing was doing which could with propriety be done at the present moment. He then desired to see me as soon as I should have satisfied the duke, and I departed, quite delighted with my reception.

The duke has in fact consented to all my propositions, and I have the entire confidence of the people in office. Lord Cathcart, Sir William Howe, and many others, yesterday at court, congratulated me on the excellence of my plan, and said I had done much for the public service. In short, God granting me health, I shall set my name high.

Mr. Huskisson to Lieutenant-Colonel Le Marchant.

December 18,1799.

Mr. Pitt has perused your papers, and appears very well inclined to give every necessary encouragement to the plans you have detailed. He is, however, of opinion, that they should be submitted to some military men, to report upon, before the whole plan is adopted and acted upon. I proposed to him General D. Dundas and Colonel Calvert, as proper persons, from their official situations, for this purpose, to which he readily assented; but expressed his regret that the general was absent, as it would be so much time lost. I mention this circumstance to satisfy you, that he feels a wish that the plan should not be delayed.

Another proof of it is, that he desires you will, either by yourself, or through Delancey, or any other channel, procure him particulars of the Duke of Newcastle's house, as it appears to him very desirable that it should be purchased immediately, if upon investigation it should be found to answer, and can be obtained on reasonable terms. I should have been glad to have seen you on these subjects, but I am obliged to go to Portsmouth tomorrow morning for some days, and must defer that pleasure until my return.

Mr. Pitt's suggestion was, of course, immediately adopted, and the business having thus travelled back to the Horse-Guards, the adjutant and quartermaster-generals were directed by the commander-in-chief to deliver their opinions upon it, for the information of the government.

The report of these officers, bearing date the 20th day of February,

1800, reviews the three departments proposed in the plan, and bestows high praise on all of them. It concludes in the following words:—

> On reviewing the whole of the subject, and the papers relating thereto, we beg leave strongly to express our sentiments of the very great importance of the former, and our opinion that the latter are so well arranged, and so entirely methodised, that it now requires nothing but His Majesty's sanction and royal approbation, to carry into immediate execution a measure long earnestly wished for, and most essentially conducive to the public welfare.

The Duke of York transmitted this report to Mr. Dundas, with the strongest assurances of his entire participation in the sentiments it contained,[8] and on the 14th of August following, his Royal Highness received a letter from that gentleman, written in the same spirit, with the report, and stating:

> That Mr. Pitt, who was equally aware of the national advantages that may be expected from the execution of this plan, had assured him of his readiness to propose to Parliament to grant whatever reasonable sum of money might finally, and after due discussion and deliberation, be found requisite for erecting the necessary buildings, and for accomplishing the other purposes of the proposed institution. Mr. Pitt, therefore, proposed that his Royal Highness should appoint a committee of general staff and other officers for examining and discussing the various plans, proposals, and suggestions which had hitherto been received upon the subject, and direct the committee, as soon as possible, to make a report upon the same, and prepare a plan, with estimates, and all necessary details of the building of the institution, and that they should also consider of proper regulations and statutes for the management thereof.

The Duke of York having taken the king's pleasure on this communication, His Majesty was pleased to nominate the following officers as a special committee for that purpose:—

President

His Royal Highness the Duke of York.

The Right Hon. Gen. Sir Wm. Fawcett, K.B.

Lieut.-Gen. the Hon. Wm. Harcourt.

8. The report dated the 10th day of February, 1801.

Lieut.-Gen. David Dundas, Quartermaster-Gen. of the Forces.
Lieut.-Gen. the Earl of Harrington.
Major-General Lord Cathcart.
Major-General Delancey, Barrack-Master-General.
Major-General the Earl of Chatham.
Colonel Calvert, Adjutant-Gen. of the Forces.
Lieut.-Colonel Le Marchant, Queen's Dragoon Guards.

The leading members of this committee had long approved of Lieutenant-Colonel Le Marchant's plan; and although their incorporation produced some modification of the opinion they had expressed as individuals, they gave him no reason for joining in the complaint which has so often been raised against deliberative assemblies of this description. The only portion of his plan that they rejected, was the course of instruction for the Legion; and this they did on the ground that it was inconsistent with the habits of the country to raise private soldiers to so close an equality with their officers, as well as from the apprehension that the measure might prove injurious to the service at large, by leading to frequent promotions from the ranks, which Sir David Dundas observed had been the case in the French army during the Revolution, when the soldiers constantly deserted, rather than be commanded by their former comrades.

Some slight alterations were made in the arrangement of the details, and before the end of the year, the committee delivered their report, in which they recommended the institution to be established under His Majesty's warrant, and submitted such a warrant, as they thought would answer the end in view, to the consideration of ministers. They showed their sense of the importance of the institution, by proposing the sum 146,000*l.* to be laid out in building a proper edifice for its reception.

The report[9] was accompanied by a letter from the Duke of York to the Secretary of War, urging immediate selection of the different professors necessary for carrying on the institution, and concluding in these words:

> The committee have farther desired me to express, in very strong terms, the sense they entertain of the ability and uninterrupted assiduity which Lieutenant-Colonel Le Marchant has displayed, in preparing and arranging the very intricate and voluminous details necessary to bring this important object to the state in

9. The report and letter are dated the 2nd of December, 1801.

> which it is now presented to His Majesty's ministers; and from a consideration of the unavoidable expenses to which he has been exposed, during the long period he has been engaged in this undertaking, they recommend that he shall receive, not less as a token of approbation, than as a just remuneration for the same, the sum of 500*l.*

Lord Hobart (Secretary of State) immediately forwarded the king's warrant for 500*l.* with expressions of his high sense of Lieutenant-Colonel Le Marchant's merit.

The warrant was confined[10] to the formation and necessary government of the Institution already established at High Wycombe, and it appointed a Supreme Board of Commissioners, consisting of the Commander-in-Chief, the Secretary at War, and the heads of the great military departments for the time being, with others of high rank in the army, to form a Board for managing and controlling the affairs of the same. It also conferred upon the Institution the title of "The Royal Military College."

The committee having approved of two branches of Lieutenant-Colonel Le Marchant's plan, *viz.* that for the instruction of officers, as well as that for the instruction of young men destined to be officers, the lieutenant-colonel was not a little disappointed at the latter being entirely omitted in the warrant. Even with this omission, the warrant was still thought by the ministry to be too extensive; and notwithstanding the sanction of one of the most distinguished committees that had ever sat on military matters, it still lingered in the government offices, and month after month wore away without any prospect of its receiving His Majesty's signature. In the meantime the Institution had begun to excite the animosity of those who regarded it as a tacit reflection on their own want of professional knowledge; it did not escape some sneers in the debate on the Army Estimates, and all the efforts of Lieutenant-Colonel Le Marchant were scarcely sufficient to keep alive the interest that had been so warmly expressed in its behalf by the members of the committee.

His own patience at last began to give way, and finding govern-

10. The committee give as a reason for the brevity of the warrant, that they conceive "that the arrangement of the details relating to the interior economy, discipline, and instruction of the College, which has been with great labour and ability prepared by Lieutenant-Colonel Le Marchant, will most properly be submitted to the Supreme Board whenever His Majesty may be pleased to give his Royal Sanction to the Warrant."—*Report*, p. 5.

ment, after an investigation that had lasted more than two years, as undecided as ever, he more than once thought of throwing up his command and returning to his regiment. These desponding purposes, however, did not render him less attentive to the Institution. No sooner had the committee been nominated, than he procured the appointment of four additional professors, one of Field Fortification, two of Military Drawing, and one of the German language; a measure that awoke the activity of the students, and led to a well-organised system of military instruction, in which General Jarry's various qualifications were exercised to the greatest effect. Fortune too, for once, favoured his zeal.

The expedition under Sir Ralph Abercrombie offered him an opportunity not to be neglected, of employing some of the officers who were most forward in their studies; and three of them were accordingly appointed to the quartermaster-general's staff of the Egyptian Army. Their conduct proved the judgment with which they were selected, and considering the short time they had passed at the establishment, they must have possessed no ordinary talent and industry to have carried so much knowledge away from it. Their merit is recorded by the historian of that short but brilliant war,[11] and his praise has been confirmed by the testimony of one of the most enlightened French writers of the present day, (as at time of first publication).[12]

The success of the Wycombites as they were termed, in Egypt, entirely changed the tone of public opinion at home. All parties now united in praising an Institution that had given such early and incontrovertible proofs of its usefulness; and the opposition which Lieuten-

11. Sir Robert Wilson, after expressing, his thanks generally to those officers of the Staff Corps and Quartermaster-General's Department, who had rendered him assistance, mentions "Major Birch, and the officers of the Military College, by whose united labours the original work was perfected during the campaign, notwithstanding the severity of their other duties. *N.B.* Major Birch was senior officer, and under his immediate and active superintendence the country was reconnoitred, and the plans traced."

12. "The pupils of this school (the Military College) were tried for the first time, in the Egyptian expedition. They were of the greatest service on that occasion, as at the time the British Staff were in total ignorance of the manner of directing the march of troops; and of choosing, on a rapid survey of ground, the most advantageous positions and routes. The success of the first pupils of the school for the staff, opened the eyes of government to the importance of such an Institution: it was rendered permanent, and united to the school which had just been founded for cadets for the infantry and cavalry, the whole establishment being termed 'The Military College.'"—Dupin's *Military Force of Great Britain,*

ant-Colonel Le Marchant had so long experienced fell entirely to the ground. The following letter shows how highly he appreciated the exertions of the first students who were employed on active service.

Lieut.-Colonel Le Marchant to Major Birch, (later Major-General Birch Reynardson), Assistant Quartermaster-General in Egypt.

High Wycombe, 9th May, 1801.

Many thanks for all your letters; the last was dated the 16th February, off Marmorice. Accept my most hearty congratulations on the very handsome manner Colonel Anstruther[13] speaks of you and the Wycombites. In his last despatches he says, "the officers sent me from Jarry's are of infinite use, and the details of the several actions fought by this army are accompanied by plans in drawing, executed by Major Birch and the officers from Wycombe, in a style of perfection that does them great credit." I saw this encomium upon you and my friends at the Secretary of State's.

Continue your exertions, and they will place you high in the most honourable rank of your profession.

The establishment is improving in science daily. I have some very intelligent officers here at present, and government is so sensible of the advantages to the country which the establishment is producing, that we receive the greatest possible encouragement. The moment an officer is qualified for the staff, he is immediately appointed, and any who have reasonable claims to promotion are attended to. In short, we are in high feather, and the credit which the world is willing to allow us exceeds my warmest expectations.

In regard to my progress in rendering the college a national institution, I have been equally fortunate. This week it is to be brought before Parliament, and the Secretary at War assures me there is no likelihood of opposition: indeed your conduct, joined to those of the establishment with you, have materially contributed to fix the opinion of the public as to its utility to the service. The poor king's illness, and the unexpected change of ministry, threw me back for the moment; but I set to work with such expedition, and found the minds of the new government so well disposed towards my plan, that I experienced no difficulty.

13. Quartermaster-General of the Expedition.

The classes, progress of studies, &c. are all better arranged than when you were here, yet notwithstanding, the establishment is more difficult to conduct; fine gentlemen cabal together and discourage the industrious, which must be the case until I have a book of statutes confirmed by order of His Majesty, and this I expect shortly.

Stuart will show you some very interesting lectures by General Jarry on the march of armies. Study them with attention, for they are of the highest importance. I have added some drawings with a stump, according to a style and plan of my own. It is reduced to a system, the effect of which is certain, and it is quick in the execution. It executes as readily with a pen.

We see no immediate prospects of peace, therefore you have a fine game to play. I have particularly recommended you to General Floyd,[14] and with Stuart at his elbow,[15] it will be your fault alone, if your exertions do not meet with due encouragement. The general is an experienced and gallant soldier, and no one is more sensible of the advantages of military instruction; so that whatever may be proposed to him of real utility, depend upon it, will be most effectually supported. You see that your interest is pushing at home, whilst you are labouring to lay the foundation of success abroad. Recollect all I have told you on the head of exertions. It is only by doing what others do not, that you are to build your hopes of preferment.

General Jarry is very well, and I hope will yet live to see the great establishment in activity."

In a few weeks after the date of the preceding letter, the warrant received the Royal Assent, and the Institution was placed upon a permanent footing. His Majesty was also pleased to direct by another warrant that the regulations prepared by Lieutenant-Colonel Le Marchant "should be observed as the Statutes for the Government and conduct of the First Department of the Royal Military College." These statutes regarded the duties of the officers: the qualifications necessary for the admission of students, the studies to be pursued,[16]

14. General Floyd had been appointed to succeed Sir Ralph Abercrombie, but the appointment was rescinded, and he was sent to Ireland. He had served with great distinction in India, in command of the cavalry under Lord Cornwallis.

15. Sir James Stuart, Bart, *aide-de-camp* to General Floyd.

16. Some account of these studies will be found in the appendix, having been drawn up at my request by one of the most distinguished staff-officers in the army.

and the manner in which they were to be conducted; and they regulated the allowances of forage, coals, and candles, to the several officers, professors, and service of the department.

About the same time, Lieutenant-General the Honourable William Harcourt was appointed the Governor, and at the special recommendation of the Committee, General Jarry, the Director-General of Instruction, and Lieutenant-Colonel Le Marchant, the Lieutenant-Governor and Superintendant-General of the Royal Military College.

The time was now rapidly approaching for Lieutenant-Colonel Le Marchant's triumph to be complete. On the 4th of May, 1802, His Majesty was pleased to issue his warrant for the formation and government of the Junior Department of the Royal Military College for the instruction of those who from early life were intended for the military profession, and who might thereby be grounded in science previously to their attaining the age that enables them, consistently with the regulations, to hold commissions in the army; and to afford a provision also for the orphan sons of those meritorious officers who had fallen or been disabled in the service of their country, as well as for the sons of those officers who, from pecuniary difficulties, might not otherwise be able to give them a proper education."

The same warrant directed the formation of a Collegiate Board, consisting of the governor, lieutenant-governor, and commandant, for the interior government and regulations of the two departments, more particularly for providing the supplies, and examining and settling all the accounts of the college. All these documents were drawn up by Lieutenant-Colonel Le Marchant, under the superintendence of the Supreme Board, and some notion may be formed of their comprehensive and complicated nature by referring to the annexed table of the strength of the establishment. Whatever changes were afterwards made in them by subsequent warrants, they continued to form the groundwork of the system upon which the Royal Military College was conducted on its most extensive scale at the close of the late war.

Chapter 3

Difficulties to Contend With

The Royal Military College being thus raised to the highest rank of the national establishments of this description, Lieutenant-Colonel Le Marchant resigned the command of the Queen's Dragoon Guards, and entered upon the duties of his new office with the sanguine hopes which his hard-earned success was calculated to inspire. In the course of a few months he had the gratification of seeing the and the professors at their respective posts, the number of students complete, and both the senior and junior departments of the college in full activity.

This was the brightest period of his life. He passed from a state divided between suspense and disappointment into one of unmingled and unqualified satisfaction. The views he had so warmly cherished, and so resolutely maintained, were, at length, realized, and his heart glowed with the consciousness that he had conferred an essential benefit upon his country. More fortunate than most public benefactors—he had received his reward. He had been appointed, without any solicitation on his part, to the most distinguished, as well as the most lucrative, post in the service that was compatible with his rank, and, to crown all, his wife and children were the witnesses and partners of his elevation.

Hitherto he had been the chief and responsible officer of the establishment, and although he ceased to be so from the date of the governor's nomination, he was too much identified with it, to allow that, or any other circumstance to produce the least intermission of his labours. They were, however, confined to a more limited sphere, and no detailed account of them could be made sufficiently interesting to do them justice. His immediate province was the charge of the senior department of the college at High Wycombe, where he had to contend with the various obstacles that are the usual accompaniments of young institutions.

He soon found the number of students that thronged to the college upon its opening, to be a very delusive test of its prosperity. More of them were actuated by a wish to escape from their regimental duties than by zeal for the improvement of their professional attainments. All were young, and unaccustomed to the restrictions indispensable for the maintenance of order in such an establishment;—indeed, the assemblage of so large a body of officers for the mere purpose of instruction, was an event wholly unprecedented in our military annals. Instances of insubordination were not long in making their appearance, and being generally directed against the professors, these gentlemen required the constant superintendence and support of the lieutenant-governor to enable them to discharge their duties effectually. General Jarry was more than once the object of this sort of persecution, and, to say the truth, his foreign habits and eccentric character would sometimes provoke a smile from the gravest of his admirers. Expecting the same deference and courtesy from the young officers about him that he had experienced in the courts and armies abroad, he overlooked the little tricks that were first played upon him, but the moment he discovered himself to be regarded as an insignificant schoolmaster, he withdrew from the society of the students, and even went so far, on one occasion, as to discontinue his lectures, which it was a considerable time before the lieutenant-governor could prevail upon him to resume.

The following extract from a letter which has been addressed to the author by a general officer who was, I believe, the earliest student at the college, gives one of the many proofs that might be adduced of the energy and good sense of the lieutenant-governor in promoting the welfare of the establishment.

> General Jarry, in order to illustrate his able Lectures on Field Fortification, had himself constructed models, and placed them in the halls of study, and they had been found of the greatest use. Among other acts of insubordination of the junior officers was the total destruction of these models. The general felt indignant at such wanton mischief, and although he said little, he did not condescend again to exercise his ingenuity for the benefit of those so little worthy of it, and these valuable specimens were never restored. To counteract this more than irregularity, Colonel Le Marchant saw at once the necessity of some

decisive step, or the establishment would have dwindled into a mere excuse for idle officers to absent themselves from their regiments. He made himself acquainted with the characters of all: ascertained who the offending parties were, did not visit them with any punishment at the time, by which he avoided cabal and ill-will, but either caused them to be recalled to their regiments, or gave them intimation on the first vacation that they were not to return to the college.

Nothing but this judicious and decisive step on the part of the lieutenant-governor would have prevented the ruin of the establishment at its earliest stage, although it was adopted to a certain degree at the hazard of his popularity; but a sense of duty and strict integrity operated on this, as in every other action of this upright officer through life. By dismissing the idle and ignorant, and retaining those in whom he discovered (in concert with General Jarry) a wish and ability to improve themselves, and in whom he could place confidence, he established the firm foundation of an establishment which has proved of so much real benefit to the army.

The insubordination was not confined within the walls of the college; and the quiet inhabitants of the neighbourhood not relishing the part they were sometimes forced to take in the amusements of their military guests, harassed the lieutenant-governor with complaint, (see note following), which it required both firmness and address to satisfy. He managed, however, to establish, by degrees, a discipline and good order which continued the subject of admiration in the place long after his decease.

★★★★★★

Note:—I cannot help noticing one of these complaints from the ludicrous circumstances attending it. Two officers happened to be sauntering on the banks of the river Wye, when they saw a rich and respectable farmer in his boat fishing; they very unceremoniously hailed him, and desired to be rowed some distance up the stream. He complied at once, and took them in, but before they had reached the spot, they suddenly seized him by the waist, and, without saying a word, flung him into the water, and then rowed away, leaving him to get to the shore as he could. Fortunately, he was not out of his depth, and escaped with a ducking. The next day he called on the lieutenant-governor, and told his tale, which, of course, excited much indignation, and he was assured that the offenders should be promptly and severely punished. The good man, who was a Quaker, seemed much distressed at this result, and begged that it might not be. "Why then," said the lieutenant-governor, "have you mentioned the matter to *me*—what could have been your object?" "Only," replied the Quaker, "that you should desire them not to treat me so again."

★★★★★★

He exercised his authority with the strictest impartiality, and although of an irascible temperament he never was betrayed into an act even bordering on injustice. One of the most marked features of his character was uprightness; not that accommodating, pusillanimous uprightness which is found in ordinary minds, but an active, inflexible, unalterable principle which actuated him in all his proceedings. It shone so forcibly, and yet so unostentatiously in every thing he did, that the students invariably entertained the deepest respect for him, and I have known him most warmly praised by those who had been the greatest sufferers from his severity. At the same time, he knew still better how to reward than to punish, and every student who had gained distinction at the college, was henceforward secure of his support; indeed the extensive patronage (in the quartermaster-general's department,) entrusted to him by government, was exclusively distributed among such students without regard to friendship or connections; and some of the first officers in the service thus owe their early appointments to his disinterestedness and discernment.

The junior department for the instruction of gentlemen cadets intended for the army, being on too large a scale to be accommodated at Wycombe, it was established at Great Marlow, as being the nearest place affording the requisite conveniences. It was under the immediate charge of its commandant, who resided on the spot, and enforced the regulations applicable to the establishment subject to the control of the governor and lieutenant-governor. The latter received weekly a detailed report of the state of every branch of it, and he never failed to go to Marlow, at least, twice every week, when he inspected the cadets, went through their halls of study, and from his own observations, and the reports of the professors, made himself acquainted with their progress.

No instance of individual merit was likely to be overlooked by him, and many young men of humble fortunes were materially forwarded by his support; whilst others were reclaimed from idleness and vice by his stern but impressive admonitions. Few persons possessed the art of reproving with such effect. The severe expression of his features, combined with the dignity of his manner and the deep tones of his voice, struck his youthful audience with an awe which some of them did not forget even amidst the stirring scenes of military life. It is right to add, that his kindness was at least equally appreciated, and produced in after times the most honourable tributes to his memory.[1]

One great object of his care, was the administration of the finances of the college. He was anxious to make the Institution as little burdensome to the nation as possible; and with this view, he was always on the watch to prevent waste or peculation in any of its departments. He examined the voluminous accounts of its expenditure with an assiduity which he never bestowed on his own domestic affairs; and many serious abuses were thus brought to light, which otherwise would have passed unnoticed. The mass of papers in his own handwriting which he left behind him on this subject, is almost incredible; and they show a knowledge of business, and a talent for economical arrangement, which men of his profession are seldom found to possess.

The office of the lieutenant-governor being subordinate to that of the governor, the constant correspondence that passed between them was a serious addition to the duties of the former. He was averse to carry on business of any importance by conversation, when it could be done in writing, which he conceived to be the best check on bad men, and the best security to good.[2] He used to say that this habit had

1. One instance of this occurred to me very recently. I wrote to an officer, whom I had understood to have witnessed my father's death, requesting him to give me the particulars of it; I also begged his acceptance of my father's portrait. The officer acquainted me in reply, that I had been misinformed, and that his only knowledge of my father was from having been a cadet at Marlow;—the close of the letter is so elegant, that I cannot help transcribing it: "Pray accept my best thanks for your offer of sending me your father's portrait, although I feel that I am not entitled to it, not having ever had the good fortune to have been under his orders: yet, should it find no more worthy destination, I shall accept, and keep it, with the sentiments that every one must have, who had, however slightly, known such a man."

2. The Duc de Bouillon, one of the most artful adventurers in the times of Henry the Fourth, had a maxim: *qu'il falloit se défier du temoignage de la main.* "*On explique,*" said he, "*comme on veut ce qu'on a dit, on n'en convient même qu'autant qu'il est à propos de le faire, on se retranche sur le plus ou le moins; on accorde ou l'on nie selon qu'il convient.*" The French commentator on Sully quotes this passage, and adds, "*M. de Sully étoit dans les maximes toutes contraires. Il pourra se trouver quelques politiques qui ne blamoient pas le Duc de Bouillon, mais il n'y aura personne qui ne loue le Duc de Sully.*"

on one occasion saved him from utter ruin. His official letters, purely relating to college matters, during the nine years he held his command, fill five massive folios.

The duties of the lieutenant-governor were necessarily increased by the declining health of General Jarry, as the lieutenant-governor became the principal channel of communication between the students and the general, and never failed to attend him in his lectures in the field.

The general's illness was tedious and trying. At the beginning of the year 1807 he grew much worse, and finding his end near at hand, he sent for the lieutenant-governor, and acknowledging in warm terms the benefits he had experienced from their friendship, he recommended his family, whom he was about to leave almost destitute, to the lieutenant-governor's protection. He shortly after expired, and the lieutenant-governor, with the assistance of Lord William Bentinck, obtained for his widow and each of his children a pension of 100*l. per annum*.

******

Note:—I find this letter among the lieutenant-governor's papers:

Letter from the lieutenant-governor to Mr. Gomme, Undertaker, at High-Wycombe.

Sir,

You will please to cause the remains of General Jarry to be enclosed in an oak coffin, and on the plate you will engrave the following inscription,

Francis Jarry,
a General Officer, Knight of the Military Order of St. Louis,
and Inspector-General of Instruction
at the Royal Military College.
Died on the 15th of March, 1807.—Aged 75.

******

The following letter is a pleasing mark of the lieutenant-governor's warmth of feeling on this occasion.

Letter from Colonel Le Marchant to General Sir James Pultney, K. B.

February 14th, 1808.

I have been honoured with the receipt of your letter of yesterday's date, and I beg to say that I shall with great readiness

General Jarry from a sketch by
Lieut.-Gen. B. Reynardson

become a trustee jointly with Lieutenant-Colonel Douglas[3] for Madame Jarry's pension; but I regret to learn that the pension in question can be granted only when the funds of the Treasury will admit of it Though Madame Jarry may thus ultimately be assured of a provision being made for her and her daughters, the period may yet be distant, whilst their necessities are most pressing.

General Jarry has been dead nearly twelve months, during which time his widow and daughters have subsisted on a trifling sum, that was left at the general's death, but which, if not entirely expended, is nearly so. I therefore entreat, that you may consider of some means of ensuring to these poor sufferers a competency from some other fund than the Pension List, waiting the period when they may become pensioners.

Lieutenant-Colonel Douglas desires me to say that he has no objection whatever to become trustee to the pension proposed to be granted General Jarry's family.

I cannot end this chapter without expressing my regret that none of the officers who profited so much by the instructions of General Jarry, should have favoured the public with any particulars of his life. He was not only a companion of Frederick the Great during the whole of the Seven Years' War,[4] in the course of which he received several severe wounds, but one of the twelve individuals whom that monarch mentions to have himself instructed in the duties of the quartermaster-general's department. Invited to France by General Dumouriez at the beginning of the Revolution, he held a high command in the army of that officer, and shared the glories of the celebrated campaign of Jemappe. The French historians have accused him of unnecessary cruelty in burning the suburbs of Antwerp; but as he has escaped the censure of the most severe military critics, he probably did no more than his duty. Be that as it may, he was one of the few emigrant generals whom Napoleon strove to recall to their native standards. Overtures of the most advantageous nature were made him in the short peace of 1803,

---

3. Later Major-General Sir Howard Douglas, Bart C.B. and K.S.C. and Governor of New Brunswick. He was at this time the Commandant of the Senior Department of the College, and after General Jarry's death he discharged the duties of the office of Inspector-General of Instruction. He is author of a well-known *Treatise on Naval Gunnery* and various other scientific works.

4. *Frederick the Great & the Seven Years' War* by F. W. Longman is also published by Leonaur.

and he would readily have availed himself of them had the English Government allowed him to do so. His value was too well known for him to be spared.

I have heard him described as a man of extraordinary quickness and decision, and one of the best staff officers of the day: (see note following), but these are qualities which I am not competent to delineate.

******

Note:—A favourite pupil of the general, to whom I owe the letter which appears in a former page of this chapter, has favoured me with the following communication.

> General Jarry was a native of France, but he entered the Prussian army very young, and served on the personal staff of Frederick the Great during the most eventful campaigns of that king's reign. At the close of the war, he was placed at the head of the Military School at Berlin, where he continued as long as his patron lived. He once, indeed, resigned his command, owing to some difference with the court, but the king could not spare him, and he was speedily recalled and replaced. To show the sort of estimation in which his talents were held, I may mention a circumstance that occurred at Harwich, when I was on duty there. General Dumouriez had just landed from the Continent, and I introduced myself to him, knowing that General Jarry had formerly served under him.
>
> I mentioned the general's name, and how I had become acquainted with him. Dumouriez observed, that I was very fortunate in having been able to avail myself of the instruction of General Jarry, for he considered him *one of the cleverest officers in any service.* Perhaps this authority is superfluous, when I add, that the general lived on the most friendly footing with Frederick the Great, as well as with his brother, the still greater Prince Henry. Many an anecdote have I heard him relate of both; but my faithless memory only retains a general impression that he raised my admiration of these extraordinary men almost as high as his own.
>
> The general, like most men of genius, had his peculiarities, and one of them was a *penchant* for cookery. He used to say that no man could be a good general without being a

good cook; for a man could not know how to feed an army who did not know how to feed himself. He told us that his old master, Prince Henry, had been of the same opinion, and moreover, was a competitor with him in this noble art; and that they often tried their skill dish by dish, when the general usually vanquished, which is probable enough; for the little dinners he gave us at Wycombe were in truth most excellent, and he always prepared them with his own hands, a superannuated old woman being his only domestic.

All his leisure hours in spring and summer he would devote to his garden, even sowing the small seeds himself. He watched with a jealous eye the depredations of the sparrows, and kept a gun loaded by his side to shoot them. He would lay his victims in a row, and say with satisfaction, '*J'ai bien tué de mes ennemis aujourd'hui.*' His labours were not thrown away, for his salads were as much prized as his stews.

I merely mention these trifles as illustrating the simplicity of his character, and to show how entirely he was free from the defects that are ascribed to the Prussian generals of his day. His manners were easy and refined, and there was nothing of "the haughty quartermaster" about them; indeed, so far from attaching any undue importance to drills and dress, he carried his indifference to the externals of discipline much farther than I should have expected from so old a soldier. I recollect a new comer at the college having written to him, in the absence of the lieutenant-governor, to know what was the necessary equipment, he forwarded the application to me with the following letter:

Cher Major,

Je viens de recevoir une lettre avec des questions si profondes, que je n'ai pas assez de science pour y de répondre. Comme vous êtes maintenant Commandant de l'Ecole Royale, de High Wycombe, je vous prie d'informer le gentilhomme qui m'a écrit de vos propres intentions au sujetdes bottes, des gaiters, et des pantalons, car sous ce point ce sont vos ordres qu'il faut prendre, et non pas les miens.

Bon jour, et les pieds chauds,

Jarry

CHAPTER 4

Treatises on Military Subjects

There are few authors whose real merit is capable of being ascertained with exactness. A French bibliographer has filled four bulky volumes [1] with a catalogue of anonymous publications, many of which would do credit to any name; and it would be impossible to enumerate the different works which being intercepted in their passage to the press, have thereby left the world in ignorance of the pains that have been bestowed upon them.[2] Thus the productions of our minds are subject to the same capricious destiny as ourselves, and whatever may be their excellence, they are often indebted to a happy combination of fortuitous circumstances for their escape from obscurity.

These observations are strictly applicable to the subject of this sketch. His life was passed in a constant and judicious exercise of his abilities; his pen was always in his hand; yet little that he wrote ever came before the public. His profession was, therefore, ignorant of his labours, and as the time is now past for them to be appreciated, I shall only notice such of his works as were composed whilst he held his

1. Barbier's *Dictionnaire des Anonymes*, 4 vols. 8vo. a work of great research and accuracy.

2. The MSS. of Alexander Selkirk are said to have assisted Defoe in his composition of Robinson Crusoe, (*The Robinson Crusoe Trilogy* by Daniel Defoe & Samuel Griswold Goodrich features *The Story of Andrew Selkirk*, and is also published by Leonaur.); and Llorente has given some specious arguments for believing that Le Sage borrowed the most interesting parts of Gil Blas from certain MSS. which he found in the library of the Marquis de Lyonne. Observaciones *Criticas sobre Gil Blas, Madrid*, 1822. *The Life of Bertrand de Mornay*, which was not published till two centuries after the death of its writer, is one of the best works extant on the religious wars of France. Mrs. Hutchinson's *Memoirs* narrowly escaped the fate to which Mr. Warburton's cook consigned Massinger's MSS. plays; and I recollect the MSS. autobiography of a great statesman in one of the most important periods of our history being sold almost as waste paper at a country auction.

post at the College, and are connected with the studies which it was the object of the Institution to promote.

In the year 1801, he submitted to the commander-in-chief, "*A Plan for Recruiting the Army*," which the adjutant-general strongly recommended the government to carry into effect; and although not adopted at the time, it served as the basis of sundry regulations subsequently issued on the same subject by the War Office. Whilst it remained under consideration, he furnished Mr. Yorke, the Secretary at War, with "*A Plan for the General Enrolment, and Effectual Discipline of the Population of the Country capable of bearing Arms*," the substance of which was introduced into an Act passed at the close of the session of 1803.

His next work was more ambitious in its design, and more elaborate in its execution. In preparing the course of studies for the senior department of the Military College, he had been led to bestow great attention on the nature and object of the *Etat Major*, and he not only examined the practice of our service, but collected and compared the different systems that prevailed in the Continental armies, and discussed them with officers who had seen them in operation. The result was a volume of 280 pages, entitled *An Outline of the General Staff of the Army*, presenting a complete system, the various branches of which were analysed with much precision, and the duties of staff officers, more particularly of the quartermaster-general's department, detailed at considerable length. His Royal Highness the Commander-in-Chief, to whom it was submitted in December 1802, expressed a very favourable opinion of its merits, as did some of the highest military authorities; but an innovation of such magnitude was too serious an experiment to be tried, except partially; and where this has been done, which frequently happened during the late war, the service has been essentially benefited.

The following remarks on this treatise have been furnished me by the distinguished officer.

> The practice of a long war had allotted to the several departments of the army their respective portions of its general business, and the correspondence and connections required for the fulfilment of their duties, had been gradually established as a system which was recognised in practice, *although no authorised written instruction existed*, to point out how that system was to be traced and maintained.

Under these circumstances, the proposal of Colonel Le Marchant was highly useful; and if its arrangements were not wholly adopted, there is little doubt of their having in a great measure given rise to many of the Orders and Instructions which have since been published, relating to the duties of departments, their correspondence, &c.

Indeed, with little variation from the plan proposed, a small corps was actually formed of officers selected from those who had studied at High Wycombe, whose duties were to be confined to the quartermaster general's department; from which corps it was intended that the army should be supplied at all times with officers competent to direct and discharge the duties of the department, and it furnished many of the officers who served in the quartermaster-general's department in Spain and Portugal.

This useful corps has become a permanent branch of the quartermaster-general's department, and is now maintained on the modified principles of a peace establishment.

But one of the most valuable suggestions of Colonel Le Marchant, and from the adoption of which the greatest benefit was derived in the field, was his plan for the formation of a "Staff Corps." The operations of the army in the Peninsula were greatly facilitated by the services of the "Staff Corps;" its assistance was always ready at hand, either for the usual duties of the quartermaster-general's department, or of those of engineers or artificers.

From constant practice, it acquired extraordinary resources in expedients; and often with very rude and slender means overcame obstacles which otherwise must have greatly delayed and embarrassed military movements. The history of the war will record the able and useful works that were conducted by the Staff Corps, and do justice to the talents and activity of the officers who superintended them.

The appointment of Mr. Windham as Secretary of State for War and the Colonies, in 1806, gave Lieutenant-Colonel Le Marchant a patron who kept his pen in constant activity. His bold views, and his independent expressions of them, were in perfect congeniality with the characteristics of Mr. Windham's own mind, but it was to another quality that he owed the confidence with which he was honoured by that great statesman. He possessed a very comprehensive understanding, capable of embracing the most minute details, and presenting them with equal accuracy and precision. In whatever he undertook, his first step was to collect all the facts that he could discover to bear upon the question before him; and he suspended his judgment until he had patiently and rigorously sifted and examined them. No multitude of facts, no complication of detail, could weary or bewilder him, and he had both a tenacity of memory and a passion for arrangement that admirably suited such investigations. Moreover, he had the prudence to confine himself exclusively to professional subjects. Hence he was a most useful auxiliary to a minister whose fertile genius would sometimes lead him to positions too startling to be admitted, without the support of more confirmatory illustrations than his employments allowed him leisure to collect.

Many of Mr. Windham's measures, previously to their being brought before Parliament, were privately submitted to Lieutenant-Colonel Le Marchant, and the latter was frequently called upon for advice and assistance, which Mr. Windham knew so well to turn to the best account.

The following letter relates to an interesting topic, which was the subject of much correspondence and discussion between them.

The Right Honourable William Windham to Lieutenant-Colonel Le Marchant.

22nd Feb. 1806.

You will easily conceive that many speculations are afloat about possible measures, if any such can be found, for the improvement of our military means of defence. Whatever may be done or thought of in that way, should be founded on a careful consideration of things as they have hitherto subsisted; and therefore I have been very desirous, before I venture to settle any thing even in my own mind, or to determine whether any thing could be done or not, to have before me as large a collection of data as possible. Many such, I understand, your active attention to the subject has procured, particularly on a point on which I have always wished for information, and which must enter much into most questions respecting the formation and constitution of our army.

I mean the ordinary duration of men's military service; in other words, the comparative number found in the army of different ages. You would oblige me much by favouring me with any communications on this, or any point which you might think useful; and I am too well aware both of your zeal for the public good, as well as your obliging attention towards me, not to flatter myself that you will excuse as well as comply with my application.

The application was complied with, and I suppose satisfactorily, as I find Mr. W's grateful acknowledgements of the answer. This circumstance probably led to Lieutenant-Colonel Le Marchant's completion of a work in which he appears to have been occupied for some years. The nature of this sketch precludes any farther notice of it here than the following transcript of the table of its contents.

Outline of a General Organisation of the Military Establishment of Great Britain.

The Army shall consist of a disposable force, to be raised by voluntary enlistment for a limited term of years, according to the Schedule No. 1.[3]

In lieu of the militia, a corps to be raised by ballot, for the service of the United Kingdoms—to become the second battalions of established regiments, and under the command of regular officers. To be regulated according to the Schedule No. 2.

The Yeomanry and Volunteers, under certain regulations, free of expense to the public, according to Schedule No. 3.

A general enrolment of the people under the denomination of the British phalanx, and according to Schedule No. 4.

A general organisation of the Staff of the Army according to a determinate principle, adverting to the number of troops embodied, and the military organization of the country as well in peace as war, according to Schedule No. 5.

An organisation of a peace establishment, in order that the country may be prepared for war without incurring the heavy expenses inci-

3. The system of limited service has been of late years much condemned, with what justice I am not competent to decide; but it must be allowed the merit of having greatly improved the character of the soldier. I have heard experienced general officers observe, that the recruits whom it attracted were of a higher class than previously enlisted; and the moral effect of this was considerable; besides, it gave an impulse to enlistment, which was very much wanted at the time, when men were obtained with extreme difficulty. Pensions were perhaps somewhat lavishly granted; but the crisis was such as to excuse the employment of any honourable means of encouraging the patriotism of the people.

dent to frequent armaments, according to Schedule No. 6.

A plan for assembling the population of the country in case of invasion, with reference to a plan of defence, according to Schedule No. 7.

CHAPTER 5

Pursuits Whilst at the College

The favourite occupation of his leisure hours was drawing, in which he was originally self-taught. His early essays during his residence at Gibraltar, are numerous and elaborate. They give a very correct notion of the places they are intended to represent; but they are not free from the stiffness and coldness which are almost inseparable from the works of the painstaking but uninstructed student. On his return to England, he was quartered for some time in Devonshire and Cornwall, where his close and unwearied observation of nature made him feel the necessity of additional knowledge. He accordingly became a pupil of Payne, and it is surprising how rapidly and happily he seized the manner of his master, especially as the only lessons he ever took were during his negotiations with government for establishing the Military College; a business one would suppose, quite sufficient to engross the attention of any ordinary man.

He belonged to this school long enough to perceive its inferiority to that of Mr. Glover, under whose tuition he proceeded upon more judicious principles until he had formed a style for himself, which bore no slight resemblance to Dewint's, having the same boldness of conception, and the same clear, distinct outline that distinguishes the works of that excellent artist. The principal merit of his drawings, however, is their fidelity, which was in some degree ensured by the mode in which they were executed. Instead of trusting to recollection or fancy, he invariably finished his drawing on the spot, at a single sitting, which gave him a knowledge of the effects of light and shade, that shed an air of freshness and reality over his compositions such as even art has it not always in its power to bestow. Indeed, he laid no claims to any thing like science; and although his drawings were correct, spirited, and faithful, they were too unadorned and unfinished to

Le Foret, Guernsey from a sketch by Major-general le Marchant

be taken for the work of a professional man. Perhaps he was as well pleased that they could be ascribed to no other than a man of genius.

His taste for drawing was favoured by many local circumstances. The village of High Wycombe, where he passed several years of his life, stands in a rich and narrow valley formed by opposite ranges of chalk hills covered with the finest beech, in the immediate vicinity of the Thames, whose tributary streams carry picturesque beauty along with them in this direction, through a district of considerable extent. These natural advantages have not been neglected. The park and abbey of High Wycombe, are among the most elegant fruits of the genius of Wyatt; and the contiguous domains of West Wycombe, are not less interesting, as a specimen of the Italian villa, the work exclusively of Italian artists, brought over for the purpose by the late Lord Le Despencer. Other seats in the neighbourhood contribute to spread cheerfulness and cultivation around; and in the approaches to the Thames, almost every spot has been dedicated to ornamental purposes, not always with equal judgment, yet with an eagerness for rural improvement that no one can condemn, who has seen the woods of Hedsor, and the "proud alcove" of Cliefden.

He studied these scenes with enthusiasm, and of course with benefit; but he did not regard them with the feelings of admiration that attached in his mind to the unfrequented islands, which still continued to be the residence of various branches of his family. The preference was not without foundation. Guernsey abounds with fine prospects. The rocky shore of the southern extremity of the island presents a succession of bays or inlets, which the violence of the Atlantic has hewn out of the cliff, in all the irregular and striking shapes that generally denote the encroachments of the ocean. Each has a distinct character, according to the nature of the soil, or the resistance originally given to the waves; but all have a wildness and desolation, as if the tempest was hushed but for a moment. No human habitations are near; and the solemn stillness of the solitude is only interrupted by the breakers, which during the equinox rise so high as to cast their spray entirely across the island.

No other inconvenience, however, is suffered by those who dwell in the interior, from the conflict of elements around them. The atmosphere is of a mildness rarely known in our northern latitude; and the productions of the earth are more varied, more abundant, and more easily obtained, than in any place of the same extent in any quarter of the globe. The Guernsey lily, and the Guernsey' pear, indicate peculiar qualities of soil; and even the common vegetables are of an excellence that makes them, whenever it is possible, valuable articles of export. The sweetness of the herbage has, in spite of the ignorance and carelessness of the farmers, given a celebrity to their race of cows, which the other domestic animals would probably share, under an improved mode of treatment; and rich harvests are annually reaped in the same fields, at a trifling expense to the agriculturist. The effect of such general fertility, is greatly increased by the singular structure of the island. The long narrow slip of high ground of which it consists is broken into numberless hills and valleys, combining within an insignificant compass all the qualities of picturesque beauty, except magnitude; and the exquisite proportions of this fairy landscape have not been disturbed by the institutions of the country; for the absence of the law of primogeniture has brought the incisures to such tiny dimensions as are strictly conformable to the reduced scale of the features of nature.

The sea view from St. Peters, (the capital) has reminded many travellers of the Bay of Naples. The Islands of Jersey, Alderney, Serk, Herm, and Jedhou, rise out of the watery waste, as Kent or Repton might have been proud to have placed them. The irregularity with which they are clustered; combined with the difference of their outlines, presents them to the eye under different lights, and gives rise to optical deceptions, which must have astonished the minds of our superstitious ancestors. Jersey may be compared to the cultivated part of the north of Devon. Serk, which is the largest and most remarkable of the lesser islands, is a mass of rock about five miles in circumference, not less fertile in the interior, but infinitely more bold and romantic on the coast than Guernsey. Many of its bays terminate in precipices of considerable height, the sides of which are richly coloured with purple, red, and yellow oxides of iron, occasionally intersected by mixtures of quartz, and chalcedony, and all the gay variety of jaspers.

The annexed plate gives a very correct view of one of these interesting spots. It is called Le Port des Moulins, though no vessel perhaps ever sought so dangerous an asylum. The only descent into it is through a narrow and steep pass of wild rocks, about 200 feet high, on issuing from which, the traveller finds himself at the foot of a precipice, that stands almost perpendicular, on a semicircular base, both ends of which extend to the sea. At some distance upon the sand, is a large wall of red granite, the end of a vein, from which the clay has been washed, so as to give it the form of a natural arch; and contiguous to it, are two gigantic columns, surrounded by fragments of rock, striped and waved of different colours. When these rude memorials of the

Port de Moulin from a sketch by General le Marchant

triumph of the tempest are irradiated by the sun, they almost answer the description of the ruined palaces, which the Danish mythologists have assigned for the residence of the tutelary deities of the deep.

Colonel Le Marchant visited these islands every alternate year, and the time he passed in them constituted perhaps the happiest portion of his life. Released from the cares and responsibility of his office, he was here at liberty to indulge without restraint his passion for, the beauties of nature; and no one could more highly appreciate the privilege. He might be seen daily with his sketch-book and colours, intensely gazing on some view that had caught his eye, or he would thread the rough and unfrequented passes along the cliffs, or sit for hours among the rocks unconscious of the contingencies of the weather, as if he had never known a more serious occupation. All these scenes had charms for him, and the attention he bestowed upon them, probably infused into his style the boldness and vigour that characterized it.

The natives often stopped to look at him with wonder; and many were proud to take a place in his drawings, a distinction they richly deserved, for they were almost as picturesque as the country they inhabited. At the beginning of the nineteenth century, the women still adhered to the short close tunic; whilst the men in their strange coloured doublets and three-cornered hats drove their high narrow carts along roads not sufficiently wide to admit of two vehicles abreast. Every market day brought an influx of petty traders of both sexes from Normandy and Brittany, where the costume has preserved its primitive simplicity amidst the change of every thing else. This motley assemblage furnished groups worthy of Teniers; and Colonel Le Merchant's representations of them are full of life and truth, and can be mistaken by no one who has seen the originals. Some of the likenesses were so striking, as to excite a regret that he had not cultivated the talent which he so evidently possessed for portrait-painting; and he probably would have done so, had he not formerly felt it to be combined with a propensity for caricature, which he had the prudence to perceive was much too dangerous to be indulged. The success of a few of his satirical sketches when a subaltern, had frightened him.[1]

1. I cannot help noticing one instance of his employing this talent with effect. Whilst he was residing at Wycombe, he was consulted by his wife on the propriety of dismissing a female servant, who lay under strong suspicions of appropriating the wine in the *celeret*. As the woman protested her innocence, and the circumstantial evidence against her was far from conclusive, he recommended a farther trial, and in the meantime, he drew a figure of her swinging from the gallows, and placed it in the *celeret*, so that it should be the first thing seen on raising (continued next page),

He was not less partial to music than to drawing, and had these sister arts been equally accessible to him, he would have attained equal proficiency in them; but his professional engagements left him so little leisure within doors, as to render this impossible. The only instrument on which he performed was the flute, and the grace and spirit of his execution were worthy of more scientific compositions than he ventured to undertake. It was a constant theme of regret with him that he could not bestow more time upon this study,[2] and it was one of the accomplishments which he was most anxious to cultivate in his daughters. He superintended their progress in it as assiduously as if he had been their only instructor.

He also had some acquaintance with architecture, and I have seen designs from his hand of considerable elegance. With the details of building, the internal arrangement of houses, and the cost of their construction, he was remarkably familiar. He was still more skilful in landscape gardening, and perhaps never paid a visit without considering the ground before him, in regard to its capability of improvement. Many of his friends profited by his taste, which notwithstanding his long familiarity with Stowe and Wilton was perfectly simple, being better calculated for displaying the beauties of nature than the resources of art.

His reading had never been extensive. An imperfect education, and an active life, were drawbacks which not even his energy could overcome. He had little taste for works of fiction either in prose or verse, though he was tolerably familiar with Shakespeare, and had studied the modern drama with Mr. Cumberland: what he knew of history he knew well, and one book in particular, the *Introduction of Robertson's Charles the Fifth* he had almost learnt by heart. *The Memoires of the Duc de Rohan*[3] *sur la Guerre dans la Valteline*, and the *Memoires de Monteculi*

the lid. It had not been there long, before the woman came to resume her depredations; but a glance at the portrait frightened her to such a degree, that leaving the *celeret* wide open, she rushed violently agitated into the kitchen, and made the most ample acknowledgment of her offences.

2. He preferred the great masters of the German school, and had studied their works with his characteristic industry. He was one of the first subscribers to Dr. Whitfield's beautiful edition of Handel, and was always ready to promote similar undertakings.

3. This work principally relates to the duties of light troops, and the employment of them in mountainous countries. It is written with spirit, and shows the author to have been a clever man, though he was an unsuccessful general. The issue of the war in the Valteline would probably have been different, had he been properly supported. He is spoken of with great respect by all contemporary writers, notwithstanding their difference of opinion on his political career.

were also very highly prized by him, and the subject of much correspondence with his military friends. There was a preciseness and exactness in his mind that best suited chronology and geography, and his attainments in the latter were considerable, especially in its connection with the military operations of the last century, most of which he had studied with great care and attention. The collection of maps that he left behind was very curious and interesting.

When it is recollected how diligently he discharged the duties of his post, and how constantly he was engaged upon his various military works, it may be wondered how he could have acquired these accomplishments. But he possessed a quick apprehension, perseverance almost unrivalled, and indefatigable industry: besides which he was a strict economist of his time. He slept little, and he was by constitution both temperate and abstemious, perhaps to an extreme. His day therefore was long, and not a moment of it was wasted. The mornings were usually devoted to the business of the college; and as this was not always equally heavy, he frequently contrived to reserve some hours for his military studies. Before dinner he rode, and in summer, he seldom returned without a sketch. In the evening, he would hear his daughters play and sing, and when they retired, his pencil or his book would employ him till bedtime.

Though tenderly attached to his wife and children, he did not take much part in their conversation. There was an habitual seriousness about him, that would not yield to the gentle influence of domestic ties. Under the excitement of society, he spoke with fluency and spirit; and none but those who knew him well, could suspect that it cost him a painful effort to break silence. He more than once astonished Dr. Parr by an exhibition of powers of argument and expression which the doctor seemed to think very extraordinary properties in a soldier. It is just to add, that the doctor, who was not lavish of his praise towards those who presumed to differ from him, pronounced the colonel a very able man. Whatever he did, was done with an intense earnestness, of which I believe he was incapable of divesting himself. His mind was never at rest, and the only refreshment of which it was susceptible arose from the variety of his pursuits.[4] These had been chosen so judiciously, that he rarely had occasion to drop any thing he undertook, and if he did, his labour usually proved in the end subservient to some purpose or other, so that it was not wholly

4. He might have truly said in the words of the great Chancellor D'Aguesseau, "*une changement d'étude me delaisse*."

unprofitable. "Perseverance," he used to be constantly repeating to his children, "perseverance," is the only sure road to success.

He did not consider himself at liberty to live in retirement. Being the chief resident officer at the college, the duty of receiving the persons who visited the establishment devolved almost entirely upon him. Many were attracted thither by having relations in either of the departments; some by the interest they felt in what they deemed a great national undertaking, and not a few by the curiosity that naturally attached to a peculiar and novel mode of education. Among those who were actuated by the most patriotic motives, were their Royal Highnesses the Dukes of Clarence, Kent,[5] Cambridge, and Gloucester; and they, as well as others of the most distinguished characters of the day, frequently honoured the lieutenant-governor with their company at his house. Every student at the senior department also dined with him upon fixed days, and as the intervals were short, and the students numerous, his table was rarely without guests.

He thus contrived to see more of the character of these young men, than he could have done in his official intercourse with them; and by gaining a stronger hold over them, secured their obedience to the discipline of the establishment. Many of them indeed, became his personal friends, and kept up a constant correspondence with him after they had left the college; so that in the course of time, no military event could occur, of which he did not receive his private gazette from some Wycombite, who happened to be upon the spot. The collection of letters of this description that he left behind him, written as they were by officers of distinguished talent, form a most valuable comment on the history of the late war. These were not the only attentions paid to him by those who had been under his command. They constantly came to see him, especially if they had been lately on foreign service.

I never shall forget the visit of a party of officers, who had just returned from the disastrous expedition to Buenos Ayres. Child as I was, I could not help being deeply interested by their narrations of the wonders they had seen, and of the dangers they had passed. The theatre of war, the people, and the mode of warfare, were all strange and picturesque. One of them, a young officer of great enterprise, had contrived during his imprisonment, to gain the confidence of some

5. The Duke of Kent kept up a constant and confidential correspondence with Colonel Le Marchant for many years. The letters of His Royal Highness are now before me, and they are, as he says, those of a friend to a friend.

of the chiefs who were then planning the insurrection against the Spaniards, which proved afterwards so successful. He was present at several meetings of the conspirators, and described their bold designs and romantic characters with all the enthusiasm that belonged to his age and temperament. I almost fancy I hear him still. The next morning he departed, and before four years were over, I listened in the same manner, at the same hour, and in the same room, to the account of his death, in his gallant attempt to defend the Tamega at Amirante, an exploit which one of his companions in arms has preserved for the admiration of posterity.[6]

Besides the social engagements that thus sprung out of his situation at the college, the lieutenant-governor had many friendships and acquaintances in his immediate neighbourhood. At the hospitable mansion of Lord Carrington in the same village, he sometimes met Mr. Pitt, and others of the leading characters of the day. The Marquis of Buckingham, whom he had known so long and so well, was within a morning's ride; and at a still less distance in an opposite direction, his Lordship's illustrious brother, Lord Grenville, was passing the evening of life amidst the elegant pursuits that had cast so much brightness over his political career. The Lieutenant-Governor owed his intimacy with Lord Grenville to the Marquis of Buckingham, and this was only one of his obligations to that excellent nobleman. The marquis brought him forward in the county as his friend, and sought every occasion to show the warmth and sincerity of his friendship.

The following note was written during the visit of his late Majesty, then Prince of Wales, at Stowe.

The Marquis of Buckingham to Colonel Le Marchant.

Stowe, Oct. 5th, 1808, half past eight in the morning.

My Dear Colonel,

6. Napier's *Peninsular War,* vol. ii.. This officer, Colonel Patrick, was a connection of Mr. Canning's, by whom he was attached when young, to the embassy at Rio Janeiro. On his return from Buenos Ayres, he was employed with the Spanish armies, which he left to enter the Portuguese service. He commanded a regiment in the army of General Silveira, in the affair at Amirante, and won all the laurels that are due to that day. I understood that the Portuguese at first abandoned the bridge at Amirante; and it was with the greatest difficulty that the colonel could collect a few of his regiment to defend it. He declared he would not leave the post; and he was so much beloved by them, that they stopped rather than lose him. By degrees, the party increased; the colonel, however, was obliged to be wherever there was danger; and he at last was marked, and fell mortally wounded. Immediate consternation followed; the French advanced, and met with no farther resistance.

I have this moment received the commands of his Royal Highness the Prince of Wales, to desire that you will come to Stowe upon the receipt of this letter. I have very particular satisfaction in this communication passing through me, to one, whom on every consideration, both public and private, I do highly honour and esteem.

Adieu, dear colonel, and believe me ever and most truly, Your very faithful and devoted friend and servant,

Nugent Buckingham.

A vacancy having occurred in the representation of a borough under the marquis's influence, his Lordship offered the seat to Colonel Le Marchant; but as his duties at the college would not admit of his being an efficient member of the House, he wisely declined the honour. The same conscientious feeling made him hesitate to become even a county magistrate. However, he was at last prevailed upon to act in that capacity; and having a more than common familiarity with the rules of evidence, from his former experience in courts martial, he soon attained a high authority among his colleagues.

******

Note:—The following letter contains a specimen of very respectable proficiency in his magisterial functions. I need scarcely observe, that the offender mentioned in it was totally unconnected with the college.

Colonel Le Marchant presents his compliments to Lieutenant-Colonel Butler; and in reply to his note of yesterday's date, begs to say that he entirely concurs with him in preferring to adopt lenient measures towards the boy detected in committing theft at the college.

If information is lodged against him with the civil power, touching any of the thefts, in which he may have forced a lock or entrance into the college, it will affect his life. Colonel Le Marchant is not sufficiently informed of the nature and extent of the depredations committed, to determine whether there are any minor points that might be brought forward, which would be deemed petty larceny; but if so, the information should be immediately lodged, and confined to those points. When the culprit is apprehended his relations should apprise him that unless he consents to become a sailor, and will of his free will propose the same to the magistrates, the whole of his guilt will be brought against him, which will change the complexion of the charge, and cause his offence to become capital.

By this means, the object of mercy will be attained, and he may become useful to his king and country.

The magistrates have no power to send him to sea against his consent on account of a petty larceny, as the Act of Parliament that enables them to send persons to sea, specifies the offences that are subject to that punishment

CHAPTER 6

Appointment to a Brigade in the Peninsula

The king said to Colonel Le Marchant, one evening on the terrace at Windsor:

> I consider the Military College an object of the deepest national importance. The Duke of Cambridge has just given me a most favourable account of it, and I hear from scientific men, that your studies are conducted by very able masters, and according to an excellent system. I entirely approve of the measures you have pursued in the late disturbances, and I think the example must lead to the improvement of the cadets; there was no expecting them to be docile at first, but the management of them will be, every day, less difficult; and you will all the while be raising a race of officers, who will make our army the finest in Europe. The country is greatly indebted to you.[1]

The approbation of his sovereign was not the only testimony paid to the merit of the lieutenant-governor. A school for the instruction of cadets, on the plan of the Junior Department of the Royal Military College, arose at Madras, during the government and under the auspices of Lord William Bentinck; and the East India Company soon after formed a similar establishment at Addiscombe in Surrey. Even Russia, possessing as it did, in the Cadets' College at St. Petersburgh,

1. Extracted from a paper in the lieutenant-governor's hand-writing, entitled "*My conversation with the King, on the 7th of April, 1805.*" The author, then a boy at Eton, was present during this conversation, which lasted nearly an hour. He recollects the king to have been very animated, and he has no doubt, from the kindness and cordiality of His Majesty's manner, that his commendation of the lieutenant-governor was far more personal than the modesty of the latter chose to record.

(see note following), the most splendid institution of this nature in the world, considered the Royal Military College worthy of imitation; and the lieutenant-governor had the honour of furnishing His Imperial Majesty, by his express desire, with all the details of its constitution that seemed applicable to the military system of that country.

★★★★★★

Note:—This college was established in 1766 for the education of upwards of seven hundred youths, the sons of nobles, or persons bearing the rank of officers in the military or civil service. The pupils are admissible only at the ages of five and six, and are not allowed to be removed for fifteen years. During the first nine years they receive the instruction which other academies in the country give to boys of the same age; but the last six years their education is strictly military, and they are not only confined to military studies, but pass six or eight weeks of the summer entirely in camp, where they are taught the manoeuvre evolutions, and other practical parts of the service. At the expiration of the fifteen years, they are dismissed with military or civil rank, according to the credentials they obtain from their superiors. The expenses are wholly defrayed by the government.

The staff of the college consists of a director, lieutenant-colonel, two majors, six captains, twelve lieutenants, and six ensigns, one police-master, one master of the horse, and sixty-five instructors, of whom some have the title of professors, several masters for drawing, fencing, and dancing, a physician, a staff-surgeon and two assistants, an apothecary, an upper and two inferior stewards, and besides the officers of the chancery, and all the people belonging to the interior economy of the corps, a Lutheran and a Roman Catholic clergyman.

Notwithstanding all the exertions of the government, the college was in a very discouraging state at the beginning of the present century. Indeed, it was admitted, on all hands, not to have come up to the expectations which the public had a right to form from the magnitude and extent of the means employed to support it. Low as the standard of intelligence was in the Russian army, the graduates of the college were rarely distinguished above other officers of the same rank, and almost all situations requiring scientific attainments were obliged to be filled by foreigners.—*Storch's Picture of St. Petersburgh*, vol. i.

The bad state of the establishment has been ascribed to the want of a properly organized system of instruction, the studies being conducted by each professor according to his own views, wholly independent of his brethren, and the lectures being delivered in French and German, and therefore not intelligible to the greater portion of the students. A better reason may be found in the limited diffusion of knowledge in the higher classes of the country. Where this is the case, the advantages of education are not likely to be appreciated, and any efforts made in its behalf by the government will not be sufficiently encouraged by the community to be successful.

★★★★★★

He gave the same assistance to the Spanish Government at the request of his friend General Whittingham, when it was in contemplation to found a Military College at Majorca. His views were also adopted on the other side of the Atlantic, and the experiment proved so successful, that the Military Academy at West Point, (see note following), in the United States, is now one of the most costly, and yet most popular of the public establishments of this proverbially economical government; being on a more extensive scale than the Royal Military College at Sandhurst.

★★★★★★

Note:—The Military Academy at West Point has for its object to diffuse through all the departments of the military establishment of America those sciences which are necessary to its efficiency and proper administration. The military instruction embraces the system of infantry tactics established for the army of the United States, commencing with the elementary drill of the soldier, including the school of the company, school of the battalion, evolutions of the line, the exercise and manoeuvres of light infantry and riflemen, the duties in camp and garrison of privates, non-commissioned officers, and officers, including those of guard and police.

For three months in the year the cadets are encamped in open field, and perform the service of an active campaign.

Instruction is given by professors in the following branches: geography, history, ethics, engineering, mineralogy, drawing,

> mathematics, and the modern languages.
>
> The number of cadets who had graduated at the institution since its establishment up to 1825, was four hundred and twenty-eight, of whom three hundred and twenty-eight had graduated since 1812. Of the whole number, two hundred and sixty-one were serving in 1825, forming more than a half of all the officers in the American Army. Thirty-three had died on service, and nine had fallen in battle.—*North American Review.*
>
> Since 1825 the establishment has been greatly augmented, and several foreign officers, of distinguished merit, are to be found among the professors.

★★★★★★

A still more flattering distinction awaited him. The Battle of Corunna having been followed by the evacuation of Spain by the English troops, all the energy of England was now employed for the preservation of Portugal. Not only were the disposable troops at home prepared to embark immediately for Lisbon, but a plan was formed for the reorganisation of the Portuguese Army upon principles entirely foreign both to its existing discipline, and to the habits and prejudices of the country.

The task of carrying the measure into execution, devolved upon the British Ambassador at Lisbon;[2] but it was necessary for him to have a military assistant, and the person on whom the Ambassador, the Secretary of State, and the general in command fixed for that purpose, was Colonel Le Marchant.

An undertaking like this must have presented every attraction to one with whom the details both of military instruction and of the formation of armies had been favourite subjects of thought and observation through life. To make it still more acceptable, it came upon him entirely by surprise; for he knew nothing of the matter until he received the notification of his intended appointment. But his joy was destined to be of short duration.

The commander-in-chief refused his consent, on the ground, as his Royal Highness informed Lord Castlereagh, "that Colonel Le Marchant could not be spared from the college." It remains only to add, that the colonel submitted to His Royal Highness's decision without a murmur, being sensible, as he said, "That the college was his chief care,

---

2. The Right Honourable John Charles Villiers, later Earl of Clarendon, to whose care the civil and military affairs of Portugal were entrusted.

and its success the great object of his life."[3]

The lieutenant-governor now conceived his connexion with the Institution to be indissoluble, and perhaps he was not sorry for it. Ambitious as he was of military honours, he felt an attachment almost paternal for the establishment, and its growing success was continually adding to his reputation. Already in 1811, two hundred officers had been educated in the Senior Department in the duties of the general staff; the quartermaster-generals both of Lord Wellington's army, and Marshal Beresford, together with most of their assistants, being amongst them.[4] Not less than 1500 youths had issued into the army as regimental officers from the Junior Department, many of whom had been most favourably noticed. The applications for admission at both departments had become far more numerous than the vacancies, and government had consequently been encouraged to sanction the purchase proposed by the lieutenant-governor of an estate at Sandhurst, on which the long projected buildings were at last commenced on the magnificent scale originally contemplated. The mansion appropriated to the lieutenant-governor was after his own design.

In the midsummer of 1811, he was raised in the ordinary course of promotion to the rank of major-general, and about the same time he went to Sandhurst, to see the progress of the works, They stood on a wild and barren heath, which had been partially cleared, to admit of a few plantations recently made under his superintendence. The walls just rose above the surface, and extended along an eminence that commanded an immense expanse of bold open country. Immediately below, were numerous groups of huts and tents for the protection of the stores and the accommodation of the workmen, several hundred of whom were employed in various capacities in the construction of the building.

It was like the establishment of an infant colony in some American desert. Masons, sawyers, carpenters, blacksmiths, and all manner of artisans were crowded within a narrow spot, so as to be seen at a single glance, when the contiguous brick-kilns and forges did not participate very actively in their labours. The constant stir of men, and the ceaseless hum proceeding from such a concentration of human

---

3. Mr. Villiers ultimately went but without any military assistant, and the Portuguese Army was placed under the command of General Beresford.

4. General Murray, later the Right Honourable General Sir George Murray, G.C.B., and General D'Urban, later Lieutenant-General Sir Benjamin D'Urban, K.C.B., and Governor of Demerara.

and mechanical industry, on a spot that bore every mark of having been condemned, by nature, to perpetual solitude and sterility, were singularly impressive. The lieutenant-governor looked around him[5] with the exultation which one too accessible to the last infirmity of noble minds was likely to feel. He observed to the author, who was then by his side, that his struggles were now at an end, the difficulties under which the college had been labouring would be removed; and he had the certainty of passing the remainder of his days where he could witness the accomplishment of the schemes that had occupied him so many years.

Thus happy and elated he returned to Wycombe. The disappointment that was in store for him was proportionably severe. The week was scarcely over, before he received a letter from the adjutant-general, acquainting him "that their Royal Highnesses the Prince Regent and the Duke of York were of opinion that his situation at the college was incompatible with his rank in the army, and he must therefore expect to be immediately removed."

This was a heavy blow to a man of strong feelings, and it was aggravated by the prospect of his separation from his family, at a time that his elder children were of an age when a father's care is the most valuable, and his wife was in a very advanced state of pregnancy. His fortitude, however, was unshaken. He assured his friend, the Marquis of Buckingham, who kindly condoled with him on the occasion, that he had no desire at any time to remain longer at the college than was requisite to entitle him to the approbation and favour of his sovereign, and he used the same language to his eldest son (then an ensign in the 1st Foot Guards), bidding him always recollect that, as a soldier, the country had a right to dispose of him and his services as might be deemed best for the public.

It was even with some difficulty that he could be induced to represent to the Duke of York, that so far from having derived any advantage from his connection with the college, "he was the only individual on the establishment who had not obtained permanent rank or been otherwise benefited, either in being brought back to the service, after

5. He had an additional reason for regarding the spot with interest. As he passed it twenty years before, on his road to Southampton, his chaise was stopped by two highwaymen, one of whom demanded his money. An event like this was then so common, that he was not taken by surprise. He pointed his pistol; it clashed with that of his opponent, who was seized with a panic, and galloped off, without having fired, as fast as his horse could carry him.

having sold out, or promoted without purchase. He might have added, what he had too much delicacy to mention, that his private fortune had been materially impaired by the expenses he had incurred, as the resident commanding-officer, at the college, a charge to which his salary was quite inadequate, and which, indeed, had been only cast upon him by the accidental absence of the governor, owing to the want of proper accommodation at High Wycombe. All these expenses would have ceased on the removal of the college to Sandhurst, and an honourable opportunity would have been afforded him of recruiting his finances. Though what may be termed a very successful soldier, he was many thousand pounds poorer than when he entered the army. He returned the following answer to the adjutant-general's letter.

High Wycombe, 9th June, 1811.

My Dear Sir,

Allow me to thank you for the early intimation that you have had the goodness to give me of my intended removal from the Military College. I would have answered your letter immediately and without hesitation, to the same effect as I am now about to do, but unfortunately there was yesterday no post.

I cannot disguise from you that this change in my situation will make a very sensible difference in my income, which must unavoidably be heavily felt by a numerous and young family. I had certainly (though without sufficient consideration) looked forward to my continuance at the college, as the more natural course that my military life would have taken, under the particular circumstances of my having given rise to an establishment, which is admitted to have been of essential service to the army, and of my having devoted my best military years to its advancement and improvement, during which time I have unavoidably lost every opportunity of distinguishing myself in common with those of my own standing, by active service in the field.

But as the appointment of lieutenant-governor is deemed incompatible with my present rank in the army, I hope that I need not say to you, that these thoughts shall never occupy me a moment; and I shall thank you to assure His Royal Highness the commander-in-chief, that I never can have any other object in view as to my professional employment, than that of showing myself worthy of that situation, (whatever it may be) in which His Royal Highness may be pleased to think my humble services may be most useful and acceptable.

Of course, I do not know whether it is to you alone that I am indebted for this early communication of what is intended, if so, pray allow me to repeat my best thanks; but if you have done it with the permission of his Royal Highness, I beg that you will express in the strongest terms, my humble acknowledgment of this mark of his condescension and kindness.

The general was not long kept in ignorance of his destination.

The Adjutant-General to Major-General Le Marchant.

3rd July, 1811.

A brigade of cavalry is ordered for immediate service in Portugal, and the commander-in-chief has selected you to take the command of it. I am persuaded that you will be gratified by this preference on the part of His Royal Highness; but I delay the official communication, till you inform me whether there are any cogent reasons that would render this mark of distinction unacceptable to you at present.

It is almost needless to add, that the general allowed no domestic considerations to divert him from his duty. Two days after he received this letter, he issued the following order at the college.

Royal Military College, 6th July, 1811.

His Royal Highness the Prince Regent, having been graciously pleased to appoint Major-General Le Marchant to the command of a brigade of cavalry, under immediate orders of embarkation to serve in Portugal; he desires, that until farther orders, all reports may be made to Colonel Butler, as senior officer at the college.

The lieutenant-governor cannot resign his command of an institution which he had the good fortune to be instrumental in forming, and to the advancement of which he has devoted so many years, without expressing his ardent wishes for, the welfare of its members; and his sincere hope and conviction that it will completely fulfil the just expectations of the army and the public, from so important an establishment.

This intimation of the general's retirement from the college was received by the students with the strongest expressions of regret, and it may encourage others to a strict and honourable discharge of their duty, to learn that one so scrupulously just and fearlessly impartial as he had always proved, carried away with him not only the respect, but, in general, the attachment of those under his command. He was immediately waited upon by a deputation of the officers, requesting him to name a day on which a public dinner might be given in testimony of their sentiments; but the urgent nature of his orders precluded his receiving so gratifying a tribute to his merit, and the dinner was not given. In little more than a week he was obliged to take leave of his family, and proceed to London, on his way to Plymouth, where he was to find the frigate appointed to convey him to Lisbon.

He visited some of his friends in town preparatory to his departure; and amongst others, the present Marquis of Anglesey, whom he requested to furnish him with any hints that a more recent experience of active service might suggest.

> The best advice that I can give to a cavalry general, is to inspire his men as early as possible with the most perfect confidence in his personal gallantry. Let him but lead, they are sure to follow, and I believe hardly any thing will stop them.

This appears to have been Murat's secret, and Napoleon could appreciate its effects, for he once observed, "I wish we had had Murat at Waterloo; one of his daring charges might have retrieved the day." Murat had, indeed, with very little science, performed some wonderful exploits, and his soldiers, conceiving themselves to be invincible under his guidance, pursued, perhaps, the best means of really being so.

The general set sail from Plymouth in the middle of August His brigade had already embarked in the transports convoyed by the frigate, and he had not had any communication with his officers, except by the following letter, which was addressed, on his nomination, to the lieutenant-colonels of the regiments under his command.

Major-General Le Marchant to the Commanding Officer of the 4th Dragoon Guards.

> July 13th, 1811.
>
> Owing to the distance that the 4th Dragoon Guards is at from town, I cannot expect to have the pleasure of communicating with you personally, previous to our meeting in Portugal; at the same time, I am desirous that you should be apprised of the opinion entertained by several officers of cavalry who have served in Spain, on the subject of the equipments best calculated to render a regiment efficient to the service of that country. In stating their

suggestions, I have to desire that you will use your discretion on adopting such parts as you may think proper.

It is recommended that the whole of the clothing, necessaries, and equipment be taken to Lisbon, where a depot may be formed for the care of such articles as will not be immediately required in the field. Two full sets of spare horseshoes should be in possession of each regiment on landing; one set for immediate use, the other to be carried in the shoe-case. According to this arrangement, there will be shoes sufficient for two months' service; as it would fall too hard upon the farriers to furnish both sets, nor would there be sufficient time to prepare them. I shall endeavour to procure an issue from the Ordnance of one set, but how far my application may be attended with success, I do not pretend to say. It will be unnecessary to take any spare iron to Lisbon, as it is stated to be plentiful there.

Each man should be provided with a bill-hook; this must also be applied for to the adjutant-general. Spare soles for boots should be taken; and materials of different descriptions, sufficient for the use of workmen employed in the necessary repair of the regimental appointments.

Eight men, per troop, are recommended to be taught to put on shoes to horses.

It would be advisable to leave behind the carbine bayonets.

Each officer should take with him a good telescope, and map of Portugal, which may be carried in a sabretash.

The forage is best carried in nets.

If there is any point upon which you desire information relative to the equipment of the 4th Dragoon Guards for service, I shall be happy in giving it you.

I should be glad to receive the names of the officers ordered on service, as soon as you have made your selection.

Chapter 7

State of the War

On the morning of the 24th of August, as Major-General Le Marchant went on deck, he found himself entering the Tagus. The rock of Lisbon, like some Alpine height, rose proudly at a distance in front, whilst the steep and rugged banks of the river, crowned with vineyards and olive-groves, formed an appropriate access to the picturesque capital he was approaching. The wind was fair, and the frigate swept fast by the towers of Fort Julian, and about noon ran close to an old Moorish castle, whose lofty towers and spacious courts showed that it must once have been a fortress of considerable importance. It was built on a ridge of rocks, at the water's edge, so as to afford a ready and secure retreat, whilst a dark mass of mountains, almost hanging over it, presented an impenetrable barrier behind.

The walls were still entire, and the sun that shone upon them—a sun so different from any the general had before seen, there being no atmospheric vapours, as in England, to intercept its rays and dim its splendour, cast so bright a hue over the whole building, that one could scarcely believe it to be the ruin it was. There it stood, silent and alone, a majestic but melancholy memorial of its original inhabitants. A brave and polished race, the noblest branch of the family of Mahomet, they almost atoned to mankind, by their conduct in the West, for the ravages which their brethren had committed in the East. The hills on the northern bank of the Tagus now rapidly developed themselves, and the villas with which they were covered indicated the neighbourhood of a great city. Suddenly Lisbon burst upon his view, like

A sea Cybele fresh from ocean,
Rising with a tiara of proud towers,

. . . . . .that spread along the adjacent shores and over the superincumbent heights, dazzling the eye by their brightness. Irregular and ill-built streets, tasteless edifices, and filthy suburbs were all "lost in airy distance," and the whole looked magnificent and rich.

In the afternoon, the frigate anchored opposite Belem Castle, and the general immediately landed.

The convoy was a large one, and having been long anxiously expected, a thick crowd was assembled to witness its arrival. The scene that thus presented itself was singularly striking, especially to him who, for sixteen years, had not been out of England, and indeed had never penetrated into the Continent beyond Flanders and France. Nothing in these countries bore the faintest resemblance to what he now saw before him. The Moorish porters, who offered their services to carry his baggage, had not yet abandoned their oriental costume, and the peasants, who had come to market from the neighbouring villages, were clad like the heroes of a melodrama. Their carts, which were all drawn by bullocks, were of a most classical though clumsy construction, being, with little variation, such as were used by the Romans. Hard by, friars, of a dozen different fraternities, and soldiers of almost as many nations, were jostling together for precedence with careless familiarity; whilst some proud hidalgos, in cocked-hats and loose shabby cloaks, the degenerate descendants of the race that once

"Beneath new skies had held their stubborn way,
To reach the cradle of the new-born day,"(Luciad)

..... looked listlessly on, as if exempted by their rank from any participation in the feelings of their countrymen.

The general, once within Lisbon, was surrounded by objects of novelty and interest. The cities of the Peninsula may not be unlike each other, but they are totally unlike the cities of any other part of Europe. Short as was the dominion of the Moors here, it has left indelible traces in the language, literature, arts, and habits of the people. Not only are the public buildings, as in Asia, most abundant, but the domestic architecture has the same light, airy, elegant, and almost theatrical character. The houses are built of white stone, and usually are much larger than is warranted by the condition of their possessors. The outside is all that is cared for, and nothing is spared upon it, so that the first *coup-d'oeil* of any considerable street is very imposing. The roofs and terraces are plentifully ornamented with tropical shrubs and flowers, which preserve all their native brilliancy in this congenial climate. A person just landed from a long voyage, coming at once on the

Portuguese Costumes.

fashionable quarter of Lisbon, almost realises his dreams of the gardens of Armida and the palaces of Tyre.

The general was immediately welcomed by a host of officers, who had been under him at Wycombe, and they set no bounds to their attentions to him. Many of them had entered into the Portuguese service, and thus formed connexions with the natives, that afforded him a ready admission into the society of the country. This was more attractive to him than to most of the English, from the beautiful music which the patronage of the court and the priesthood has made so common there; whilst it gave him an insight into the national character, which proved very useful to him in the following campaign.

With these advantages he not only saw all that was worthy of observation in Lisbon, but in the neighbourhood, which, unlike the desert that surrounds Madrid, contains much to be admired. He was a frequent visitor at Ciñtra, the Tempe of Portugal, that gifted spot, where so many features of the picturesque,

Mixed in one mighty scene, with varied beauty glow.

His sketch-book abounds with proofs of the diligence and delight with which he studied it; nor was he less successful in his delineations of many of the Moorish ruins that are scattered along the banks of the Tagus, in situations which even the founders of some of our most famed English abbeys might have envied. The warrior and the monk had different pursuits, but each, in that ruder age, had a familiarity with nature, which is incompatible with the habits of the children of refinement.

He remained at Lisbon the more readily, as it afforded him the means of receiving more frequent tidings of his wife. The state in which he had left her, caused him great anxiety, and he could not always entirely subdue his misgivings, at being away from home at a time that she was in such need of his support. Every letter, however, assured him that all was going on well. The last was most encouraging. Two days after its receipt, in the midst of his gratitude and hope, the news arrived, that the object of his affections, the mother of his children, was no more. She had gone to bed in perfect health, but the pangs of labour had come on during the night, and, after giving birth to a fine boy, she had expired.

The arrow had now gone too deep into his soul to be ever extracted. All his previous trials were as nothing compared to this; and, for the first time in his life, he bowed his head, and would not be comforted.

Nor was his grief ill-founded. His wife had gained his heart by her beauty, but she had kept it by more substantial qualities, for few women approached her in soundness of judgment or prudence of conduct. She had been the partner of all his fortunes, from his youth up, and she had not only participated in, but aided all his plans for advancement. In fact, she frequently assisted him with her pen, as well as with her advice. The most perfect community of thought existed between them; and, whether it were joy or sorrow, hope or fear, it came upon them both alike. Their loves, their interests were one.

He recollected also the state of his family. Five daughters and three sons, the eldest of whom had barely reached sixteen, were left in the house of mourning, and he knew not what to do with them. His first impulse was to return to them immediately, and the Duke of York, anticipating such a resolution on his part, had by the same packet that brought the melancholy intelligence, sent to Lord Wellington to request leave of absence for him. This act was entirely spontaneous, and adds another instance to the many upon record of the warm-heartedness of his Royal Highness. It is the more striking, as General Le Marchant, conceiving himself harshly used by his sudden removal from the college, had, for some time, avoided every opportunity of coming under His Royal Highness's notice.

It became unnecessary, however, for him to avail himself of the leave of absence that was accorded to him. His relations in Guernsey undertook the charge of his children, and it was represented to him, on all sides, that he should best consult their interests by remaining in Portugal. He prepared himself, therefore, to join the army.

His brigade was such as to afford him every prospect of distinguishing himself. It consisted of the 4th Dragoon Guards, commanded by Lieutenant-Colonel Sherlock, the 5th Dragoon Guards, by Lieutenant-Colonel the Honourable William Ponsonby, and the 3rd (King's Own) Dragoons, by Lieutenant-Colonel Mundy. The whole body mustered near two thousand men and horses of no ordinary calibre. They were the admiration of the Portuguese, who had not seen any English heavy cavalry before, and the most confident predictions were expressed of their approaching triumphs, though, strange to say, there were not half a dozen individuals amongst them who had ever been before an enemy. Captain the Earl of Euston and Captain Gabriel were his *aides-de-camp*, and Captain Hutchins, of the 3rd Dragoons, was his brigade-major.

The main body of the army was, at this time, in winter quarters, in the northern part of Portugal, and General Reynier, who lay with a large force at Alcantara, threatened to avail himself of its absence by marching against Lisbon by the roads on the right and left banks of the Tagus, and by the Estrada Nova, being the route taken by Junot when he entered Lisbon in 1808. General Reynier was an adversary of too much importance to be overlooked by Lord Wellington. His Lordship no sooner discovered his intentions, than he directed Major-General Le Marchant to occupy the points by which the French were likely to advance, and to keep the most vigilant watch over their movements. The general, therefore, marched from Lisbon in the middle of September to Faudao, a little town on the mountains, commanding the Estrada Nueva, and there he fixed his own headquarters, with the 4th Dragoon Guards. He posted the 3rd Dragoons at Castello Branco, and in the villages on the right bank of the Tagus, and the 5th Dragoon Guards at Thomar, on the other side, and within reach of the Zezere.

The country thus occupied by the general's brigade is the most picturesque part of Portugal. The three towns that formed the headquarters of his respective regiments are all within view of the Estrella, that long succession of mountains which travellers have described in such glowing colours. The general had abundant opportunities of admiring it, for he examined every pass in it, but general Reynier, happening to receive little or no support from Marmont or Soult, and being moreover far more distinguished for skill than for enterprise, gave him no further trouble, and nothing of importance occurred during his stay either within his own sphere of operations, or with the main body of the army.

The greater part of his time was spent at Castello Branco, the principal town in the province of Beira, and the usual residence of its lieutenant-governor, General Le Cor. With that accomplished and able officer, who was then little known, but who has since acquired just celebrity by his exploits in Brazil,[1] he contracted the closest intimacy. He was by birth a Portuguese, but his parents were French, a circumstance to which he owed an education that saved him from the ignorance and superstition too common in the higher classes of the country. He resided in the bishop's palace, a handsome pile, which was also the usual quarters of General Le Marchant, and it was doubtful which of the two was most the favourite of the bishop; a worthy and amiable man, not perhaps quite so well informed as his military guests,

1. An animated account of one of these victories is given in Dr. Walsh's tour in Brazil.

but very superior to most of the dignitaries of his persuasion. Their society afterwards received a most agreeable accession in General Don Miguel de Alava, a young Knight of St. Jago, attached by the Cortes in a diplomatical capacity to the British forces.

Few names are more familiar than his to the ears of our countrymen who served in the Peninsula. He had then but recently joined our army, or indeed embraced, a military life. He was a captain in the navy, and had served with distinction, especially at Trafalgar, where he was wounded. Naval and military rank in Spain are synonymous. The French war broke out, and Don Miguel was transferred from his ship to a staff appointment on shore, He displayed equal courage on both elements, and his example in the field contributed to raise the character of the Spaniards in the estimation of the lower ranks of our army. Bold and daring, however, as he was before the enemy, he was calm, collected, and statesman-like in negotiation; whilst he was frank, honest, and high-minded in everything.

He had heard of General Le Marchant before they met, and, as might be expected of men of such kindred spirit, their acquaintance soon ripened into friendship. They shared together the dangers of the following campaign, which, more fortunate than his companion, Don Miguel survived; and he continued with the English Army until the end of the war., He then went as Spanish Ambassador to Brussels, and fought by the Duke of Wellington's side at Waterloo. His last service to his ungrateful country was as commander in chief of the forces that accompanied the Cortes, when they retired to Cadiz. On the downfall of the constitution, he went into exile, and remained there ever since.

The following letters were written by the general during his command in the mountains. Artless as they are, and entirely on domestic subjects, they show the goodness of his heart so truly, that I venture to insert them. The first is addressed to his eldest son, a very fine young man, who had just joined his regiment at Cadiz, after a year's tour in Greece and Asia Minor:—

Major-General Le Marchant to Ensign Le Marchant, 1st Foot Guards.

Nov. 23,1811.

Enclosed is a letter that I take it comes from ——[2] I hope you do not neglect the attentions of this good-hearted fellow. You

2. An orphan and soldier of fortune, for whom the general had lately obtained a commission.

have done well in writing to the individuals from whom you received acts of friendship during your tour; and let me entreat that you will hereafter give this matter the consideration which the importance it is of to your welfare absolutely requires. You will say that I am always impressing this upon you; and, in truth, I mean to do so; for, as long as you regard writing as burdensome, so long you will be without friends. Nor is this all. Until you have brought writing to be even agreeable to you, business will be irksome, and you will be ill calculated for the staff, the duties of which are so much connected with correspondence; for, whether as an *aide-de-camp*, or in the quartermaster-general's department, an officer has much to write. In a letter to a friend the heart dictates, and the composition might be supposed to be at all times a pleasure; if it is not, official correspondence must be detestable.

Whatever money you find necessary to your living as the reasonable part of your corps do, you will, in course, draw for it. There is no medium between a father and his children in regard to the confidence that should subsist between them. If the children are right-thinking, which they cannot avoid being if they are well-principled, a parent should implicitly confide in them. I have always done so towards yourself, trusting that, from a candid exposure of my finances, and the many calls that are made upon me, you will studiously endeavour to live at as moderate an expense as possible; and with this impression I have ever refused you nothing, though I have frequently been hard pressed to answer the demands made by the different members of the family.

I told you my reason for not naming you to my staff: the money that would be saved to me by it is no light consideration. But I have never, through life, hazarded my credit for any personal advantages; and in this instance I could not take you without endangering your good name, of which I am as jealous as my own. I had likewise, by laying by for so many years, greater cause to seek an intelligent and experienced staff. I repeat this to show that other generals can and must naturally be actuated by similar motives in the appointment of their staff. Therefore the first and principal recommendation in a young officer is the faculty of rendering himself useful. You have not had the means of experience, but you have had opportunities of cultivating languages, the French, Italian, and now the Spanish. I hope I am correct in the opinion that you are tolerably strong in your knowledge of the two former, and are making considerable progress in the latter. As soon as you assure me that you speak and write all of them sufficiently to interpret and be serviceable to a general, I can ensure you an appointment on the staff of this army. The means are in your power: study hard, and you will be rewarded by seeing service in a manner creditable to yourself, and enabling me to appropriate your present allowance for the benefit of your brothers and sisters.

Life, my dear son, is short and uncertain. You see yourself now with only one support left. How soon that may be taken from you it is impossible to anticipate. What a different situation would you be in without parents! My ambition was and is to see you in a line of service in which you might push your way with distinction; and with this view I gave you the education that you have received, and for this reason I encounter the expense attendant on the Guards. You have had advantages that very few young men possess, in adding the knowledge of other countries to that of your own. Let me entreat that you will profit of the moment when I can serve you by acquiring the attainments that would secure to you, after I am gone, the support of others, in consequence of your merit and utility. These are the only sure means of advancement. A few persons may have got on by accidentally falling into the way of men of powerful interests, possessing weak minds and less knowledge than those whom they take by the hand; but the instances are few, whilst, on the other side, generally all those who make any figure, or fill high situations, possess genius and superior acquirements.

To Denis Le Marchant, Esq. Lincoln's Inn, London.[3]

Castello Branco, Christmas-Day, 1811.

I have received one letter from you on your leaving Wycombe for Guernsey; one announcing your arrival in the island, and, latterly, a third, on your establishing yourself in town.

I feel great affection towards my children, and consequently I am doubly mortified and distressed when anything appears like neglect or indifference on their part. So little could I have supposed that you could have been unmindful of me, and at such a

3. The general's second son, a student-at-law.

moment, that I have been regular in writing, taking it for granted that your letters were on their way. My dear Katherine,[4] who at the same moment, and in your presence, joined with you in promising to write to me every fortnight, has most strictly adhered to her word; and I owe the more to her for it, as she had not been in the habit of writing, therefore the exertion on her part was the greater.

This is a day to forgive, and I will even forget what has pained me so much. If you are closely occupied, which I understand to be the case, it is not a long-studied letter I require; for what you can express in half an hour will be amply sufficient to satisfy me that I have not lost my place in your affection.—The entrance upon any new course of study is somewhat discouraging, but it is no more than what most of your schoolfellows and friends daily encounter, and without it there is no arriving at independence, be the profession what it may. Happily, our profits and advantages are generally proportioned to our industry. God grant that you may have sense enough to see your interest in this its real point of view, and by your attention and acquirements recommend yourself to the esteem and protection of those who have already attained the eminence to which you aspire.

Recollect you are now working for yourself, and God knows how soon you may be left with no other dependence than your own industry. At this period last year the whole family were assembled at Wycombe; since then, what a change! Let it be an example to us, and a warning of the events of time. As long as I live, you will be certain of my most affectionate support in every rational undertaking——but let me entreat of you to make the most of the time present.

I do not know whether you recollect Captain White at the Military College; he is now attached to my brigade, as assistant quartermaster general. Last year, he happened to be detached with a troop of the 13th Dragoons and some Portuguese cavalry. A party of the enemy, consisting of sixty men, attempted to surprise him: but the biter was bit; he advanced on them with his troop, leaving the Portuguese to support, and in a dashing charge took every soul of them. Lord Wellington thanked him in public orders. I have likewise obtained, as my commissary,

4. The general's eldest daughter.

an old acquaintance of yours in the island, Mr. Tupper Carey, the son of Mr. Isaac Carey, of Hauteville, who is likely to prove a great acquisition. He appears very well up to his duty, and is gentlemanlike.

Several deserters from Valladolid arrived here yesterday; amongst them are two surgeons and many non-commissioned officers belonging to the Imperial Guard. They report, and there is ground to believe them, that at the time of their departure, about a month ago, forty thousand men were detached from the army in Spain and actually marched for France; and it was understood that they were destined to act against Russia. We also have learned, within the last few days, that the enemy is in motion towards Talavera and Valentia; if there is any thing going on, I am so situated with my brigade that, in all probability, I shall be employed, whether on this or the other side of the Tagus.

Tomorrow I shall remove my quarters to Thomar, where a regiment of my brigade is stationed, and there I shall pass the rainy season, unless actively employed: of this we know nothing, so properly are all Lord Wellington's movements kept secret.

I am happy in having so far enjoyed my health, and I hope the climate agrees with me: how I may bear the wear and tear of service is another thing, but I am inclined to think very well.

God bless you, my dear son; may you have many and many returns of the season in happier times than the present. Do not let me have to complain farther of your silence.

The Same to the Same.

Faudao.

Your last letters have come to hand.[5] I am sorry to have given you pain on this head, but when I reproached you with neglect, I felt doubly the pangs I was inflicting. My affection for you made me the more miserable to believe neglect from you possible. Had I been indifferent, I should have been silent. I need not tell you the pleasure that I receive at the favourable accounts that reach me from different quarters of your general conduct and application to your studies. You may thank God for having endowed you with an understanding capable, in early life, of

5. These letters, the absence of which gave rise to the complaints in the general's former letter, had been trusted to private hands, and were not delivered till very long after the arrival of the post.

> discriminating between the right and wrong path: that of virtue and religion insures the possession of honour and honesty. Continue as you have begun, and you will contribute to render my latter days those of contentment.

The inactivity of the French at the time these letters were written, allowed the general to visit the headquarters of the army, which then were at Freneda, on the frontiers of Spain. His journey was short, but not shorter than he wished; the destitution of the country through which he passed frequently occasioning great difficulty in procuring even the coarsest food. He expected to find matters better at Freneda, but he was disappointed. The town is dull, dirty, and poor. Lord Wellington's house, which was perhaps the best in it, would hardly have satisfied an alderman in one of our provincial cities, and the most distinguished officers of the staff were reduced to accept the meanest accommodations. Some of them are said to have borne these privations rather reluctantly, but Lord Wellington used always to observe that it was one of the best quarters he was ever in:—alluding, no doubt, to its position, which enabled him to obtain constant intelligence of the movements of the enemy.

The general having established himself in a chamber worse than "the worst inn's worst room," proceeded to pay his respects to Lord Wellington. His Lordship, to whom he was already no stranger by reputation, gave him a cordial welcome, which was heightened by his finding many of his oldest and most valued friends under His Lordship's immediate command. Some of them, who had been constantly in active service, he had not seen for years, and it may be imagined how delighted he was to refresh his remembrance of old' times in such society. No persons after a long separation can have more to say to each other than military men of rank, and amongst these few could be found who had run a more eventful career than the general's companions at Freneda.

Their services had not been confined to Europe, for some of them were lately returned from the capture of the French West India Islands, whilst others had, like their illustrious commander, reaped laurels in the wide field of Eastern warfare, which at one time was the only school of tactics that Napoleon had left us. The stations they held in the army attested their professional merit; and many of their names are now associated with the honours awarded by a grateful nation to the successful heroes of the Peninsula.—Alas! the survivors of this cheerful circle would be soon told. War had its victims, and peace has proved that it can be as destructive as war.

One of these officers, whose name I should be proud were I at liberty to mention, has favoured me with the following note:—

> I found the general as active and energetic as when I had first known him fourteen years before. I was happy, also, to perceive that his temper had greatly improved; and indeed he seemed to have spared no pains to get it under his control. He once said to me, 'I have been all my life squabbling and quarrelling, and unable to get out of troubled waters: I am determined henceforward that no one shall have any just ground of complaint against me.' I thought this was being too hard upon himself, and could not help telling him, that it was not so much from defect of temper that he had fallen into these difficulties, as from expecting all men to be as eager and able to do their duty as himself, and treating them, in case he happened to be disappointed, as if they were the very reverse of what he had supposed them. If he would but adopt a more humble standard, he would form a more accurate estimate. I afterwards observed that my advice had not been thrown away; for no general could show more judicious indulgence than he did to his officers and men, or in return be more beloved by them.

It may be observed, that the defect of judgment which is here justly imputed to General Le Marchant is more commonly found in powerful minds than in weak ones, and, like other generous errors, is not without its advantages. The equal distribution of natural endowments is only a dream of philosophers; but the existence of such a notion is a strong argument against the opposite doctrine, which would become the worst enemy of all improvements, being pushed to an extreme. There is no trusting to appearances. Circumstances often call forth strength of character where there is the least visible sign of it, to the astonishment of none more than its possessor, and it is one attribute of genius to discover and avail itself of these resources; some of the most extraordinary triumphs of modern times having been gained by an application of means which it required a very sanguine opinion of the extent to which human energy might be carried to pronounce adequate to the occasion.

It was fortunate for the cause of Spain that Lord Wellington possessed this faculty in an eminent degree. While his sagacity saved him from placing any trust in the Spanish levies, there seemed no limit to his confidence in his own troops. It was the fashion of the day to regard the military profession as uncongenial with our national habits, so that the superior merit which attached to the character of our seamen was not claimed for our soldiers. This distinction met with no favour from Lord Wellington; he assumed the moral and physical qualities of Englishmen to be the same in either service, without reference to the element on which they were employed.

Accordingly, he led his troops to enterprises which no previous commander would have dared to contemplate, and which nothing but the confidence that existed between himself and his men could have made successful. In one of the many engagements in the Pyrenees, a battalion of English infantry was on the point of yielding to a very superior force of the enemy, when the sight of Lord Wellington galloping towards them, waving his hat, produced a sudden burst of enthusiasm, under the influence of which they charged their opponents with an irresistible fury, and in a few minutes remained masters of the field. Nor is this a solitary instance: his presence never failed to impart to his followers a moral force, such as made the French armies so formidable when fighting under the eye of Napoleon himself.

At no period during the whole war were the great qualities of Lord Wellington of more use to his country than at the close of 1811, whilst General Le Marchant was staying at Freneda. The army was then in a state of unusual despondency. All those bright visions of glory that cheered our entrance into the Peninsula had vanished—the character of the contest was entirely changed. We were no longer an auxiliary force, co-operating with the Spanish armies, in the midst of a friendly country, to resist the aggressions of the French: the Spanish armies, broken by repeated defeats, had, one by one, disappeared; all the fortified towns of importance were either in the possession of the French, or under siege; and the English were left to cope single-handed with the mighty host which Napoleon had sent from his tributary nations to form the garrison of Spain.—The Anglo-Portuguese Army did not exceed 80,000 men, whilst the French were not less than four times that number, and had, besides, the advantage of all the resources to be derived from their occupation of the country. To move them from their seats appeared hopeless; and it was even apprehended that, on their first advance, we should be compelled, by retiring within the lines of Torres Vedras, virtually to abandon the whole of Portugal, excepting Lisbon.

This last resort being necessarily of a temporary nature, many of the best-informed officers in the army regarded the entire subjugation of the Peninsula by the French as not far distant, and accordingly wrote to their friends in England to prepare them for their speedy return home. Some of these letters, describing in a most melancholy strain the situation of the army, found their way into the public prints, which afterwards passing into Portugal, could not fail to confirm the bad impression already prevailing there. Lord Wellington wisely issued a general order, containing one of these letters, and pointing out its impropriety in forcible terms. The result of this was, that more caution was used by his officers in their communications with England; but their language among themselves continued the same, and it was impossible for an individual like General Le Marchant, recently arrived in the country, entirely to escape its influence. Without yielding to all these gloomy forebodings, though they were shared by several officers of deserved distinction, he certainly had no hopes of our being able to maintain for any length of time an effectual resistance to the overwhelming forces of the French.

Still, whilst the contest lasted, he desired to see it fought with a spirit worthy of the British name. He could not, therefore, fail to appreciate the great qualities of Lord Wellington, whose mind was capable, amidst such difficulties, of preparing and maturing an offensive movement, calculated to bring upon him the combined armies of Soult and Marmont, yet with an object fully proportionate to its danger. Lord Wellington's design upon Ciudad Rodrigo had for some weeks been suspected by his officers, but nothing transpired until he communicated his orders to his superior officers when the time was come for their immediate execution. This happened in the first week of January 1812, and caused General Le Merchant's departure from Freneda, to join his brigade at Castello Branco.

Chapter 8

Capture of Ciudad Rodrigo

The investment of Ciudad Rodrigo commenced on the 8th January of the new year; and General Le Marchant being ordered to bring up his brigade to cover the operations of the besieging army, he marched from Castello Branco early on the morning of the 13th. It was a march of only three days, but many circumstances combined to render it unusually harassing and fatiguing. The weather was bitterly cold and raw, the snow was deep upon the ground, and the road, owing to long neglect and the severity of the season, had become almost impassable. At every step the horses plunged nearly knee deep, and they could not pass the ravines, through which their course frequently lay, without floundering in sloughs of sleet and mud, which made the seats of the horsemen so precarious as to cause constant confusion in the line of march.

The district had been utterly exhausted by the contending armies: and poor as the villages in the Peninsula proverbially are, their former condition was prosperity itself compared with that into which they had now fallen. Most of them had been abandoned. The few inhabitants that yet remained looked miserably squalid and ghostlike. The houses were without doors or windows, and indeed, in most instances, without roofs, the troops being in the habit of taking the rafters for fuel, which was the only comfort they procured on their march: everything else they carried along with them, and each trooper being provided with five days' rations for himself and his horse, the bundles of straw were necessarily very large, and no light burthen to the horses, as well as very embarrassing to the men. An officer present says:

> It was surprising how good-humouredly the poor fellows bore their inconveniences, which to men accustomed to the comparative ease of home service were sufficiently trying. I repeat-

edly heard them jesting on their own grotesque appearance. One of them I recollect observing to his comrade—'Call this dragooning! why it looks more like waggoning!' All, however, were in the highest spirits, when on the 17th we, for the first time in our lives, saw the French flag as it waved on the citadel that crowns the ramparts of Ciudad Rodrigo.

The brigade now joined the besieging army, and its headquarters were established within a league of Ciudad Rodrigo, at Aldea da Ponte, a straggling town on the Portuguese side of the Agueda. It had been too long in the habit of changing masters to have anything left in it, and the neighbourhood was in a similar condition, so that not without extreme difficulty could any forage be procured there. When the bundles brought from Castello Branco had been consumed, the horses were often reduced to oak-leaves,—a fare very ill suited to constitutions formed in the luxury of an English stable: several died, but the losses were less than in other brigades of the army, which was mainly owing to the great exertions of the general, who showed an attention to this branch of duty seldom found in officers of equal rank. He felt, as he once observed to the commissary of his brigade:

> . . . .that in providing for cavalry, the supply of forage to the horses is of as much, if not more, consequence than provision for the men, as the latter are inefficient to the service unless their horses are well fed.

These privations became more serious than they would have been at another time, from the nature of the service in which the cavalry were employed, it being their office to keep a vigilant watch on all the roads by which the French could possibly advance upon the besiegers; and they were thus obliged to be always on the alert, as none supposed that Marmont would allow so important a fortress to be wrested from him without a struggle.

It had been generally believed that the siege would occupy from two to three weeks. Massena had been kept a month before the place in 1810, although the fortifications were only in moderate repair, and the garrison consisted principally of new levies. The fortifications had since been put into excellent order by the French engineers, and the efficiency of the garrison secured by the visit of the French so late as the end of September. General Banier, the governor, was an officer of Marshal Marmont's own selection, and chosen under a full sense of the importance of his post. This was, therefore, no unreasonable calculation; but the activity of Lord Wellington was not to be measured by ordinary rules. He knew he was running a race in which it was very improbable that his adversary should be far behind him; and so it proved. Marshal Marmont had marched from Old Castile, with what troops he could collect, on the very day that he was apprised of Lord Wellington's design; but he had a journey of eighteen days to perform, through bad roads and a hostile population, and his army being in separate cantonments, and not in a condition for a long and unexpected march, it was obliged to move in separate bodies, as it received and happened to have the means of obeying his orders.

All this while the siege was pressed with an ardour equal to the occasion, suffering no interruption either from the incessant fall of sleet and rain which had poured down upon the troops from the first hour of the investment, or yet from the efforts of the garrison, whom we had permitted, in the course of a few days, to fire above 11,000 large shells, and nearly an equal number of shot, without discharging a single gun against the defences in return; so intent were, the besiegers upon their first object of completing the works. Still, it is doubtful whether they were not too few in number to have done so within the very short space of time before them, had not the Spanish peasantry in the neighbourhood caught some portion of their zeal.

General Alava having represented to these good people, that the fall of the fortress would leave the province free, and allow them for the future to pursue unmolested their agricultural labours, they readily came forward in great numbers to assist the soldiers in the trenches, where they worked most assiduously, notwithstanding the tremendous cannonade to which they were constantly exposed, and by which many of them were killed or wounded. The exertions made were so extraordinary, that on the day of General Le Marchant's arrival, being but the ninth from the commencement of the siege, not only had the batteries been brought to bear upon the walls, but the breach was actually pronounced practicable.

Had not Lord Wellington been better informed of the movements of Marshal Marmont than the marshal was of His Lordship's, the assault would, of course, have taken place without delay, and must, from the preparations being necessarily still imperfect, have been attended with immense bloodshed. Happily for the English, they could now avail themselves of the great moral advantage they possessed over the enemy. There was scarcely a French civil or military department throughout the country, into which some Spaniard had not contrived to insinuate himself, solely for the purpose of conveying information to his countrymen; and one of these agents being in Marshal Marmont's camp, despatched a messenger every night to Lord Wellington, to acquaint him with the march of the French during the day. He thus ascertained, on the 17th, that he had yet two days to spare,—and at such a moment they were invaluable.

General Le Marchant employed the 18th in examining the country, for the purpose of determining how the cavalry could be turned to most use in the event of any attack from the enemy. On the following day, he learnt that the assault was fixed to take place the same evening, when his brigade was ordered to be present. He accordingly collected his men and having ranged them along the plain in such a position as appeared to him best suited to protect the infantry, he returned to dine with Lord Wellington at Gallegos, where he met Sir Thomas Graham, who had the direction of the siege, with some of the other generals and the principal staff of the army.

I have been informed by one of the survivors of this entertainment, that it was a most cheerful and agreeable party. The guests were sanguine in their anticipations of success in their approaching enterprise. The failure at Badajos in the preceding June, instead of causing despondency, was treated as a wholesome lesson, likely to supply the want of experience of the troops in this branch of warfare, which, from the close collision and personal encounter that it involves with the enemy, seems particularly adapted to the British soldier. Besides, a siege is always an unpopular service, from the constant labour it imposes on the men, and the close attention which must necessarily be paid to them by their officers, whose duty in the trenches consisting principally in the superintendence and direction of the workmen, sometimes in a very hot fire, is far more perilous than interesting: all ranks of the army, therefore, rejoice when it is over.

On this occasion, they felt an additional satisfaction at the disappointment they were preparing for the French, who had been long accustomed to say, that although the English might win battles, they would never take a town,—an assertion which had hitherto not been disproved. The evening thus wore pleasantly away, the party only breaking up when the time arrived for the generals to go to their respective posts. They then, as their *aides-de-camp* announced that their troops were ready to advance, dropped off almost one by one. General Le Marchant would have followed to take charge of his brigade, but Lord Wellington told him that there was little probability of his men being engaged, so that he need not join them, but should remain with him during the assault. Shortly afterwards his Lordship rode to the works, accompanied by the general, and many other officers.

Two breaches had been pronounced practicable, and they were fixed for the points of attack, an escalade in another direction being projected merely as a feint.[1] The limited time that could be given to the works did not admit of their being completed so as to afford the usual protection to the assailants, and hence the breaches being still difficult of access, the task of forcing them became proportionably formidable. This was entrusted to the two individuals, who would, perhaps, of all others, have been chosen for that purpose had the selection rested with the army at large; the main breach being committed to General Picton, and the lesser one to General Crawfurd—officers alike distinguished by gallantry and talent, but most opposite in disposition and deportment, and, it may now be not uninteresting to add, in person.

Picton, when wrapped in his military cloak, might have been mistaken for a bronze statue of Cato, and was equally staid, deliberate, and austere: whilst Crawfurd, of a diminutive and not imposing figure, was characterised by vivacity almost mercurial both in thought and act; his eager spirit and his fertile brain ever hurrying him into enterprises of difficulty and danger, which he loved the more because they sometimes left him at liberty to follow his own view of the crisis of the moment. Others shunned responsibility—he courted it. He had served on the staff of the Austrian armies during the revolutionary war, and was well versed in their tactics, as he had shown by his translation of one of their best military histories: but this knowledge was of very questionable benefit to him, for it occasionally led him to try experiments which were hardly consistent with the comparative insignificance of his corps.

In short, he was too much disposed to aim at objects which were the province of the commander, rather than of a subordinate general. Picton had no such ambition, but he was slow to execute orders of which he disapproved, and the quickness of his perception was not equal to the soundness of his judgment. Crawfurd had the faults incidental to a hasty temper—Picton to a morose one. Each was possessed of indefatigable industry, and perfect familiarity with all the duties of his profession; and last, though not least, both were men of the highest

1. The author has entered into no details of the storming of Ciudad Rodrigo, beyond what appeared to him necessary for the consistency of his narrative. It has been admirably narrated by Colonel Napier.

integrity and honour. Next to Lord Wellington, none stood higher in the estimation of the army; and they were the rival candidates for his truncheon, in the event of its falling from his hand.

Both these officers were the friends of General Le Marchant. He had known Crawfurd long and intimately; and there existed between himself and Picton a degree of affection, which the latter did not often show, but could most strongly feel. He was a man much more generally admired than beloved, though he possessed in an eminent degree qualities calculated to inspire attachment. In this respect, as well as in his military talents,—and in some degree his person—a resemblance might be traced between his friend and himself.

Soon after Lord Wellington had reached the works the assault commenced. It was then about seven o'clock, but the glare of innumerable fireballs thrown up by the garrison made it as light as day. Our troops met with every opposition which skill or courage could offer. Picton, however, crossed the ditch with less difficulty than had been anticipated, and it was in ascending the breach that his principal loss was sustained. Here boards were strewed covered with spikes; and large masses of stone and brick work were rolled upon his men, numbers of whom were swept off by a well-directed fire of musketry and grenades from the summit of the breach. An officer[2] who distinguished himself on this occasion said to the author, describing the scene:

> The carnage was terrible until we attained the summit, and were near enough to close on them with the bayonet; we then made short work of it, and the place was virtually won.

Crawfurd was mortally wounded early in the attack, before his division reached the breach. He was struck down in the act of encouraging his men, as he led them, under a heavy fire from the ramparts along the glacis; yet such was the admirable discipline into which he had brought them, that notwithstanding his fall, and that of their other principal leaders who fell shortly afterwards, they forced their

2. The late Major-General Sir William Williams, K.C.B. and K.T.S. formerly lieut.-colonel of the 60th foot, which he commanded at Fuentes de Honor, Ciudad Rodrigo, Badajoz, and Salamanca, in all of which engagements he was wounded. He also distinguished himself at Corunna. He had entered the army in early life, and having served for some years in the West Indies, where he was employed in that destructive warfare against the Charibs in St. Vincent, he accompanied Sir Ralph Abercrombie to Egypt. He was highly esteemed both by Sir John Moore and Lord Wellington; and there was perhaps no officer whose name received more frequent or honourable mention in His Lordship's despatches.

way through the breach, and were even the first to gain possession of the citadel. His death was lamented by all ranks in the army, and from his peculiar excellence in his own branch of duty, as a commander of light infantry, it occasioned a void which none could expect to see adequately filled up.

General Le Marchant remained by Lord Wellington's side during this hard-fought and eventful struggle, which he afterwards ever cited as one of the most brilliant exploits of the war; and it is to be regretted that a detailed description of it, which he wrote for the information of one of the highest military authorities in England, and which was at the time greatly praised, cannot now be found. When Lord Wellington entered the city to take formal possession of it, the general accompanied him, and witnessed with equal pain the excesses committed by the troops upon the unfortunate inhabitants, which he used his most strenuous efforts to repress. He was also present at His Lordship's first interview with the French governor, General Banier, who was for a while placed under his charge, and appears to have made no favourable impression upon him.[3]

The loss of Ciudad Rodrigo caused the immediate retreat of the French, whilst Lord Wellington, having committed the fortress to the care of the Spaniards, suspended for a time all active operations. General Le Marchant accordingly received directions to retrace his steps from Ciudad Rodrigo on the 31st, and the troops were again established in their former quarters along the Portuguese frontier.

3. General Banier, though of some character as a soldier, was a man of ordinary capacity, and entirely destitute of anything approaching refinement. So little used was he in the common courtesies of society, that the British generals, with all their anxiety to show attention to an officer of his rank whom the fortune of war had thrown into their hands, could not help rejoicing when the order was issued for his removal to Lisbon. This was the more noticed, from the contrast it afforded to their recollection of his predecessor, General Reynaud, who on his capture by the guerillas had been delivered over to Lord Wellington, and remained long in the English camp, where the frankness and urbanity of his manners made him an universal favourite.

CHAPTER 9

Return to Portugal

The month of February passed without any offensive movement on the part of either of the contending armies. The English lay quiet in Beira and the Alentejo, whilst the French were again scattered over the interior provinces of Spain, as if they calculated on a long period of repose after the extraordinary efforts made by Lord Wellington for the reduction of Ciudad Rodrigo. Both Soult and Marmont had withdrawn to a distance from the scene of operations, leaving the task of watching the frontiers to officers of subordinate rank.

Major-General Le Marchant, who was at this time quartered as before at Beira, now began to feel the benefit of that constant intercourse he had enjoyed with Lord Wellington at Freneda and Ciudad Rodrigo: it had made them thoroughly known to each other, and henceforward the general's brigade was maintained in a condition adequate to any enterprise within the province of an officer of his rank, and was always employed where opportunities of distinction seemed most abundant.. One of his regiments (the 4th Dragoon Guards,) being after the capture of Ciudad Rodrigo greatly reduced in numbers and efficiency by sickness and hardships, Lord Wellington substituted for it the 4th, or Queen's Own Dragoons, who were in full strength, and inured to the climate, and whose lieutenant-colonel (Lord Edward Somerset) would alone have been an important acquisition. But what no less gratified the general, was the entire independence he was allowed to enjoy in his command.

The interior economy of the brigade, and all matters of detail and management relating to it, whether they concerned either officers or men, were left wholly to his own superintendence, instead of being regulated by other authorities: for Lord Wellington was free alike from that dread of encroachment on his power, and that puerile love of interference in the lesser points of discipline, which have been no uncommon defects in officers of considerable military reputation. Wholly free from jealousy himself, he required only to be well served; and if, making little allowance for negligence or incapacity, he exacted a strict performance of duty, yet, when he found ability and activity in those under him, he ever turned such qualities to the best account by giving their possessors every facility for their exercise.

A new field was also opened to General Le Marchant by his being appointed President of the Board of Claims; an office the duties of which could not be properly discharged without great knowledge of business, and more than common sagacity, tact, and discernment. All the applications made to Lord Wellington by his officers or soldiers for compensation on account of the loss of horses, mules, accoutrements, or other military necessaries, were referred at once to this board for adjudication; and as no claim was admitted where the claimant could be justly charged with neglect, omission, disobedience of orders, or where the loss was occasioned by the ordinary occurrences of service, investigations were frequently thrown upon the board involving very nice and difficult points with reference to the conduct of individuals, the responsibility of which mainly rested with the president; and the business of the board increasing proportionably with the activity of the campaign, the pressure upon the general became very severe, and often, after a hard day's march, abridged the few hours that remained for repose. His decisions, however, were so carefully made, that they materially contributed to the high estimation which he gained in the army.

It was still the middle of winter; a season which, in the Peninsula, usually compels a suspension of hostilities; but the large draughts from the French armies preparatory to the war with Russia, and the weakness of their forces along the frontier, determined Lord Wellington to carry into effect his long-concerted plan for the reduction of Badajoz.

Major-General Le Marchant's brigade was one of the first that moved forward to accomplish this daring design. He marched from Castello Branco on the 21st of February, and proceeding across the Alentejo, halted on the 5th of March at Villa Vicosa, a handsome, well-built town, lying a little out of the high road from Elvas to Lisbon. The kings of Portugal had a pleasant hunting-seat here, with a park ten miles in circumference, laid out with taste, and admirably adapted for the chase, which has long been the favourite amusement of the courts of Portugal and Spain. Churches and convents, the usual appendages of these courts, abound in the town; and there is also a royal chapel, whose music was formerly a great attraction to amateurs; but the choir, like other departments of the arts, had sensibly declined during the war. The brigade was dispersed over the neighbouring villages, which were populous and flourishing, owing to their vineyards, which are noted for producing some of the best wine in the kingdom. It is exported far and wide, and gives employment to a vast number of individuals. Estremos, once the principal town of the district, was, in the rich days of the trade, supported by manufacturing wine-coolers.

The general secured comfortable quarters at Villa Vicosa, and was detained there several days by the incomplete state of the preparations for the siege of Badajoz, which made it impossible for the army to advance. On going over to Elvas, he found Lord Wellington deeply mortified by the delay, and trying with his usual energy to put an end to it.

This, however, was no easy task; and nothing short of his Lordship's personal influence could have overcome the tardiness of the Portuguese authorities, whose conduct on this occasion had well nigh proved fatal to the success of the enterprise; and as it was, the time thus uselessly consumed greatly increased its hazard.

The different departments of the army set an honourable example to the Portuguese, by emulating the activity of their chief; and the exertions of General Le Marchant were afterwards felt in the excellent condition in which his brigade took the field and went through the ensuing campaign.

They who saw him labouring early and late, with a mind always collected, vigorous, and apparently at ease, little guessed what anguish lay concealed under this calm exterior. The kindness of friends, change of scene, the excitement of war—nothing availed to subdue or even mitigate the intense grief with which he still mourned his departed wife. Her name never escaped his lips; nor did any one venture to allude to it before him, for there was a reserve in his nature that made him nearly inaccessible to sympathy; but a tone of melancholy breathed through his correspondence, and showed the feeling predominant in his breast. The following letter but too plainly proves how he

Strove to hide
Beneath the warrior's vest affection's wound.

Major-General Le Marchant to Colonel Birch (Later Major-General Birch Reynardson), Quartermaster-General, Edinburgh.

My Dear Birch,

I am satisfied of your friendship for me, therefore your silence needed no apology. Your kind letter reached me a fortnight ago; and I assure you that it gave me great pleasure to hear from one whom I have so long and highly esteemed, and in particular to learn that you had inherited so considerably,[1] although I regret the loss you experienced in the death of a valuable friend: may you and your amiable wife enjoy your very ample fortune with every degree of happiness that this life affords!

As for myself, my days have been woefully embittered by misfortune, and discouraged by disappointment: I have now little to look forward to. From Carey [2] you will have heard how my poor children have been disposed of: it is impossible to express what I owe to his friendly care of them, and to the unexampled kindness of his sister, Mrs. Mourant. Whenever I allow myself to think of my family in their present dispersed and dependent state, I am made truly wretched. Still, whatever may be my lot, I feel that I shall have done my duty to my country and to my family; and if I have not been more successful, it will not be owing to any want of exertion on my part to merit a more fortunate issue. But I will not, my dear Birch, dwell on this gloomy topic; you know already everything that relates to my most private concerns, and I am confident no one participates more than yourself in my grief.

I have now been six months in Portugal, during which I have constantly been on the march. I am now just arrived here from the North, having been present at the storming of Ciudad Rodrigo, the most spirited enterprise that has been undertaken this war, and nothing could exceed the good order and judgment with which it was conducted. The troops are collecting fast on the left banks of the Tagus, with a view to the attack of Badajoz. It is expected that we shall find the works considerably strengthened since we last sat down before it, added to the probability of a general action. I am in command of what

---

1. Colonel Birch had lately received a large accession of fortune by the death of his father-in-law, Jacob Reynardson, Esq. of Holywell, in the county of Lincoln.

2. Major-General Thomas Carey, of the 3rd Guards, a brother of the late Mrs. Le Marchant.

is considered the finest brigade of cavalry in the army, consisting of nine large squadrons: rely upon it, they will make a hole wherever their exertions are directed.

I expect my son Carey to join me from Cadiz. I have not seen him since his tour in the Mediterranean: it is now two years since we parted. What unforeseen events have occurred in this interval! My time is exceedingly taken up between the duties of my brigade and the Board of Claims, of which I am president; and this is not to be regretted. I meet with great kindness from all quarters—not a single controlling hand from any in this army; and I have reason to hope and believe that I shall make it out well with all whom I have any concerns with, which is no small degree of consolation and comfort. In the course of a few days it is supposed that the cavalry will be posted forward, beyond the Guadiana, as far as Villa Franca. I am told it is a fine country for the movements of that arm, where it will probably have much to do.

I congratulate you on the flattering appointment you hold; the more so from the manner in which your promotion took place. Many thanks for your friendly invitation, and I shall be glad to profit of the first opportunity to accept it.

Adieu, my dear friend, &c.

All obstacles being at length removed, Marshal Beresford invested Badajoz on the 16th of March; and in order to cover the operations of the siege, a corps, consisting of the first, sixth, and seventh divisions of infantry, and two brigades of cavalry, under the command of Lieutenant-General Sir Thomas Graham, were directed to march upon Llerena, to keep in check General Drouet, then lying at Villa Franca with 5000 men; whilst another corps, under Sir Rowland Hill, advanced on Almandralejos, above which, at Zalamea de Serena, near Medellin, was General Darican, with a force of equal strength with Drouet's. These were the only French troops of whom any immediate apprehensions could be entertained.

Major-General Le Marchant, whose brigade formed part of Graham's corps, quitted Villa Vicosa on the morning of the 15th, and having crossed the Guadiana, proceeded by forced marches through Estremadura towards Villa Franca: but before he could reach that place, Drouet was ascertained to have fallen back upon Hornachos; and although the French cavalry lingered on the plains, and occasionally showed a disposition to contest the ground, they always retired as the general advanced upon them, and the British were allowed to establish themselves without opposition at Zafra, a large and well-built town near the northern frontier of Estremadura.

The general continued at Zafra and in the neighbourhood from the 21st to the 25th instant, during which interval the following letter was written.

Major-General Le Marchant to Denis Le Marchant, Esq. Lincoln's Inn.

Zafra, 24th March.

I received your letter of the 8th instant when in the field, and at a moment that I was in expectation of falling in with the enemy; notwithstanding which I had great pleasure in its perusal, which I did not delay. For nearly a month I have been constantly moving; and the result has been, that the army has reached this place by forced marches from the north of Portugal, and is now busily employed in carrying on the siege of Badajoz. Everything is going on well, and we entertain the most sanguine hopes of ultimate success. The enemy retired as we advanced; but it is supposed that he will return in sufficient force to give us battle. The army is in high spirits, and confident m the gallantry and experience of their leader.

Tell —— that I am expecting to hear from him, and that should he write, I wish him to inform me of the state of parties, and what is likely to turn up in the way of politics during the winter. A war with Russia is certain: very many of the best French generals have already left Spain to join the army in Poland, and also some troops.

General Drouet's corps, after moving for some days along the mountains, halted at Llerena; and Sir Thomas Graham, who was fond of bold strokes in war, collected all his forces, in the hope of surprising them there on the morning of the 26th instant. The attack was well timed; for Graham had received intelligence that the French officers had invited the ladies of Llerena to a ball on the 25th, preparatory to the departure of the army on the following morning; so that there was every probability of the absence of some of the officers from their posts, as well as of a general relaxation in their usual vigilance and discipline. General Le Marchant set out from Bienvenida on this expedition at eleven on the night of the 25th, and, by a rapid march through Villa Garcia, they found themselves close upon Llerena before any alarm had been given: so near did they approach, that the lights in the town were distinctly visible.

But at this moment one of the baggage-horses broke loose and dashed into a column of Hanoverian infantry, some of whom, believing the enemy to be upon them, fired; and whether this gave the alarm, or the French had otherwise been apprized of their danger, the British had the mortification, as day dawned, of seeing them file over the hills behind Llerena, their bands playing as if on parade, and with every sign of order and regularity. Pursuit was useless, and they escaped without loss or difficulty.

Major-General Le Marchant returned on the same day to Villa Garcia, in the neighbourhood of which the enemy's cavalry gave him ample employment, being equal in number to our own, better acquainted with the country, and no way behind us either in activity or enterprise. They also claimed to be our superiors in discipline and skill,—qualities which they had now frequent opportunities of exhibiting, as the extensive plains of Estremadura, uninterrupted for miles by any enclosure, are admirably adapted for manoeuvring. These lofty pretensions, however, were very ill supported, as in all the affairs they had with the general's brigade, which was frequently opposed to them on the 27th and 28th, the loss and the consequences on either side were equally unimportant.

On the 28th General Le Marchant was at Berlinga, from whence he wrote to one of his sons:—

> Nothing can be more active than the operations of this small corps under General Graham, and I hope that the object of our endeavours will be ultimately accomplished,—namely, to prevent the junction of the enemy's force without obliging them to make a detour, that will occasion a delay, before which the garrison of Badajoz would probably fall.

Thus far the British had carried all before them; and the two marshals, as if paralysed by the boldness of Lord Wellington, appeared to have abandoned Badajoz to its fate. Various reasons have been assigned for their inactivity; of which the most plausible is, that each relied too much on the resources of the other, whilst from some personal misunderstanding they did not possess that knowledge of each other's views which was indispensable in such an emergency. A fortnight had the town been under siege, yet not a soldier marched from either of the grand armies to its relief; and it was only on the 3rd that Soult's advance from Cordoba was decided.

Late as this demonstration was, it necessarily obliged the English forces to concentrate; and General Le Marchant had already retreated on the 1st of April to Albuera, followed, as might be expected, by the French cavalry, who during the day pressed him vigorously on several points, especially before La Granja, where, through the information given them by a deserter, they had almost cut off a squadron of the 3rd Dragoons, under Major Hugonin. The major had gone there on the preceding evening to collect forage, of which the troops stood in great need; and as the French were not known to be in the vicinity, he had no reason to apprehend an attack from them. They had marched, however, all night, and at noon were seen issuing in great force from the woods that crown the hills immediately above La Granja; and descending very rapidly into the town, they came on Lieutenant Johnstone, as he was bargaining for corn with the daughter of the *alcade*, and he only escaped by the swiftness of his horse.

When they had pushed through the streets, they found our dragoons prepared to receive them, and a charge took place, in which neither party gained much advantage; but we lost half a dozen men killed or wounded, and, from our inferiority of number, might have been handled severely, had not Sir Stapleton Cotton and Major-General Le Marchant opportunely come up with the main body of the cavalry, and secured Major Hugonin's retreat without further molestation. To compensate for this little disaster, the French were on the same day worsted in an encounter with a detachment of the 6th Dragoon Guards at Assuega, when a sergeant of that regiment behaved with distinguished gallantry, and killed a French officer in single combat, for which he afterwards, through the general's interest, obtained a commission in the line. Nothing else of interest occurred during the remainder of the week, by which time the brigade had joined the army at Albuera, where a general engagement was expected, as the French troops were all marching hastily in that direction, Soult himself having reached Llerena on the 4th.

There he was joined by the subordinate corps of Gazan, Drouet, and Darican, with which he resumed his march on the 7th; and as he advanced on the following day towards Albuera, and was only a few hours distant from it, some horsemen, despatched by General Philipon, brought him the unexpected intelligence of the storm of Badajoz on the night of the 6th; an exploit which called forth the strongest expressions of amazement[2] even from the old soldiers of Napoleon, versed as they were in the daring tactics of their leader.

It was now Soult's turn to retreat; which he did with such expedition, that he got back to Seville by the 11th to oppose the Spaniards, who were already before the gates of that city. The English cavalry were no less alert; for General Le Marchant pushed on the 8th as far as Los Santos, and consequently beyond the posts which the French had occupied in the morning. Here the marshal seems for a time to have baffled his pursuers, who must have had great difficulty in tracking him over these boundless and solitary plains, whose utter desolation gave him all the advantages of a march through a desert. It was but on the evening of the 18th that information of the cavalry of his rearguard being posted between Villa Garcia and Usagre reached Sir Stapleton Cotton, who thereupon instantly determined to attack them.

The forces selected for this enterprise amounted to somewhat under 1900 men, consisting of the heavy brigade of General Le Marchant, and the light brigade of General Anson, then under the command of Lieutenant-Colonel the Honourable Frederick Ponsonby, who had distinguished himself at Talavera and Barrossa, and was destined in after days to raise his name high in the annals of military adventure by his romantic escapes at Waterloo. The French cavalry numbered about 2,300, all old soldiers; and General Lallemand, one of the brigadiers, was a favourite pupil of Napoleon, and had already established a brilliant reputation. The commander-in-chief, General Peyremmont, was a soldier of acknowledged gallantry, who prided himself on his knowledge of his profession; but he was of a vainglorious disposition, and entertained an utter contempt for the English cavalry, whose officers he was constantly holding up to ridicule as unworthy opponents, and entirely ignorant of their duty. The coils, however, which they had contrived to weave around him, showed them no such despicable foes.

The French position was accessible by the roads from Villa Franca, Bienvenida, and Llerena, being at a short distance from the junction of the Bienvenida and Llerena roads. The country about it is flat, but intersected by ranges of hills, and it had been the scene of some sharp encounters between the cavalry of the hostile armies during former

2. General Lery, an officer of great experience, and the chief engineer of the Army of the South, and therefore necessarily knowing thoroughly the condition of Badajoz, mentions the capture of it (in an intercepted letter) as "a very extraordinary event."

campaigns. It was not unfavourable for a surprise, and Colonel Ponsonby was accordingly directed to march from Villa Franca in time to fall upon the French in front at daybreak; while General Le Marchant should push round the hills to Bienvenida, to be ready to intercept their retreat on Llerena. In the event of the enemy being prepared for Ponsonby's attack, or being in very superior force, the general's movements were left to his own discretion.

The troops accordingly set out that night from their respective stations, Sir Stapleton Cotton accompanying Ponsonby's brigade.

General Le Marchant accomplished his march without meeting any of the French picquets; but on approaching the ground he had been directed to occupy, he had the mortification of perceiving that one part of the plan had failed. All hope of surprising the enemy was at an end. Ponsonby's brigade had by some mistake arrived before the appointed hour, and his skirmishers had been for some time engaged; whilst the enemy, who had retreated when he first appeared, and afterwards returned, on seeing the weakness of his force, were concentrating their squadrons in order to make a signal and decisive charge.

This design was baffled by the skilful manoeuvring of Sir Stapleton Cotton, who contrived to engross the enemy's attention and enable General Le Marchant to approach un-perceived. The delay thus obtained, however, was but short; and Sir Stapleton then stood as if patiently to await the onset of the enemy. His defeat appeared inevitable, and they were advancing in the expectation of overwhelming him, when suddenly General Lallemand descried a small body of British cavalry emerge from an olive-grove in his rear, and push boldly towards him across the plain. They were evidently no more than three or four hundred men, and he could not see any troops near to support them. For a moment he supposed them to be a detachment who had mistaken their orders or lost their way; but on closer observation, the compactness and precision with which they moved, aroused in his mind suspicions which he deemed it prudent to communicate to General Peyremmont.

The troops that had thus attracted General Lallemand's notice, were four squadrons of the 5th Dragoon Guards, with which General Le Marchant was about to make a daring effort to gain the day. One glance had satisfied him that the French might still be advantageously attacked, and since a defile that separated him from the enemy necessarily would take some time for his whole brigade to pass, he only waited for these three squadrons, and then set off with them, although their horses were apparently spent by having marched sixty miles almost without intermission, and having stolen through an olive-ground which lay beyond the defile, he was bringing his little band upon their rear, whilst the rest of his brigade hastened by the road to support him.

A few minutes elapsed before Lallemand could find Peyremmont; and when he did, his suggestions were ill received. Peyremmont insisted that the officer commanding the British detachment must be a blockhead, and was throwing himself upon certain destruction. To Lallemand's more experienced eye, the disposition of the British denoted anything rather than want of skill, and he could not help observing, that if the commander were not a blockhead, he must be no ordinary soldier. Peyremmont smiled contemptuously at a supposition which he treated as absurd, and turned away.

They then parted; but almost ere Lallemand could return to his men, Peyremmont's resolution was shaken. General Le Marchant approaching still closer, and presenting a very formidable front, Peyremmont checked his movement against Ponsonby, in order that he might prepare for attacking his new opponent In the midst of this operation, and whilst the French were in the confusion inseparable from the act of suddenly changing their position, General Le Marchant dashed upon them with desperate impetuosity at the head of his brave followers, whose close and serried array, undisturbed by the extraordinary speed with which it moved, went as one unbroken mass into the ranks of the enemy, who, unprepared for so rude a shock, and already in disorder, were unable to avail themselves of their superiority of numbers, and made a very ineffectual resistance. Such was the violence of the onset, that many of their dragoons were absolutely ridden down, and their ranks pierced through and through.

The *mêlée* which ensued was bloody, owing to the opportunities it afforded of personal conflict, and many were the wounds given and received by the victors. Its duration, however, was brief; for Sir Stapleton Cotton having charged the enemy's front with success as soon as he saw General Le Marchant engaged, and the general's two regiments having come up to support him, the enemy gave way in all directions; the rout was complete, and the plain was soon covered with fugitives. The French officers had fought with their accustomed gallantry, and some of them were taken prisoners whilst vainly endeavouring to rally their men, whose flight, however, became at last so general as to oblige them to join in it.

Lallemand could hardly repress a smile when a horseman caught his eye, urging his steed along the slippery sides of a hill which afforded but an insecure footing, some English dragoons following at a distance, with a certainty of capturing him in case the animal fell. His dress, though soiled and disordered, showed him to be an officer of high rank; but danger levels all distinctions, none stopped to help him, and he was left to escape as he best might. This proved to be Peyremmont himself; who, doomed to witness the fatal effects of his presumption, had been involved in his own broken bands and hurried off the field.

The pursuit continued for more than four miles, and was pushed up to the suburbs of Llerena.

The loss of the French was stated by deserters, and generally estimated at little less than five hundred men in killed, wounded, and missing; of whom one lieutenant-colonel, two captains, and one hundred and twenty-eight privates, were made prisoners. That of the English was only fifty-six killed and wounded; of whom forty-five being of the 5th Dragoon Guards, furnished that regiment with too sure a title to the greatest share in the laurels of the day; and that these were hardly earned, is perhaps best proved by the fact that almost all the wounds were found to have been inflicted by the sabre.

The engagement being fought in the vicinity of both armies, received an ample share of attention, and established General Le Marchant's military character. Lord Wellington, in his despatches, mentions it as highly creditable "to Sir Stapleton and General Le Marchant, and the officers and troops under their command:" thus coupling the general with his chief,—an unusual distinction, which plainly showed the sense that Lord Wellington attached to his services on that occasion. The merit which he claimed for himself was very moderate; for, in a letter to a friend, he merely observes:

> The affair, though of no great consequence, brought myself and my brigade acquainted on essential points, and I have reason to believe that we are mutually well pleased with each other.

The day after this engagement, the general was joined by his eldest son, who had obtained permission to quit Cadiz, (where he was quartered with his regiment,) that he might serve in future under his father's eye on the staff of Lord Wellington's army. His arrival was the source of unmingled delight to his father, who had always rather distinguished him above his brothers—partly, no doubt, on account of his being much older than any of them, and possibly not less from the fact that, although of the same profession and pursuits with himself, their natures were totally dissimilar. He was, however, a youth of whom any parent might have been excusably proud. Unassuming in manner, mild and gentle in disposition, yet so bold and intrepid, that he seemed in battle to have no sense of personal danger: his character could hardly fail to win the affection and respect of those around him. Without possessing his father's depth of intellect or searching penetration, he was noted for the soundness of his judgment, and surpassed by few of his comrades in general accomplishments.

His talent for drawing, which he had diligently cultivated during his travels through Sicily, Greece, and Asia Minor, was scarcely inferior to his father's; and although under twenty, he spoke French, Italian, Spanish, and Portuguese with correctness and fluency. In external advantages he could have few competitors; for his figure, though slender, was tall and well-proportioned, and realising the description given by a great modern writer of one of his heroes:

> An oval face, a straight and well-formed nose, hazel eyes, and a complexion just sufficiently tinged with brown to save it from the charge of effeminacy, contributed to form such a countenance as limners love to paint and ladies to look upon.

The general and his son first met at Zafra; where the latter had the happiness almost at the same moment to receive his father's embrace and to hear of his success. He observes in a letter describing the engagement:—

> Everybody says it was a most brilliant and gallant affair.

And it may be added, that this opinion was not confined to the English camp; for there is reason to believe that the general impression produced by the day on the French was very discouraging. It probably accelerated Drouet's retreat, for he immediately quitted Llerena and withdrew his division behind the Guadalquivir, which he was allowed to do unmolested, the attention of the English being now engrossed by the operations of Marmont. That marshal had made an irruption into the North of Portugal at the time that Soult marched upon Albuera, with the view of diverting Lord Wellington from the siege of Badajoz; and although he had failed to accomplish his object, he still remained in the country, committing the most dreadful ravages, and apparently seeking to strike a blow that might redeem his damaged reputation.

The inhabitants were flying before him in all directions, abandoning everything that could hinder their escape. The country was left entirely at his mercy, and great fears were entertained for the safety of the fortified towns; their only garrisons being the militia, who had been hastily and compulsorily brought under arms. Lord Wellington, therefore, hastened to attack him as soon as Drouet's retreat was ascertained; and it was most eagerly wished in the English camp, that he would either be found ready to accept battle, or be forced to fight before he had recrossed the frontier.

The British Army having moved towards Portugal on the 13th, the general, now accompanied by his son, left Zafra, and reached Nozales the same evening. In three more marches they arrived at Badajoz, which, after all the horrors of the assault, presented a most cheerless spectacle. The breaches in the fortifications had indeed been partially repaired, but the streets were encumbered with the ruins caused by the fire of the besiegers; and the general appearance of the houses, defaced, as most of them were, and exhibiting marks of violence, corresponded but too well with the condition of the inhabitants. Within little more than a year they had undergone three regular sieges; and deeply as they must have felt the oppressive exactions of the French, these evils were insignificant compared with the price they had paid for their deliverance by the English.

After halting a night at Badajoz, the brigade crossed the Guadiana on the morning of the 17th, and at a league distant passing over the Caya, entered Portugal. This little stream, the boundary between the two nations, was no longer regarded with the interest that had attached to it in their happier days, before the success of their common enemy had swept away all such conventional distinctions, and left them with no other landmarks than military posts. Portugal began, in effect, two leagues further, at Elvas, which had escaped the fate of Badajoz only by the strength of its citadel,—a virgin fortress, built by the celebrated Count de la Lippe, when he commanded the Portuguese Army. This town enjoys the reputation of being the dirtiest in Portugal; which is the more inexcusable on the part of its inhabitants, as the streets, being steep, narrow, and plentifully supplied with water, might be kept clean without much labour or expense. When the brigade arrived, the rain was falling in torrents, and flowed down the streets as if a number of sluices had been let loose on them, carrying every sort of filth along with it, and spreading far and wide, incontestable evidences of the universal impurity, which, after floating from street to street, found a resting-place within the walls, owing to the want of proper ducts and channels for its removal.

It was with no small satisfaction that the general and his companions, after a night's confinement in this fetid atmosphere, breathed again the pure air of the country. They rode out of the gates at daybreak, and came at once upon an extensive plain, which increased in fertility and cultivation as they advanced. The orange-groves were in full beauty, their exquisitely delicate and fragrant blossoms mingling with the bright golden-coloured fruit, which was now quite ripe, while both stood out in strong relief from amidst the dark branches that shaded them. Towards noon they halted some hours at Borba, to supply themselves with wine, for which the village has long been famous. The approach to it was embellished by plantations of olives, oranges, and almonds, interspersed with fruits and flowers, all glowing under the mild influence of spring. Being out of the high road to Lisbon, it had suffered less from the inflictions of war; which fall with comparative lightness on rural districts, especially in a country whose extraordinary qualities of soil and climate render it almost independent of the labours of man.

The houses were many of them well built, and there was an air of comfort and prosperity in their exterior very delightful to men whose recollection of Badajoz was still fresh. The general and his staff were billeted in a mansion that passed for the best in the village, belonging to a noble lady, whose family had long been the principal proprietors in the district. Although her age and circumstances might have dispensed with her appearing before strangers,—for she was more than seventy years of age, and a widow,—she received the party very courteously, and gave them as good an entertainment as a Portuguese country-house afforded. Her conversation was interesting, and showed that she bad been much in the world; though there was a marked sadness in her countenance, which was sufficiently explained when she told them part of her life. She and her only child, a daughter, unhappily of weak understanding, were the only descendants of the illustrious Vasco de Gama. Within two years she had lost her husband, her brother, and her only son, the last having been mortally wounded at the gallant but unsuccessful defence of Evora.

After dinner they took leave of their venerable hostess, and resumed their march along the plain, which brought them late in the evening to Estremos,—a walled town of some importance, where a spacious and well-built square and clean streets bespoke moderate prosperity in the inhabitants. A large house, tolerably furnished, and not without pretensions to architectural beauty, was appropriated to the general and his staff, who had entire possession of it, the owner being absent at Lisbon, where he usually resided. He had great estates in the neighbourhood; though, like the other Portuguese nobles, he manifested little if any interest in their management, and seldom or ever visited them.

The general could not quit Estremos on the following morning without visiting the castle, which stands on a high hill, rising abruptly above the town, which is itself built on an eminence. It was formerly a place of no mean strength; but the works have been neglected since the construction of the citadel at Elvas, and it is now chiefly remarkable for the boldness of its position, and the extent of country it commands. This extent sinks into insignificance when compared with the "illimitable wastes" of Estremadura; but there is more variety in the prospect than is usually found in the scenery of this part of Portugal, and few spots display to equal perfection the wonderful diversities of cultivation of which the soil of Alentejo is susceptible.

All the productions of a Portuguese farm are here collected in the richest abundance;—grain of every description, vineyards in endless succession, whole tracts of oranges and olives, with a profusion of almonds, figs, laurels, and garden shrubs, surmounted by well-grown timber trees. Nothing is wanting to prove the extraordinary powers of this favoured land; nor are more picturesque features entirely denied to it. Innumerable streams, at once its brightest ornaments and the sources of its wealth, intersect the fields in every direction; and if the ornamented mansion, with its cluster of dependencies, be absent, the want is in some degree supplied by the spacious premises of the wine-growers; and here and there on a rising ground may be seen the remains of a Moorish castle, more interesting in ruin than in the gaudy days of its ancient lords.

Descending from "this proud eminence," the general proceeded on his march towards Beira, and soon found himself in the midst of the scenery he had been previously contemplating. His route lay for some time through these fertile vales, which continued equally luxuriant; but it was melancholy to observe how little human good resulted from so liberal a distribution of the bounties of Nature. Resident gentry there were none. The peasantry, a simple docile race, frugal and industrious, were in a state of the grossest ignorance, and, content with the bare necessaries of life, were surrounded by all the accompaniments of poverty. Their labours yielded a very inadequate return, owing to the difficulties of transport and the want of mechanical contrivances; obstacles which might have been easily removed by a moderate outlay of capital under judicious management.

Their landlords, however, being little more enlightened than themselves, were blind to such considerations; which, in truth, were not likely to occur to them, as they for the most part resided in the capital, or some of the other large towns, and being engrossed by frivolous occupations, were utterly indifferent to the condition of their tenantry. Deeply had they paid for such a dereliction of duty; for with the decline of their taste for rural pursuits, and the consequent abandonment of their estates, their own character had rapidly degenerated. They were no longer the brilliant chivalry whose exploits by land and sea, and whose attainments in science and literature had given Portugal, in spite of her narrow limits, a distinguished place among the nations of Europe. All their great qualities had disappeared under the blighting influence of the government and the priesthood: even their love of war seemed extinguished, and unmindful of their ancient glories, they now idly looked on while their own countrymen were fighting for independence on their native soil under foreign chiefs.

As the brigade approached Beira, they learnt that Marshal Marmont, after suffering a disgraceful check at Guarda from an insignificant corps of militia, had concentrated his forces in a strong position between Sabugal and Penmacor. Upon that point therefore they were directed to march; and such was the sense entertained of the importance of the object, that they did not halt for a single day until the 23rd of April, when they reached the village of Zebras, a few leagues beyond Castello Branco, and within a march of Sabugal. Had it been possible for them to arrive a little earlier, they would have either found Marmont in his camp, or been able to intercept him in his retreat.

The hope of cutting off a convoy which he knew to be expected at Almeida, had detained him longer than he intended; and when its safe arrival left him without a reason for risking a battle, his route was closed by the rains, and he was reduced to remain and fight, or to make a detour, in which he would inevitably have encountered the English, flushed by recent success, in a country where their superior numbers and great local advantages gave him no chance of escape. Fortunately for him, the rain ceased as suddenly as it had commenced; and, to the extreme disappointment of the English, and still more of

Bridge between Niza and Villa Velha

the Portuguese, he recrossed the Agueda and got back into Spain, leaving behind him a name which is still pronounced with execration in every valley of Beira.

The following extract from a letter from Ensign Le Marchant to one of his brothers in England gives some particulars of the march of the brigade on this expedition, and of the state of the country through which they passed.

> Our road from Estremos was flat and uninteresting until we arrived at Niza, a small town, whose wretched condition is quite unaccountable, since it has always had the luck to escape falling into the hands of the French. Here the scenery assumes a bolder character, and we entered a defile about two leagues in length, formed by opposite ranges of mountains, at the extremity of which we reached the Tagus. The sands, I am sorry to say, have lost their golden hue; but the river is not unworthy of the praises it has received, and the view of it from the heights is very striking.
>
> We crossed it by a bridge of boats at Villa Velha, where the course of the river makes a slight bend, and the mountains opening for it to pass, form an enclosure, whose lofty sides, rising boldly and precipitously around, seem to shut it out from the rest of the world. I never saw a more still and sequestered spot, and there was a solemnity in its repose that made our small party feel like intruders when we disturbed it by our presence. We had scarcely time to admire the silent and savage solitude of the scene, before a regiment of cavalry appeared in the defile; and the effect of the troops spread along the road, and then the bustle and noise they caused in crossing the river, were altogether perfectly dramatic.
>
> We observed an abundance of cork-trees in these mountains. The tree resembles the oak. Its bark is converted into the cork which is in such use with us. The Portuguese have not invention enough to take advantage of so precious an article; for you will be surprised when I tell you that corks for bottles are not to be procured in any part of the country.
>
> We were quartered at Castello Branco, in the house of the vicar. He complained of having been dreadfully pillaged by the French; and if they left him any linen and plate, he kept them out of our sight, perhaps from fear of being pillaged by us like-

wise. My father's friend, the bishop, who, poor old man, is above seventy, had fled into the mountains on the approach of the French, and was not returned.

We then proceeded to Alcaniz, where we got into a famous good quarter, with an excellent garden; the proprietor of which had fled, leaving a single domestic in charge of the place.

The next day we marched to Zebras, a pretty little village, standing on a hill covered with cork-trees; every cottage having its own vine, which formed a shady seat before the cottage door. The situation is most romantic, and at a little distance it gave every indication of peace and happiness; but on a closer approach we found the French had been there, and had broken and destroyed all they could not carry away. We established ourselves at the house of a Fidalgo, who had retired with his family and flocks into the neighbourhood of Thomar when the French entered the district. The boards of the floors had been taken up, to discover if any thing was concealed under them, and the whole house turned upside-down in a very wanton manner.

We contrived to make ourselves tolerably comfortable, and got some dinner. Shortly after our meal, we observed two persons on horseback enter a wood in the valley; and in about half-an-hour a man and woman arrived at the door, who told us they were the owners of the dwelling. It seems they had just returned from the mountains, and had left their family in the wood which we had seen them enter. We offered them half the house, which they thankfully accepted, and soon brought their family to take possession of it; when they presented us with a couple of lambs as an acknowledgment of our kindness. They had been fortunate in saving some of their effects; which was not the case with many of their neighbours.

You cannot conceive the wretched condition of the people in the North of Portugal; forced as they are to fly from their homes whenever the enemy advance, and often in such haste, that they are content to get off only with their lives. Every thing they leave behind them is of course plundered or destroyed; which I think would hardly happen if they remained at home, for it must be against the interest of the French to render the country incapable of yielding them any supplies.

But such is the hatred the Portuguese bear to them, that they submit to any sacrifice rather than come in contact with them. The scenes of misery that thus constantly occur are most distressing; and indeed the destruction is almost universal, for the villages are half in ruins; and we think ourselves exceedingly fortunate in getting under a house with a roof, as very few have that appendage.

We did not advance beyond Zebras; but at that time the brigade had been constantly marching, either in pursuit of, or retiring from the enemy, since the 13th March, the day it left Villa Vicosa; so that we have been pretty hard worked.

On our road from Zebras, we met in the mountains a family nearly related to the minister-at-war, returning to their homes, which, like others, they had abandoned on the approach of the French. The party consisted of three pretty women, attended by their brother and two or three soldiers, with a greasy old monk, who seemed to be father confessor and sole manager of the establishment, for he helped them to mount and dismount their asses, and evidently regulated all their proceedings. They were obliged to use asses, as all mules and horses belonging to individuals are seized for the use of government.

The excesses of the French Army in the province of Beira during this expedition have been indignantly described by all the historians of the Peninsular war, and it is extraordinary that such gross inhumanity should have been sanctioned by a marshal who was distinguished from many of his comrades by having had no concern in the sanguinary atrocities of the revolution, and was not only a man of birth and education, but bore a high character for private worth and amiability of disposition. In the English camp the feeling against Marmont was universal. Lord Wellington briefly states in his despatches, that "the French, as usual, had robbed and murdered the inhabitants of the country." The following letter enters more into detail.

M. General Le Marchant to Denis Le Marchant, Esq. London.

Southeiro, near Castello Branco, 26th April, 1812.

I was too much engaged to write to you by the last packet, but Carey undertook to give you a few lines. I have now to thank you for your letter of the 28th. I am always happy in hearing from you, and the length of your letter makes it proportionably more acceptable.

My return to the North of Portugal is accompanied with the

deepest regret at the melancholy effects of the ravages committed by the enemy on the helpless inhabitants during our absence: not a vestige of clothing, furniture, meat, grain, wine, or oil, have they left them; everything carried away or destroyed. Little do you, who have never witnessed the horrors of war, comprehend its destructive effects. I returned yesterday from my old quarters at Fundao, where I went to see the lieutenant-governor of the district.

He and his family had just come back from their emigration to the mountains, and found nothing but an empty house perfectly gutted, their cattle driven away, and, in fact, themselves left entirely destitute. A respectable inhabitant apologised, through a friend, for not calling upon me, having no clothes. Others of the most opulent proprietors, my acquaintance and friends, are, I am afraid, equally sufferers. Whole villages emigrated; indeed, not a soul remained wherever the enemy advanced. The distress of these poor people during their emigration, from want of provisions,, as well as on their return, cannot he expressed. 1 have not been more melancholy throughout the whole campaign than at beholding these scenes.

The enemy has retired, and we are provisioning Almeida: what is to follow no one knows; to conjecture would be a waste of time.

Carey gets on famously, and will make me a most useful *aide-de-camp*. We both enjoy health and strength, and stand well the fatigues of active service.

It was impossible for troops to traverse a country so exhausted and spoiled without suffering great privations; and these were rendered more trying by the fatigue attendant on long and unintermitted marches during several successive weeks. The cavalry thus often found themselves in the plight so quaintly described by Froissart in his account of the unhappy adventures of their countrymen, when fighting under John of Gaunt in the Peninsula some 500 years before:—

> They wold gladly haue bene in some towne to haue refresshed theym, for their forayers wheresoeuer they wente coude fynde no thing; and somtyme whan they sawe a village on a hyll, or on the playne, than they rejoysed, and wolde say, Go we thyder, for there we shall be all ryche and well prouyded: and thyder they wolde ryde in great haste; and whan they were there, they founde

nothynge but bare walks, and the howses broken downe, and nether catte nor dogge, cocke nor hen, man, woman, nor childe there; it was wasted before by the Frenche-nien. Thus they loste their tyme; and their horses were leane and feble, by reason of their poor norisshyng: they were happy when they founde any pasture, and some were so feble that they could go no further, but died for great heat and povertie.—*Froissart*, vol. ii.

Lord Wellington, not thinking it expedient to follow Marmont into Spain, again distributed his army over the north of Portugal. General Le Marchant was ordered to proceed by easy marches into the Alentejo, and to put his men into cantonments in that province. He accordingly returned to Castello Branco, and, after despatching his troops to their respective stations, fixed upon Crato, a small town lying between Castello Branco and Estremos, for his own residence during the ensuing month. Some military business detained him a few days on his route amidst the splendid scenery of the Estrella, a portion of which he has represented in the accompanying sketch of a bridge over the Sal, a small river in the mountains near Castello Branco.

It is only in the Peninsula that bridges of a structure so elegant are to be found over obscure streams in districts little frequented; but in a country where a mountain torrent is often swollen by one night's rain into a river sufficient to arrest the march of an army moving to battle, as had been witnessed by the English in the war, bridges are necessarily numerous, and their construction becomes a most important branch of national architecture. How successfully it was here cultivated by the Romans, and subsequently by the Moors, numerous proofs are still extant; and with these models before them, the Spaniards, notwithstanding their general neglect of the arts and sciences, have produced works of the same description not unworthy of their masters.

The general arrived at Crato on the 1st of May. Part of his brigade he kept under his immediate eye; the rest were quartered only a few leagues distant, at Cabeco de Vide and Fronteira, which admitted of his superintending them without inconvenience. The position of Crato in this respect could have been its only recommendation, for it was one of the most wretched places in the Alentejo. Formerly, indeed, this town had enjoyed some importance, and it was still surrounded by walls of considerable thickness, which had probably been erected by the Knights of Malta, to whom it for ages belonged.

The Prior of Crato was a candidate for the throne of Portugal

Bridge over the Sal

upon the death of Don Sebastian; and he must have been materially assisted by the interest of his order, for they held large estates throughout the kingdom; the policy of the Portuguese government having favoured all military orders, as a means of providing for an over-grown aristocracy. In the palmy days of knighthood, the distribution of a number of gallant high-born soldiers, many of them necessarily of superior attainments, over rural districts, could not be otherwise than beneficial to the community; but those times were long gone by, and the residence of some impoverished and superannuated courtiers was all that of late years had resulted from such institutions. Crato, like the neighbouring town of Aviz, which belonged to the knights of the illustrious order of the same name, had long fallen into insignificance and decay.

The headquarters of the brigade continued at Crato for the whole of May, which month they passed as quietly as if they had been in any village in England. The district is exclusively rural, being divided into small farms that yielded a bare support to a thinly-scattered peasantry, whom the neglect of their landlords, followed by the exactions and cruelty of the French, had reduced to such a state, that to almost every dwelling might be applied the words of the prophet Joel, "*The garners are laid desolate, the barns are broken down; he hath laid waste my vine, he hath barked my fig-tree*." Sometimes in his rides the general fell in with families driven by the destruction of their dwellings to take refuge in the hills, where they found temporary habitations in the holes they excavated, or in the quarries which nature or art scatters over districts abounding with stone.

A sketch taken by the general in the neighbourhood of Crato, on the 21st May, represents a group of this description. It consists of two females, one in the bloom of youth, and the other not far beyond it. A boy of five or six years old is at their feet. They are sitting at the entrance of a cave, under the shade of some poplars, which conceal their hiding-place until closely approached. The dress and demeanour of both, and especially the care which each has bestowed upon the arrangement of her hair, prove them to belong to the higher classes. The younger has retained some relics of finery, which she is employed in repairing, and seems to ply her task with tolerable cheerfulness: but her companion, whose countenance even in a rough sketch denotes "a matron of Cornelia's mien," is evidently unequal to any exertion. The sorrow stamped upon her brow is no less evident in her bent and pensive attitude.

Portalegre

Perhaps she was a mother, thinking of the children from whom she had been forcibly separated, or of the brutal atrocities of the French soldiery which she had seen perpetrated within her own household. A man, probably her husband, is standing over her, wearing the loose cloak and broad hat of the country: his face is turned towards her, as if uttering words of comfort which her wounded spirit is unable to receive. Such scenes were not unfrequent, and many were the victims who perished through want in those miserable abodes; others were only kept alive by the charity of the English. They bore their sufferings with admirable fortitude and resignation, and on every occasion showed a kindliness of disposition and readiness to oblige which is seldom to be found in the abodes of misery. These qualities invested even the lowest class with an interest which their appearance was not calculated to excite; for few of either sex had any pretensions to personal beauty.

The women, indeed, were not without the dark expressive eyes and long coal-black locks that seem the heritage of the females in the Peninsula; but they lose their bloom at an early age, being employed in field-work like the men, and subjected to the same fatigue and privations; nor are they less active and laborious. The burthens which they habitually carry are out of all proportion to their slight forms. Another sketch of the general's represents a group of milkwomen, each bearing two massive pitchers on her head, one placed on the top of the other, which must have made the party look at a distance like a troop of Patagonians.

At a distance of about three leagues from Crato is the city of Portalegre, whose lofty spires are seen for miles in that direction, and gladden the heart of the traveller when he catches the first glimpse of them. Weary of a route which there is nothing to enliven, sick of the filth and wretchedness which characterize the Portuguese villages, he hails with delight the prospect of finding himself once more among the comforts and enjoyments of a wealthy and well-regulated community; and these are more easily attainable in Portalegre than in any other town in Portugal. It is well-built, and has some fine churches, which were abundantly supplied with ecclesiastics, over whom the bishop of the diocese presided, even in these bad times, with becoming state. A number of respectable families had retired thither for safety or convenience during the war; and as they were partial to the English, with whom it was a favourite quarter, the society was excellent.

In addition to its other advantages, Portalegre, lying as it does under the Sierras Aronches, is on the verge of mountain scenery which offers a most agreeable contrast to the plains of the Alentejo. This splendid chain, which stretches from the Guadiana to the Tagus, is the chief ornament of the country it traverses; indeed there is scarcely any other high ground through the whole of this immense tract. The hills just beyond Crato detach themselves from the Sierra at Castello Vide, but are only remarkable for the abundance and variety of the shrubs with which they are covered. The *cistuses* were then in full bloom, and the brightness and delicacy of their pink yellow and white flowers formed a galaxy of colours not unworthy of the richest garden. There, and only there, were no traces to be seen of the ravages of war. Every description of cultivated land had suffered more or less from the incursion of the spoiler; but no impress of his foot remained on these wild wastes, which, "blossoming as the rose," seemed to exult at their escape from the desolation that surrounded them.

A few weeks' rest had the desired effect of bringing the brigade into excellent condition; and on the 26th instant, the 3rd Dragoons, who had been quartered at Cabeco de Vede, were able to march, under Major Clewes, in support of General Hill's attack on Almaraz, and accordingly advanced for that purpose as far as Puebla Cevada, after which they returned to the headquarters at Crato in full strength and the best order.

The following is an extract from a letter addressed by the general's son at this period to his brother in London.

Crato, 27th May.

> We are heartily tired of our present quarters; for a Portuguese village is not the most delightful place in the world, especially in the Alentejo, where the scenery is flat and uninteresting. Our best comfort is, that we must soon be on the move; and as no one knows Lord Wellington's future operations, there are plenty of guesses at them, and the prevalent opinion is, that a grand and last effort is in contemplation; after which, should it be found that the Spaniards continue in the same indolence and jealousy of us, we shall leave them to their fate. What part we are to take in this business is of course, like the rest of it, a mere matter of speculation. Some say we are to go to Madrid; whilst Castanos, with the Army of the North, consisting of 25,000 men, is to advance on Marmont, and Ballasteros, with 15,000 men, will cooperate with the garrison and raise the siege of

Cadiz, which now confines at the Isla a brigade of Guards and some other excellent troops, including two regiments just arrived from Sicily.

Should all these movements be simultaneously made, and skilfully executed, the French can hardly fail to be driven beyond the Ebro. They are not in sufficient force to resist such a combination of attacks. Soult, before the fall of Badajos, could only bring 20,000 infantry and 2500 cavalry into the field; so that should we make an attempt on Madrid, he would be obliged to fall back on either Marmont or Suchet, and thus leave Andalusia clear of the French. Nothing would give me greater pleasure than to write to you next month from Madrid. However, it is but fair to add that I am speaking only on my own authority, which certainly has not much experience to back it; and I fear that, like all raw soldiers, I may be too sanguine, for the older heads are much less ambitious in their expectations.

My father, among others, seems to think that we have not strength enough to guard the northern frontier against Marmont, and at the same time to carry on any extensive operations in the south. Time will show. Whatever may happen, it is clear that we are not to be much longer stationary. The bridge across the Tagus at Alcantara is repairing,[3] and magazines are forming at Niza. General Hill has succeeded in taking the bridge at Almaraz, with all the enemy's stores, boats, and 1200 prisoners. It is a most complete thing, and another proof of his being an excellent officer, as well as, what is of some consequence, a lucky one; for this is the second affair in which he has surprised the enemy.

I am just returned from coursing, but without any sport. The day before yesterday we killed four hares; but the same luck is not to be expected every day, as the game is but scanty, and the ground being broken and covered with brushwood, furze, and stones, the dogs don't run well over it. I understand that we are likely to find much better sport in Spain; and certainly while we were in the neighbourhood of Zafra we had some capital runs, and saw abundance of hares. Altogether, I like the life I am leading in this country excessively: the constant change of scene is delightful, after having been cooped up so long in

3. This was done to give a more ready communication with the corps in the south than by Villa Velha,

Cadiz, with nothing to do but garrison duty, which is, if possible, more tiresome abroad than at home.

The speculations noticed in this letter were not altogether ill founded; although Lord Wellington had a better right to success than was generally known, for he had private information of the approaching arrival of the Anglo-Sicilian army, which was on the point of sailing, and would be soon ready to prevent any diversion from the French armies in the South for the support of their forces in the North. The capture of Almaraz had also cut off all communication between Marmont and the Army of the Centre, and the British thus had the prospect of fighting the enemy on more equal terms than the great numerical superiority of the latter often admitted.

Caria

Chapter 10

Conclusion

On the 1st of June, Major-General Le Marchant, having received orders to join Lord Wellington, left Crato, and proceeding through Castello Branco and Alcaniz, as in his march in the preceding April, halted on the 7th at the foot of the Estrella, in the small town of Caria, which he has accurately represented in the accompanying sketch. It may be taken as a fair specimen of the provincial towns of a lower order that are to be met with on the high road in the north of Portugal, being supported partly by the transit of goods and passengers, and partly by supplying the wants of the rural population. One of the great roads from Lisbon into Spain passes through it, and it is commonly made a resting-place to travellers: yet, with these advantages, it had a very wretched appearance, the houses being only one storey high, and most of them out of repair, and the shops as ill provided as if they had just been plundered. The total absence of cleanliness was still more remarkable here than in the large towns, for the poverty of the inhabitants would not admit of their disguising it.

The neighbourhood of the town, however, has charms sufficient to atone with the lover of Nature for these and worse imperfections. All the country is hill or mountain: even the most rugged crags are covered with clusters of trees overhanging the narrow defiles, and darkening them by their superincumbent foliage. The pass of Alpedrinha, on the road to Castello Branco, is pre-eminent for the lonely and savage character of the scene it presents, and a more appropriate spot, to be consecrated to the god of battles it would be difficult to conceive. In the opposite direction, towards Guarda, "Alps over Alps arise" in the ranges of the Estrella, which are here seen in all their magnificence. No young painter burning with zeal for his art could be more eager in his admiration of these scenes than was the general; and the following description, contained in a letter which he addressed to his eldest daughter, now Mrs. Fanshawe, bears such evident marks of this feeling, that it is inserted here, notwithstanding the defects of composition inseparable from the haste and pressure of business under which it was written.

22nd Feb. 1812.

I am just returned from a tour, the object of which was to visit that beautiful mountain the Estrella. I was five hours in reaching Manteigas, the principal town in the Sierra, the greater part of which time was employed in ascending, such is its extraordinary height. The wildness of the scene exceeds all description. The tops of the mountains are seldom visible from below, being usually capped with clouds. The road is narrow, and only fit for mules; indeed horses would be unsafe. I can only compare it to riding on the cliffs at Serk, where a false step, as you know, would not be without its consequences.

On my journey there it was a clear day, and generally the whole of the mountain was visible, and the view from it could be supposed scarcely to have an equal. The valley below—the beautiful river, the Zezere, and an immense extent of country, were brought together in one *coup-d'oeil*, where the largest hills and features of ground were apparently lost in regard to size, owing to the height from which they were seen, and the vast expanse of the horizon embraced. You who have never been on the Continent can form no idea of the different scale of country between England and this: there is not a greater contrast between our little islands and England.

The Zezere, the most beautiful, though not the largest river in Portugal, takes its rise in the Estrella. It is not supplied so much by springs as by the mountain streams, arising from rain: half an hour's heavy rain having been known to sweep away above forty houses situated on the banks of the river. The rapidity of the current is quite wonderful, and in consequence, its ravages are great, and the country it passes through bears ample proof of its ruinous effects. Innumerable are the cascades that I passed in my journey, falling from very considerable heights among rocks and forest-trees the most majestic that can be imagined; indeed, for miles are seen continual cascades from the summit of the mountain to the Zezere, into which the water comes

Pass of Alpedrinha

rolling down with a tremendous roar. I have but little talent for description, and even of a less extraordinary scene I should find myself unable to convey a proper idea; but the scenery of the Estrella is quite beyond the powers of my pen or my pencil.

Many parts of the mountain are of massive rocks, covered with moss of different colours. The heath and aromatic plants are in the greatest variety and abundance. Chesnut-trees self-sown, growing to an enormous size on spots where there seems hardly soil enough for the most slender shrubs—the evergreen oak—the firs, and the mountain ash are scattered about in equal quantity and luxuriance.

The woods and caverns are frequented by wild-boars, who feed on the chesnut; wolves, and foxes, as well as a small tiger. I have bought a skin of the latter, which I will send you as a curiosity. I saw none of these animals; but in very cold weather, when they are pinched for food, they descend from their haunts to the great annoyance of the villagers, and carry off cattle, and any domestic animals that have the misfortune to be within their reach.

Manteigas is the principal town in the Estrella. The houses are all cottage roofs, and only one story high. No regularity; no two in the same line on the same level. The streets are so ill paved, that you cannot walk and look another way without being tripped up by the large stones that are strewed about in all directions; for the Portuguese pay little or no attention to their streets. They are, in truth, the most slovenly people upon the earth; and their dirtiness both in their persons and houses is almost incredible.

On my return from Manteigas the day was not very clear, so that in the course of an hour I got sufficiently high into the mountain to lose sight of the valley, the clouds being very low. The weather continued very hazy for three hours, and I pursued my way in a thick fog, along a route covered with snow, until I approached the Zezere, when the mist suddenly broke, and I again came in sight of the surrounding country. It was like looking upon another world. Standing as I was in a region of the most dreary winter, a forward spring burst upon my view with all its gay and beautiful accompaniments. The climate and vegetation here on the 20th of February are as advanced as you have them in the month of May.

At Caria the brigade quitted the Almeida road, and turning to the right, in the direction of Ciudad Rodrigo, left the Estrella behind them. In the evening they halted at Castelheira, an insignificant village among the hills by which the district is intersected, and on the 9th reached the headquarters of Lord Wellington at Gallegos.

All that the late Mr. Twiss, in the ponderous volume describing his travels through Spain, could find to say of Gallegos fifty years ago, is, that he saw two storks on the steeple of the church. In the stationary condition of Spain during the last century, fifty years is as one day; and Gallegos had not been increased or diminished by half-a-dozen houses in this interval. Its streets, however, now presented a scene of extraordinary animation and bustle, being crowded with troops, of whom not less than 40,000 were assembled in the camp formed in the immediate vicinity of the place, or otherwise dispersed over the district; and the weather being fine, and provisions abundant, everything conspired to keep the men in the best health and spirits.

Here the three regiments of the brigade reunited on the 10th; and it may be convenient to repeat, that they consisted of the 5th Dragoon Guards, commanded by Lieut.-colonel the Honourable William Ponsonby; the 4th Dragoons, commanded by Lieut.-colonel Lord Edward Somerset; and the 3rd Dragoons, commanded by Major Clewes. These officers were all of acknowledged merit. Lieut.-colonel Ponsonby afterwards rose to be a major-general, and Knight Commander of the Bath, and was killed at Waterloo, where he was second in command of the cavalry; Lord Edward Somerset is now a lieutenant-general and Knight Grand Cross of the Bath, and Colonel of the 4th Light Dragoons; and Major Clewes would probably have attained, or at least merited equal distinction, had he not quitted the service on his promotion before the end of the war.

On the 12th the brigade bivouacked on the Agueda, and there was a review of the cavalry in the camp, when the brigade was inspected by Lord Wellington, and received his warm commendations. It was in truth a remarkably efficient force. Other armies might produce equally fine men, who could perhaps go through the ordinary manoeuvres with the same neatness and precision; but these are only the externals of good soldiers, and sometimes disguise very bad ones. The Austrians during the revolutionary war were beaten by the French in almost every battle, although they were the finest, and their opponents the worst parade soldiers in Europe.

It is necessary to look deeper for the qualities that constitute the strength of armies; and thus only could the merit of General Le Marchant's brigade be justly appreciated. The men were by this time well-seasoned, hardy, and equal to uncommon exertions; bold, resolute, and daring to the full extent of their national character, success had inspired them with perfect confidence in their personal prowess, and they worked as coolly and steadily in the face of the enemy as at a review. Their discipline found favour even with Sir Thomas Picton, who viewed the cavalry too much with the prejudices of an old infantry officer to allow that branch of the service any praise that did not unequivocally belong to it. After relating, on one occasion, how he had found an unfortunate officer of Light Dragoons with his men all fast asleep on their post close to the French, he added, "I always feel easy when General Le Marchant's men are between me and the enemy; they do their duty, and can be trusted; and I heartily wish the rest were like them."

In no one instance had their posts been cut off by the enemy. The officers attended closely to their men, who in return looked up to them with a confidence that never sunk in hardship or danger; whilst both placed implicit trust in their general, and considering him as infallible, there was nothing that he found any difficulty in prevailing on them to undertake. He absolutely identified himself with his brigade, in which he appeared like a parent amongst his children. The hardest day's march could not prevent his walking through the bivouac to see whether the comforts of the men had been properly provided for; and, to the surprise of those who had known him in early life, if ever there was a complaint raised against him in these campaigns, it was of overindulgence to the men, who in return almost idolized him.

On the 13th the brigade crossed the Agueda, by a ford about two leagues from Ciudad Rodrigo, whose citadel, standing boldly and prominently above the plain, is seen from a great distance, and has a very picturesque effect. They were now on the ground they had so often traversed during the siege in the preceding January; but the change from winter to summer had entirely altered the aspect of the country, imparting to it a degree of improvement of which it had not appeared susceptible. The immense plain on which they had entered, bounded only by the horizon, was clothed with the richest verdure, amidst which large tracts of ripening corn gave promise of an abundant harvest. The troops, as they advanced, were surprised to find in the villages a cleanliness and comfort that reminded them of England.

The cottages were in good repair, and the peasantry a fine robust race, very superior in mien to the Portuguese, being better clothed and better fed; which was probably owing to the easier terms on which they held their farms, as well as to their having suffered less severely from the French; who, instead of laying the country waste as they had done in Portugal, had been satisfied with levying contributions; and even these were discontinued upon the capture of Ciudad Rodrigo, it having been found more profitable to carry on this system of plunder in another direction.

Two days the British marched without seeing an enemy. Marshal Marmont's force was too weak for him to seek a battle on the plain, or to risk his men in desultory engagements which could be followed by no important result. The want of provisions had obliged him to spread his army over a considerable extent of country, and he remained at Salamanca with only three battalions, not making a show of opposition to Lord Wellington until the morning of the 16th, when the British cavalry in advance, of which the general's brigade formed a part, came in sight of some French *chasseurs* on the banks of the Valmusa, about six miles from Salamanca. The French being out only for the purposes of observation, retired as soon as they had ascertained the strength of their adversaries; and the British, pushing forward, speedily found themselves on the heights above Salamanca, where the French cavalry, having received reinforcements, halted, and the English following their example, both threw out their skirmishers, who were in action during the remainder of the day.

The loss on either side was very trifling, neither having any object but to maintain the ground it covered; but there was enough of movement to make the scene most animated, especially to the British, who saw beneath them clearly and distinctly the city of Salamanca spread like a long black cloud along the banks of the Tormes, with the multitude of domes, towers, and spires that distinguish the old Peninsular cities. The river appeared about the breadth of the Thames at Richmond.

Towards evening the French cavalry returned to Salamanca. Lord Wellington, who had joined the advance at noon, did not think it prudent to press more forward that day, and the cavalry therefore bivouacked for the night on the heights.

On the following morning some Spaniards brought intelligence that Marmont had abandoned the city in the night, with all his troops, except a battalion, which he threw into the forts, in the hope that it would be equal to hold them until he could return in sufficient strength to their relief. As these forts commanded the only bridge across the Tormes, the English were obliged to cross the river by fords above and below the city, which was effected without difficulty; and about noon, Lord Wellington, with some squadrons of the 14th Dragoons, entered Salamanca.

Never was a conquering hero received with warmer transport: high and low, rich and poor—without distinction of sex or age, rushed forth to greet their deliverers. Overcome with joy, they seemed unable to control their feelings. Some of the first English officers that made their appearance were literally pulled off their horses by the crowd, and almost stifled with embraces. The outpouring of national gratitude knew no bounds, and can only be understood by those who are acquainted with the effervescence of the Spanish character. Nor did it seem to have suffered abatement on the following day as the general marched through the city with his brigade; and the younger officers, partaking of the excitement they witnessed, could not help exclaiming, that surely the French must soon be beaten when such enthusiasm existed among the Spaniards. The general, however, only remarked, with a smile, that he wished the enthusiasm were more actively directed against the French; and he feared that where a people were thus elated at receiving assistance, they would do very little for themselves.

The brigade did not stop at Salamanca, but moved at once three miles beyond it to the village of Cabrerizas, in the neighbourhood of which the whole of the army was collected in the course of the following day.

The 19th passed off peacefully. On the morning of the 20th rumours of the approach of the enemy were afloat, which proved well founded. Marshal Marmont had not fallen back further than two leagues from Salamanca; and having collected four divisions, he was seen towards the afternoon marching towards the British, evidently courting an engagement. Lord Wellington ranged his army along the heights of St. Christoval, his left resting on a deep ravine close to Villares de la Reina, and his right on an eminence above Castellanos de los Moriscos. General Le Marchant's brigade were stationed in the centre.

From this position, which was one of great strength, Lord Wellington would not be tempted to descend. Marmont in vain paraded his troops before the British lines; and ostentatiously took possession of the village of Castellanos. His artillery also kept up for a couple of hours a very sharp cannonade on the centre; which might have done great execution, had not the ground been so moist from the recent rain that the bullets lodged where they first fell. General Le Marchant's brigade, against which it was chiefly directed, lost a few horses. The only hostile demonstration in return on the part of the British, was confined to some skirmishing by the light cavalry on the plain. The day closed under the general expectation of a fierce conflict on the morrow.

On the 21st the troops were under arms at daybreak, and they saw the enemy below them equally prepared. The order to engage was awaited with impatience; and as the hours passed without its coming, murmurs were very distinctly heard through the line at such an opportunity of crushing the enemy being allowed to escape. Ensign Le Marchant, in writing on the subject afterwards to his brother, observes:—

> If we had attacked the enemy, we must have annihilated him; we were so greatly his superior in numbers.

All this ardour was destined to be disappointed. The sun set in peace as on the day before—Lord Wellington was immovable.

Some military critics, especially the author of *Annals of the Peninsular War*, have blamed Lord Wellington for not fighting on this occasion. On the other hand, it is believed by many of equally high authority that Lord Wellington decided rightly. A general action was not what he wanted. The capture of the forts of Salamanca was his primary object, and of this he was secure if he maintained his position. A battle could not be fought without quitting his position, and without losing such a number of men as would leave him unable even after a victory to cope with the French armies which he knew to be collecting for the purpose of overwhelming him. Marmont had everything to gain by a battle; Wellington had everything to lose.

During the night of the 21st, the French possessed themselves of an eminence opposite Castellanos, from which they were dislodged by Sir Thomas Graham in the morning of the 22nd. In the night they withdrew, and marching several miles, towards the evening took up a position on the heights of Cabeza Vellosa, extending their left to the Tormes at Huerta, with the view of crossing the river there, and thus gaining possession of the road to Ciudad Rodrigo.

On the following morning (the 24th) they began to put their plan into execution. Owing to a fog, they crossed the river without opposition; and General Bock's brigade of heavy German cavalry being obliged to retire before them, they marched boldly towards the heights as if to attack the British. In the mean time General Le Marchant had arrived to support General Bock, and the vigilance of Lord Wellington had secured his army against any risk of surprise.

Marmont saw that he was again foiled, and withdrew, after a heavy cannonade, which was principally directed against General Le Marchant's brigade, and carried off some men and horses. This was the last effort he made to relieve the forts; for on the next evening the besiegers contrived to throw red-hot shot into the principal redoubt, and the conflagration that followed caused an immediate surrender. The flames were visible for miles round, and were the signal for the retreat of Marshal Marmont; and he marched off so precipitately that at break of day nothing of his army was to be seen but the last ranks of his rear guard.

Salamanca was now entirely rid of the enemy, and the inhabitants gave way to fresh rejoicings. With a very praiseworthy feeling of devotion they celebrated their deliverance on the same day, by a solemn service at the cathedral, which was attended by Lord Wellington, and most of his generals and their staff. The magnificence of the building, which is a very fine specimen of the modern Gothic, the pomp of the worship, and the picturesque and varied attire of the vast multitude present, made the scene impressive and singularly beautiful. Ensign Le Marchant observes in a letter to his brother:—

> What surprised us most, however, was, that the monks had contrived to keep their splendid Communion Plate. How it escaped the rapacity of the French, I know not.

The manner in which the English had been welcomed at Salamanca and the neighbourhood enraged Marmont to such a degree, that his retreat was marked by the same atrocities that disgraced him in Portugal. Ensign Le Marchant observes in the same letter:—

> He burnt and destroyed the houses and villages as he retired, sparing nothing that he could injure; which has of course operated in our favour, and wherever we go the people receive us with enthusiasm; they curse the French, and show us the dilapidations they committed; and when a straggling Frenchman is unlucky enough to fall into their way, they never fail to cut his throat.

The following letter from Major-General Le Marchant to his friend Colonel Birch was written whilst the general was with the advance in pursuit of Marmont.

Fuente le Pena, six leagues from Toro,
on the Douro, 30th June, 1812.

It is impossible for me to allow your most friendly letter to remain unacknowledged even for a single post. Fatigued to death, I take up my pen after a tedious day's march, to thank you for the kind interest you express in me and mine. At the same time I wish to congratulate you on your late increase of family, which is well-timed, coming so soon as it does after your receiving an estate, and taking a name that you were intended to perpetuate. May you enjoy for many years to come the happiness of your present domestic life, and may your children return your care of them with gratitude and dutifulness of conduct!

Since the 1st of this month the army has been constantly on the march. It was on that day I left Crato in the Alentejo; but on our marching on Salamanca, Marmont retired across the Tormes, and as we supposed towards Zamora, leaving a garrison in the fort of Salamanca, which covers the only bridge on the river, the fords being very uncertain. To our surprise he returned; and we then took up a position on the right bank of the Tormes, commanding the heights that cover the town, and fronting towards Zamora. Marmont placed his army at the foot of our position, and so near that the two armies were within half the range of a six-pounder, and perfectly in view of each other, there not being a tree or a single impediment to obstruct it. The outposts were in constant communication. As you may suppose, we entertained no doubt of a sanguinary conflict. On the first day that he took up his ground I had thirteen horses killed in two of my regiments from a cannonade, without a man having suffered. The singularity of the case leads me to mention it.

The fort of Salamanca, contrary to all expectation, held out. Marmont on the second day of his return retired his left flank. It is nonsense to give you the names of the villages, as none of the maps contain them.

On the day succeeding he made a movement on our right, which, had he not failed, would have given him a complete view of our disposition, and facilitated his attack. The affair that followed was short but sharp. We lost some valuable officers.

Before daybreak both armies were constantly ranged in order of battle opposite to each other; the bands and trumpets of the enemy playing: ours preserved a solemn silence.

On the third day, when the morning set in, we found to our astonishment that Marmont had retired during the night; and, upon pursuit, we traced him to a position two leagues on our right, *appuyé* on the Tormes. The next day he began to cross considerable bodies of troops by a ford, with the view of compelling Lord Wellington to leave his position and fall back to protect his line of operation, his resources being mostly drawn from Ciudad Rodrigo. In proportion as Marmont detached, Lord Wellington did the same; for his lordship was on a height that commanded the ford of Alba de Tormes, and the enemy could not make a single movement without its being distinctly seen.

This attempt to draw us off failed of success. He was not in force on our left bank to fight with advantage, and to fight with the Tormes in his rear was risking more than he chose to do; the day therefore passed off with a cannonade of the cavalry, in which we lost a few men and horses, and at night the enemy retired to his position on the right bank, where he continued to make demonstrations for a couple of days, when he heard that we had reduced the fort of Salamanca, which was done by means of red-hot shot. The enemy's works caught fire, and the fear of being blown up induced them to surrender, though not until we had made an unsuccessful assault, in which General Bowes was unfortunately killed. He immediately commenced his retreat in two columns; one towards Toro, the other towards Valladolid. Tomorrow we shall come up with him, or he must pass the Douro. I rather think it will be the latter.

What Lord Wellington's movements may be beyond the Douro, no one but himself knows. *Adieu*, my dear friend. I would say more, but am too much fatigued to do more than offer you my best wishes.

On the day after this letter was written, Marshal Marmont began to pass his army across the Douro. The infantry crossed the river at once, but the cavalry waited till the next morning, when General Le

Marchant found them in considerable force on the plain. They retreated immediately upon his advance in the direction of Tordesillas, where they crossed the bridge over the river, and entered the town. The bridge is of singular construction, for it rises gradually from the left bank to the right, so as partially to overcome in the passage of the stream the superior elevation of the terrace on which the town is built. It had thus been easily converted into a post of sufficient strength to arrest the pursuit of the British cavalry, who accordingly had no further employment during the day.

It being considered unadvisable to force the bridge of Tordesillas, especially as the parapets of the town appeared well defended, Lord Wellington proceeded to try the neighbouring fords. This operation, which is attended with serious difficulty in the presence of an enemy, was entrusted to Colonel Williams of the 60th, and he conducted it with skill and success. General Le Merchant's son was with him the whole time, and in a letter written on the occasion, is warm in his praise.

Colonel Williams has been already mentioned in these memoirs; but his friendship for General Le Marchant claims some additional notice of him. He belonged to a class of officers that constituted the main strength of our army in the Peninsula; the commanders of regiments under Lord Wellington being among the best of those of any age or nation. Like the colonels in the old German wars of Gustavus Adolphus, they enjoyed to the fullest extent the confidence of the soldiery, and the names of Barnard, Blakeney, Cameron, Colborne, Ross, and Inglis, are still remembered at many a veteran's fireside, as associated with deeds of glory. They had all been trained beneath the eye of Lord Wellington; most of them, indeed, having been selected by him. Formed by long practice, they were perfectly familiar with their duty, and within their own limited sphere displayed qualities worthy of their instructor. The improvements they effected in regimental discipline, their attention to the comforts of their men, and the skill with which they handled their corps, either in subordinate or separate commands, unspeakably raised the character of the service.

But to return to Colonel Williams. He was of that small, slight, but well-proportioned figure, in which strength is usually combined with activity, and his disposition, wary and collected, yet ready, resolute, and decisive, admirably qualified him for a light infantry officer. He had served in this war from its commencement with distinguished reputation. The three great generals of those days, Abercrombie, Moore, and

Wellington, had each in their turn borne public and private testimony to his merit. Picton loved him as his son. Yet with all these unequivocal proofs of talent, so little was apparent in the intercourse of social life of the abilities that had marked his career as a soldier, that he gained very inadequate credit for them out of his own profession, and, in fact, bore no higher character than that of a worthy, obliging, kind-hearted man. He was the younger son of a country gentleman in Surrey, and being in easy circumstances, which were much improved by the death of an elder brother who had acquired a very large fortune as a solicitor in London, he retired on half-pay on his marriage, and died a few years since much regretted.

On the 3rd of July, two regiments of General Le Marchant's brigade, the 3rd Dragoons and 5th Dragoon Guards, were detached to join the fifth division at Polios, in the expectation of being able to force the ford there; and Marshal Marmont has thought it worth while to notice that operation in his report to the Minister at War of the proceedings of his army. It was an insignificant matter, being nothing but a cannonade on the part of the French, which their opponents had not the means of returning; and, as the marshal observes, the fire from the French battery soon proved the attempt to be impracticable. The brigade was then stationed between Polios and Nava del Rey to watch the ford, which continued to be guarded by a large body of French infantry, with several pieces of cannon. General Le Marchant established himself with the headquarters at Nava del Rey. The three towns are within a few miles of each other, Polios and Rueda being near the Douro, and forming the base of the angle which meets at Nava del Rey on the river Trebancos.

The two armies now remained stationary for nearly a fortnight on the opposite sides of the Douro, without undertaking any hostile movements. During this interval, Lieutenant-General Sir Thomas Graham being reduced almost to blindness by a disorder of the eyes, which likewise materially affected his general health, was obliged to go home for advice, "to the deep regret," General Le Marchant observes, in a letter of this date, "of the whole army." The general had seen enough of Sir Thomas Graham during the recent campaign in Estremadura to form a high estimate of his merit. In an army where few are otherwise than brave, mere courage could not be held in high estimation, but the man who at the outset of his professional life had, as a simple volunteer, under all the disadvantages of a foreign name, won the admiration of the Austrian Army by his signal valour at the siege of Mantua,[1] and in mature age fought the Battle of Barossa, had proved himself possessed of a moral intrepidity equal to great undertakings.

This quality seemed in Sir Thomas Graham to be beyond the reach of years, for his boldest exploit, the assault of Bergen-op-zoom,—which, it may be observed, did not fail from any fault of his,—was undertaken at an advanced age. It is now more than a quarter of a century since Napoleon, speaking of him with reference to Barossa and Bergen-op-zoom, styles him, "that daring old man;" and he yet lives, to all appearance, quite able, as no doubt he would be willing, if necessary, to resume active service in the field.

Another officer of great distinction, of whose services the army was deprived at this time, was Lieutenant-General Sir Thomas Picton: a bilious fever,—occasioned not less by his anxious temper than his indefatigable exertions,—compelled him much against his wishes to remain at Salamanca, where he long lay in a very dangerous state.

Various opinions were held in the army as to the policy of Lord Wellington in thus keeping the troops so long unemployed during the finest season of the year. Vague rumours of the strength and progress of the Spanish armies, led many officers to believe that it only required a bold effort to break through the French, and march to Madrid. General Le Marchant, on the other hand, distrusted the co-operation of the Spaniards, and so far from calculating on future conquests, considered a retreat to Portugal inevitable, as soon as Marshal Marmont should have collected sufficient strength to resume the offensive; and he wrote to a near relation in England that he should return home in the autumn, and pass the winter with his family.

Marshal Marmont's prospects were certainly such as to justify the alarm of his opponents. The accession of General Bonnet's division on the 9th, had increased his army by six thousand men. He had reason to expect aid on every side. Three divisions of Caffarelli's army were to join him from the north. Soult was diverted from the conquest of Andalusia to threaten the British left, and Suchet was directed to reinforce largely the army of the centre, which already amounted to seventeen thousand men, and was preparing to march under Joseph himself to his assistance. In fact, the movements of Lord Wellington

1. During this siege Colonel Graham undertook to convey intelligence of the distress of the garrison to the Austrian Army, from whom relief was expected. He succeeded in passing through the camp of the besiegers, and having crossed the river, he reached the Austrian camp in safety, after a most perilous journey.

had become the pivot of the military operations of France, from Cadiz to the Pyrenees, all being now combined for his destruction.

Under these circumstances, General Le Marchant heard with astonishment on the morning of the 16th that Marshal Marmont had crossed the Douro at Toro, a town some miles beyond Tordesillas at the confluence of the river with the Guarna. It appeared almost incredible; and indeed the marshal afterwards but feebly excused himself to Napoleon on the plea that the Galicians, in his rear, threatened to cut off his supplies. General Le Marchant moved instantly from Nava del Rey to Fuente del Pena, but on his road he met orders from Lord Wellington to follow him to Alaejos, as the French, after a false passage at Toro with the view of drawing the English from Toro and Tordesillas, had afterwards crossed the river at those places without difficulty, and occupied General Le Marchant's quarters at Nava del Rey.

In the confusion that ensued, the British army had been drawn rather widely asunder, and two divisions under Sir Stapleton Cotton were attacked at Castrejon on the morning of the 18th by a very superior force, which, however, they gallantly repulsed. In the afternoon the combat was resumed on the banks of the Guarena, where the German horse, under General Alten, were severely handled by the French cavalry under General Carrier. They might have suffered more had not Major Clewes come opportunely to their assistance with the 3rd Dragoons, and driven the enemy back in confusion. The regiment lost one officer, eight men, and twelve horses, killed and wounded in that affair, which added to the reputation of the brigade, and was mentioned with warm praise by General Le Marchant in his orders on the following day.

On the 19th, General Le Marchant having rejoined the army, was employed all the morning with his brigade in marching and countermarching in the neighbourhood of Canizal; but no movement of the main body of the army took place till the afternoon, when the French established themselves on some high ground near the village of Tarazona; and Lord Wellington united his forces on the opposite hills of Vallesa and St. Elmo. The hostile camps were only divided by the narrow streams of the Guarena, and it was hoped that Marmont would not be able to resist so tempting an opportunity of bringing on a general engagement.

On the 20th, as the English were eagerly expecting an attack, they beheld the French moving rapidly up the Guarena, and soon afterwards crossing the stream before a sufficient force could be collected to contest the passage. The English rapidly followed; and the two armies continued throughout the day to march along opposite ranges of hills, which brought them at times so close as to exhibit to each other the most minute dispositions of their respective forces. The weather was beautiful, and the vast assemblage of soldiers, amounting to more than one hundred thousand, moving at full speed without the slightest disorder or irregularity, their respective masses being always so connected as to be ready for battle every moment, gave no slight proofs of the ability of the two chiefs, whilst it presented one of the most brilliant spectacles that had been witnessed during the war.

At the close of the day, the British halted on the heights of Vellosa, and along the adjacent valleys; whilst the French fires gleamed from the opposite heights of Babilafuente and Villaruela; and it was ascertained that they had secured the pass at Huerta, so that Marmont had so far out-manoeuvred Lord Wellington, that he had not only gained the command of the Tormes, but re-opened his communication with Joseph by securing the road to Madrid, whilst the English had fallen back to the ground which they had occupied a month before.

On the 21st the same splendid scene was repeated; columns of both armies having crossed the Tormes, and again encamped opposite each other, the English being in their old position of St. Christoval, and the French behind Cavalrasa de Ariba. The dragoons were kept in constant motion, but proceeded only a short distance during the day. As the infantry kept the high ground, the cavalry scoured the plain, and it was beautiful to behold the latter performing the various evolutions of their arm, sometimes in large bodies, sometimes in small, constantly on the point of engaging, yet seldom coming into serious collision. The skill with which the general directed his brigade on these occasions was much remarked, as was his noble and imposing mien, enhanced in no flight degree by his admirable horsemanship.

The Spaniards and Portuguese, who set a high value on all external advantages, watched him with admiration as he rode along the field with his men; and indeed there were none amongst his followers who surpassed him even in the ordinary qualifications of a soldier. It is said of Pompey, by Sallust, that in running, leaping, and feats of strength, he was excelled by no soldier in his army.[2] In like manner, the general was perfect in all martial exercises; and in spite of his grave deportment, he could not always keep himself under restraint sufficiently to

2. *Cum alacribus saltu, cum velocibus cureu, cum validis recte certabat.*—Sall. fragment, quoted in Montesquieu, *Grandeur et Decadence des Romains*, 2 C.

withstand the temptation of displaying his proficiency in them.

Once in particular, when in Estremadura, seeing a party of German Horse give way before an equal force of the enemy, he hastily collected a few of his skirmishers, at the head of whom he fell furiously on the victors, cut down two of the foremost with his own hand, and speedily routed and dispersed the whole body, after which he returned to his former position with his usual composure, as if nothing had happened. He was, however, far from partial to such exhibitions being made by officers of superior rank; and so little did he contemplate the probability of these occurring in his own case, that during the whole campaign he was not possessed even of a pair of pistols; and upon being recommended to provide himself with them, merely answered that a general officer had always abundance of protection, and that he almost considered his sword an unnecessary appendage.

The brigade halted for some hours this afternoon at Caberizos, a village on the banks of the Tormes, within half a league of Salamanca, from the mill of which place he took the accompanying sketch:—The prospect is not remarkable, except from the extent and richness of the country it embraces; but the sketch derives a melancholy interest from its being the last record of his attachment to his pencil. He used to say that his portfolio would be the best journal he could keep for the information of his family at home; and this proved strictly true, for it was thus carried up to a very few hours of his death. Whether at that moment, when seated on the retired spot from which the sketch is taken, any thought of his approaching separation from all that was dear to him on earth entered his mind, it is difficult to ascertain; but his letters to various friends at home furnish ample evidence of the impression that continually hung over him that he should fall in battle. It was subsequently recollected how many of those friends had entertained the same impression, and vainly combated it

One of them, a person in humble life, but of a particularly sound judgment, on seeing him drive off in his carriage to Plymouth for embarkation, shed tears, and observed that he felt an irresistible conviction that he would never return to England. His own family, from the anxiety inseparable from his exposure to the dangers of war, were sensibly alive to such apprehensions, and from them he carefully concealed whatever prescience he might have had of his fate. He repeatedly urged that the risk must be slight, when not one cavalry general had been killed during the whole contest in the Peninsula,—and why should he be the first? This certainly was an encouraging circumstance;

View from the mill at Caberizos

but where they had so much at stake, it was impossible to subdue deep and constant anxiety; and certainly if ever the life of a parent were precious to his family, it was his. Independently of the inestimable value of a good father in a family of motherless children, the eldest of whom had barely reached manhood, there happened to be at that moment peculiar reasons to make his life indispensable to their welfare.

It has been already mentioned that he never was rich; the purchase of his regimental commissions, which in the cavalry are very costly, the expenses incident to a large establishment, and the proper maintenance of his post at the Military college,—where, it may be observed, that his high honour and scrupulous integrity, were the only obstacles to his enriching himself, as others holding similar situations often did in those times,—had made him poor. He had, however, considerable expectations from relations closely connected with him by the ties of blood and attachment; but he had reason to know that these were, to a certain degree, dependent on his life; so that the wealth which would be his if he survived, might be diverted from his family by his premature death.

General Le Marchant's spirits were much depressed this afternoon by receiving very unfavourable accounts of his friend Sir Thomas Picton, whose illness had assumed a more dangerous character. Indeed he was delirious all the day.[3] It being impossible that he could resume his command for the present, his division was committed by Lord Wellington to the charge of his own brother-in-law, Sir Thomas Pakenham, who then filled the office of adjutant-general in the absence of Sir Charles Steuart. The substitution did not give satisfaction to the old officers. General Pakenham was unquestionably esteemed inferior to General Picton, both in natural abilities and professional skill. He was little more than thirty years of age, and owed his rapid rise in the army to his high connexions; but he was popular from his brilliant bravery and engaging manners: and those who disapproved of his appointment were afterwards the foremost to rejoice at his successful

3. Sir Thomas Picton soon became sufficiently convalescent to be removed to England. The author had frequent opportunities of meeting him at the house of a common friend, and can vouch for the seriousness of his illness. His complexion was of the dark sallow hue of organic disease, and the expression of his features was sad in the extreme. He rarely joined in general conversation; but when he did he never failed to be clear and precise, and his remarks showed much sagacity and intelligence. He was a severe military critic, but an honest one. His praise had always been well earned. Whatever his personal feelings towards Lord Wellington may have been, he certainly often mentioned him in general society in terms of warm admiration.

career, and to deplore its abrupt termination. By a strange coincidence, he and Picton fell in battle within a few months of each other, being the last generals of divisions who perished in the war.

In the evening, the brigade crossed the Tormes by a ford at Santa Martha, and having marched through the village bivouacked on some rising ground in front of it for the night. Their encampment formed one extremity of the position taken up by Lord Wellington, which extended from the Tormes about half a league into the plain, the other extremity being marked by its vicinity to two rough isolated hills within cannon-shot of each other, whose precipitous sides and flattened summits gave them somewhat the appearance of truncated cones: they bore the name of the Sister Arapiles, and are the subject of some legendary tale of very inferior interest to the real history with which they have since been connected. The French occupied detached points on the opposite heights, being about the same distance from one of the Arapiles that the British were from the other.

General Le Marchant with his staff found shelter in the village. As he was retiring to rest at about ten o'clock, a flash of intense brilliancy suddenly passed before his eyes, and in a moment afterwards he heard a crash resembling the simultaneous discharge of a large park of heavy artillery,—indeed all the artillery of both armies united could not have produced a louder explosion. This had scarcely ceased before shouts and shrieks and the trampling of horses at full gallop, mingled with fresh peals, caught his ear, and he almost feared lest the enemy might have surprised the camp, when some officers came in with the intelligence that a thunderbolt had fallen hard by among the 5th Dragoon Guards. Happily no one was struck by it; but its consequences threatened to be serious, as the troop horses of the regiment, which had been linked together in column for the night in the usual manner, terrified almost to madness by the shock, had made such violent efforts to disengage themselves, that a portion of the front squadron broke from their ranks, and after trampling upon and wounding several dismounted troopers, who lay asleep beside them, started in one body at full speed across the plain, and by degrees separating from each other were quickly out of reach.

The horses of the other regiments, which were in contiguous columns on the left, advanced in the same manner; but having the artillery guns, and other impediments in front, and being also better secured, they were stopped without much difficulty. Indeed, order had been restored before General Le Marchant could reach the spot.

The storm, however, continued with little abatement for some hours, during which the thunder rolled in peals with the distinctness and precision of military firing; and to such an extent were the clouds charged with electric fluid, that the lightning at times seemed to fall in showers, which, as they reached the earth, were broken into an endless diversity of forms by the attraction of the various martial implements scattered over the plain. The Spanish officers said that they had never known so furious a tempest even in the Sierra Morena; indeed it is still recorded as one of the most remarkable that has happened in the Peninsula for many years. In a superstitious age it would have been regarded as prefiguring some great event; and certainly no portent could have been more appropriate to the scenes which the coming day was destined to witness.

Daybreak found General Le Marchant already busy inspecting his camp.[4] The air was thick and chilly as in a November morning in England, and the clouds threatened another tempest. The vast plain of the Tormes presented a most dreary prospect; the troops were slowly resuming their accustomed duties; officers and men might be seen in their long cloaks thoroughly saturated and dripping with wet, standing or lying on the bare ground, which was thickly interspersed with pools of rain, looking cold and cheerless; many of them anxiously watching their horses, which were still galloping wildly over the plain between our troops and those of the enemy, having baffled the efforts made by the soldiers they passed in their flight to catch them; and these were never recovered.[5]

The French occupied some of the distant heights, whilst here and there a picket of their cavalry was exploring the plain below. The mass of their army lay out of sight, in the forest where they had passed the night.

About seven o'clock the trumpet sounded, and the brigade marched

4. The ordinary duties of the general officers in this campaign appear to have been severe. General Le Marchant says, in a letter of the 20th June, "I have not halted a day in position since the first of last month: up at two every morning, sleeping constantly in the open air, with only a tree to shelter me from the heat and the dew; but this life does not disagree with me, and, thank God, I am so far in good health."

5. The loss of the 5th Dragoon Guards, notwithstanding the exertions of both officers and men from the general downwards, eventually proved to be twenty-eight horses. These had escaped into the French lines; and, although no great number, they must have been very acceptable there. Marshal Marmont had recently been driven from absolute necessity to seize all the horses in his camp not belonging to mounted officers for the use of his cavalry; a measure that made him very unpopular.

with the general at their head, to take their post in the line of the army. As soon as they ascended the high ground above Santa Martha, they found a very different scene before them from that which they had beheld earlier in the morning. The plain was all animation; both armies were again in activity; the Arapiles, no longer bare and solitary, glittered with arms, one being now occupied by the British, and the other by the French; and they had evidently become the points on which the operations of the day were to turn. The British were leaving the position in which they had passed the night to take up another along a succession of low irregular heights, beginning close to the Arapiles in their possession; whilst the French were forming on the opposite heights, behind and beyond the other Arapiles. General Le Marchant's brigade moved by the rear towards the right of the position of the allies, and when the troops halted they were formed behind the line of infantry on the right of the centre.

After an hour's rest, the brigade was called to escort Lord Wellington in a reconnoitre of the enemy's position. They paused awhile on a hill near the enemy's left, where Lord Wellington dismounted, and examined the ground for some time with great care, till a discharge of artillery interrupted his observations. A shot carried away Lord Edward Somerset's stirrup as he rode within a few paces of General Le Marchant; but no other harm was done, and the troops were then withdrawn, though not before it was evident to General Le Marchant that the French were too strongly posted to be attacked with much chance of success. Indeed, Marshal Marmont usually showed considerable skill in the choice of his positions, his former practice in the artillery being of use to him in this respect.

The brigade had scarce returned to their position behind the infantry, when General Beyer's cavalry came sweeping down the plain at a smart pace, in such force, that our Light Dragoons were obliged to fall back until a detachment of the brigade came by General Le Marchant's orders to their support. General Boyer retired shortly afterwards, and the movement proved to have been only in aid of a feint made by Marshal Marmont with the view of diverting the attention of the allies from their right wing; but so far from succeeding, it appears to have suggested to Lord Wellington one of the most skilful of his military operations during the war; for he now brought the third division, under General Pakenham, and General D'Urban's Portuguese cavalry, in some haste from Cabrerizos, and placed them under cover of a hill at Aldea Tejada, somewhat beyond the extremity of his right, so as to command entirely the road to Ciudad Rodrigo. He thus both strengthened his position, and secured his retreat, while he gained additional means of acting on the offensive, if necessary.

The whole of the allied army was now in the field, and drawn up in order of battle. According to the official returns, it consisted of above forty-two thousand British and Portuguese; of these there were seven divisions of British infantry, amounting to twenty-two thousand men, and four brigades of cavalry amounting to between three and four thousand men. The latter were commanded by Generals Le Marchant, Anson, Bock, and Alten, and formed the division of Lieutenant-General Sir Stapleton Cotton. The train of artillery had fifty-four guns.

The French had eight divisions of infantry, and only two brigades of cavalry; but they had a train of seventy-four guns. Altogether they numbered rather more than the allies. Among the generals of division were Clausel, Bonnet, Foy, Brennier, (see note following), and Maucune, all of whom were officers of established reputation. Boyer,[6] who commanded their cavalry, was an *elève* of Marshal Lannes, and like his master an enterprising officer.

******

Note:—

General, later Marshal Clausel, was regarded by the British as the most able of all the French commanders opposed to them. The only speck on his escutcheon is his late reverse before Constantine.

General Bonnet entered the army as a private soldier before the Revolution; but he became a brigadier as early as the Flemish campaigns of Marshal Jourdan, under whom he served with distinction. He was made a general of division in 1802. He defeated the Spaniards on several occasions in the Peninsular War; but his military reputation derives greater lustre from his conduct at Lutzen and Bautzen, in which, as in other battles of the Grand Army in 1813 and 1814, he bore a most honourable part.

General Foy began his military career as a subaltern under Dumourier, and was constantly employed on active service through

---

6. One of the brigades was commanded by General Curto, who was also considered a good officer, and has been employed frequently since. He was Governor of Oran some years ago.

the wars of the Revolution and the Empire up to the Battle of Waterloo, in which he received his fifteenth wound. His reputation as a soldier, high as it deservedly stood, is comparatively eclipsed by the fame he acquired in the Chamber of Deputies after the restoration of the Bourbons, and he still ranks as one of the most accomplished orators that France has produced since the Revolution.

General Brennier rose from the ranks. He was taken prisoner at the Battle of Vimiera, in which he served as brigadier. Having effected his escape from England he returned to the army in Portugal and became Governor of Almeida: his escape from that fortress with the whole of his garrison, passing through the British lines with trifling loss, is one of the most daring and masterly enterprises of the kind during the war. He served in Germany towards the close of Napoleon's reign, and distinguished himself at the Battle of Lutzen. According to the Duchess of Abrantes, who was well acquainted with him, he "was in stature scarcely taller than a boy of twelve years of age; but with this diminutive appearance he combined all the nobler qualities of an officer of the Grand Army, who had fought the battles of the Republic."—*Memoirs*, vol. vii.

★★★★★★

The two armies thus for some time regarded each other in silence. Impatient as the British were for battle they scarcely dared to hope for it. Intelligence had been brought during the night by the Alcade of Polios of the approach of General Chauvel [7] with the cavalry and horse artillery of the Army of the North, whose junction with Marshal Marmont might be expected within a few hours, and Lord Wellington had in consequence, about noon, moved the heavy baggage towards Ciudad Rodrigo. The troops felt that they must soon follow, and when the third division marched upon Aldea Tejada the retreat seemed already begun. There was too much reason to apprehend that the only result of Lord Wellington's march into Spain would be to

7. General Chauvel arrived at Polios on the evening of the 20th. The *alcade* had run considerable risk in bringing this intelligence, as General Chauvel was lodged in his house. His mule sank under him from fatigue as he entered headquarters. It is a remarkable circumstance that, backward as the Spaniards often were in battle, they braved death cheerfully in enterprises of this description, it being an inaptitude in the higher classes for military discipline rather than any apprehension of death that made them bad soldiers.

expose the feeble means of the British, and to bring down upon the unhappy Spaniards the increased vengeance of their adversaries.

Under these impressions the British saw the day fast waning without any improvement in their prospects. Everything being perfectly quiet, some of the infantry were allowed to cook their dinners, and General Le Marchant sent the 3rd Dragoons into the village of Aldea Tejada to rest and feed their horses. They had not been long absent when, at about two o'clock, a violent cannonade opened along the whole of the French line. The general immediately rode forward to see what it could mean, and finding the enemy descending the heights in great force, he collected his men and ranged them in front of the infantry on the right of the centre. From this point he had a distinct view of the operations of both armies in that direction, which increased in interest as the French, issuing from the rear, successively formed into column as they reached the undulating ground into which the heights were occasionally broken. Still the interval between the two armies did not materially lessen.

They continued slowly moving down the plain in parallel lines; the French all the while indulging in complicated manoeuvres, for which it was difficult to assign an adequate object. General Le Marchant believed that nothing could be intended beyond turning the right of the allies, as had been threatened for several days previously, and this was the explanation which Marshal Marmont himself is known to have given more than once in private conversation when the battle was discussed in his presence after the downfall of Napoleon. It appears, however, from his official report, that he was not without hopes of outmanoeuvring Lord Wellington, so as to bring the allies into a position where they might be attacked with success.[8]

The fact is, that he was proud of his skill in tactics, perhaps, not without reason; for Napoleon used to say, that of all his generals none entered into his plans so thoroughly as Marmont; and on this occasion he was drawn into a maze of strategetical combinations far beyond his abilities to conduct with effect, especially in the face of a bold and

8. The same day I passed the river in two columns, taking my direction by the skirts of the woods, and establishing my camp between Alba de Tormes and Salamanca. My object in taking this direction was to continue the movement by my left, in order to drive the enemy from the neighbourhood of Salamanca, and fight them with greater advantage. I depended upon taking a good defensive position, in which the enemy could undertake nothing against me, and, in short, come near enough them to take advantage of the first faults they might make and vigorously attack them.—*Report.*

clear-sighted opponent.

The issue of these manoeuvres was, that at half-past three o'clock the fifth division, under General Maucune, suddenly advanced from the centre of the French line towards the centre of the allies, whilst a seventh division, of more than six thousand under General Thomieres, (see note following), with a large train of artillery, moved rapidly along the heights in the direction of the British right, with the obvious design of outflanking it.

★★★★★★

Note:—General Thomieres had accompanied Marshal Junot in the first invasion of Portugal. On the third expedition he joined the eighth corps while the Marshal was at Burgos. The Marshal esteemed him highly, and had in 1808 entrusted him with the command of Peniches in Portugal, one of the most important points in the army.—(*Memoirs of Duchess d'Abrantes*, vol. vii.) General Thomieres was also highly considered by Marshal Soult, under whom he served as a brigadier in 1810. He appears to have been raised to the command of a division not long before the Battle of Salamanca. His wife, who appears to have been a very interesting person, accompanied him in his first campaign. She wished to remain with him in this; but to this, says Madame d'Abrantes, "the general would not consent; he foresaw another campaign in Portugal more terrible than the two first, and he would not expose his wife to the horrors of a precipitate retreat like that of Oporto, or a retreat attended by famine and assassination, like that which we had just made. She wept bitterly on leaving Spain. 'I never shall see my husband more,' said she, 'I feel convinced I never shall.' She had lost her only child not long before."

★★★★★★

The immediate cause of these movements has never been exactly ascertained.(see note following), Marshal Marmont subsequently asserted, that General Maucune, a daring soldier,[9] flushed with success

9. Colonel Napier, in describing the movements of General Maucune on the eve of the Battle ofVittoria, terms him "proverbially daring:" and he bore that character in the French army. His gallantry at Austerlitz was particularly noticed and rewarded by Napoleon. He had served in the Peninsula War from its commencement, and having been always employed against the Spanish armies, he had shared in the success which almost invariably attended the French in the battles in which the British were not present. One of the few defeats, however, (continued next page),

in the German and Spanish wars, undervaluing the British, against whom he had never served, and considering their formation very imperfect, ventured on this step without orders, in the hope of piercing their centre and flank before effectual preparations could be made to resist him, General Clausel, on the other hand, admitting the plan of attack to have originated with Maucune, has said, [10] that it was approved and authorised by Marmont, notwithstanding his own strenuous opposition, which went so far as to point out all that eventually happened.

******

Note:—The following is the account given by Marshal Marmont in his report:—There was in front of the ridge occupied by the artillery, another vast ridge easy of defence, and which had a more immediate effect on the enemy's movements. The "possession of this ridge gave me the means, in case I should have manoeuvred towards the enemy, of carrying on myself the communication on Tamanes. This post, which was otherwise well occupied, was inexpugnable; and in itself completed the position which I had taken. It was besides indispensably necessary to occupy it, seeing that the enemy had reinforced his centre, from whence he might push forward *en masse* on this ridge and commence his attack by taking this important point.

In consequence I gave orders to the fifth division to take position on the right extremity of this ridge, the fire from which exactly crossed that from Arapiles;—to the seventh division, to place itself in a second line to support this;—to the second, to hold itself in reserve to the latter; and to the sixth, to occupy the ridge at the head of the wood, where a large number of pieces of artillery were yet remaining. I gave like orders to General Bonnet, to cause the hundred and twenty-second to occupy a point situated between the great ridge and the point of Arapiles, which defended the entrance of the village of Arapiles;

---

sustained by the French was his own, he having been completely beaten in 1809 at Campo Estrella, near Corunna, by Carrera and Morillo, with the loss of six hundred men and several guns. General Maucune fully maintained his high reputation at the Battle of Vittoria and the subsequent retreat, in which he conducted his division with equal skill and courage through a hostile country in the face of a very superior force of the enemy. He also distinguished himself in the battles of the Pyrenees.

10. These sentiments are ascribed to Marshal Clausel, upon authority which the author believes to be indisputable.

> and, finally, I gave orders to General Boyer, commandant of the dragoons, to leave a regiment to clear the right of General Foy, and to push the three other regiments to the point of the wood, on the flank of the second division, in such manner as to be able, in case the enemy should attack the ridge, to attack them by the right of this ridge, while the light cavalry should charge his left.

★★★★★★

General Le Marchant being on the ground nearly opposite the point from which Thomieres' division moved along the heights, saw their march from the outset; and, indeed, his brigade was intended to be one of the first objects of Thomieres' attack. When the movement was decided he naturally expected a corresponding disposition of the whole of the French line; but, to his surprise, none followed, and Thomieres' division pursued its course towards the Ciudad Rodrigo road single and unattended, every step that brought them nearer the enemy carrying them further from their friends, until they became a completely isolated body. It was plain to him at once, as to many other officers, that the French had fallen into an irretrievable error.

The intelligence of the approach of the French was communicated to Lord Wellington from several quarters at the same moment;[11] the emotion he displayed upon receiving it has been described as very remarkable, but it could not be more than the occasion called for. To be thus unexpectedly extricated from all his embarrassments, and instead of the reverses which he had anticipated to find the path to victory with all its glorious results thus suddenly opened to his view, must have affected his feelings deeply. He rose from the spot, where he was taking some refreshment, and hastened to a neighbouring eminence whence a glance was sufficient to satisfy him that the French were in his power. He might almost have said with Cromwell as the Scotch were descending the hill at Dunbar, "*The Lord hath delivered them into my hands.*" With his usual promptitude and decision he immediately gave his orders for battle.

These were simple and precise. General Pakenham, with the 3rd

---

11. The late General Sir John Elley was one of the officers here alluded to. He told the author, In a conversation they once had upon the battle, that he was taking some refreshment (if the author's memory is correct) with Sir Stapleton Cotton, when he saw the movement of the French, and it appeared to him so important that he immediately mounted his horse and galloped to Lord Wellington to acquaint him with it.

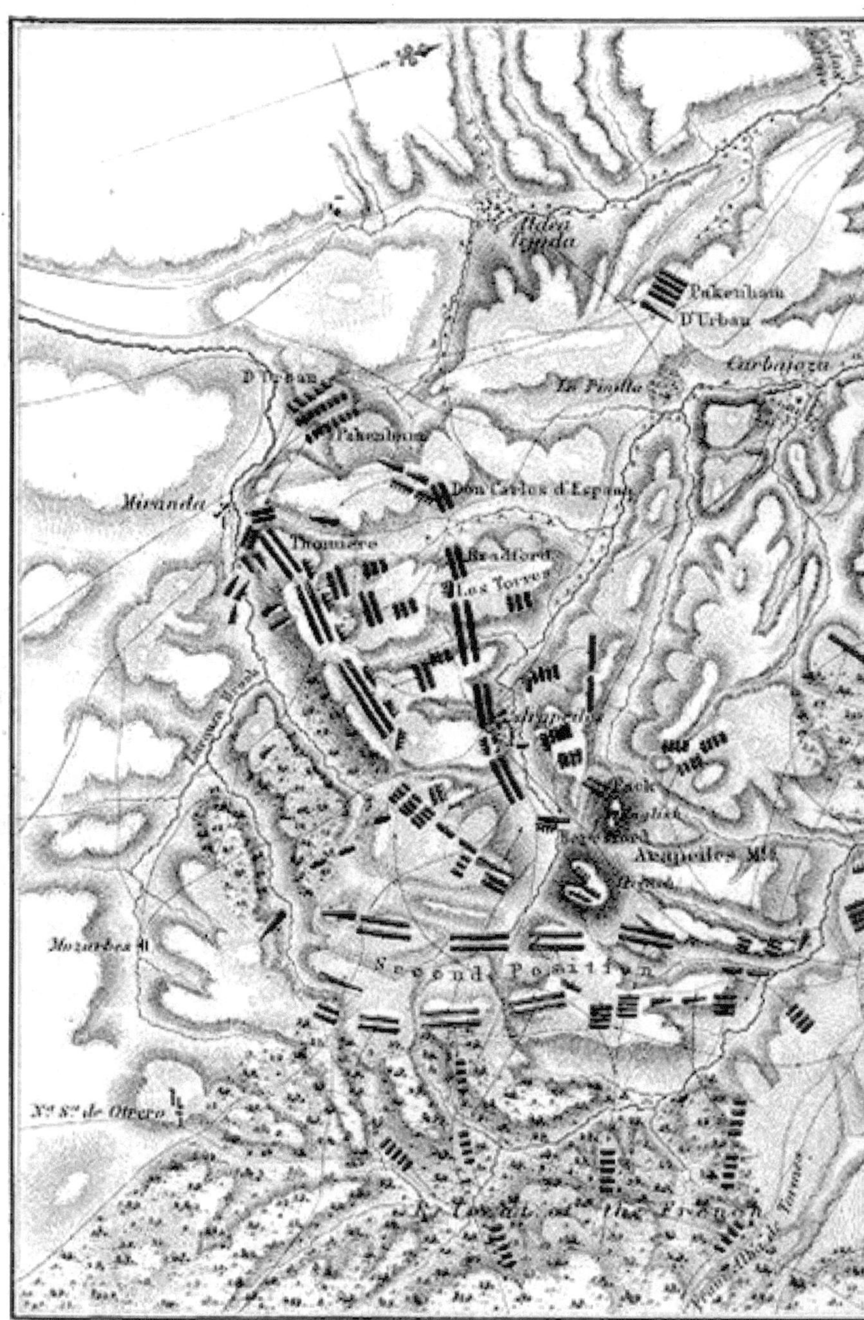

Aldea Tejada
Pakenham
D'Urban
Carbajosa
La Pinilla
D'Urban
Pakenham
Don Carlos d'España
Miranda
Thomière
Bradford
Los Torres
Pack
English
Arapiles
Second Position
Mozarbes
Nª Sª de Olvero

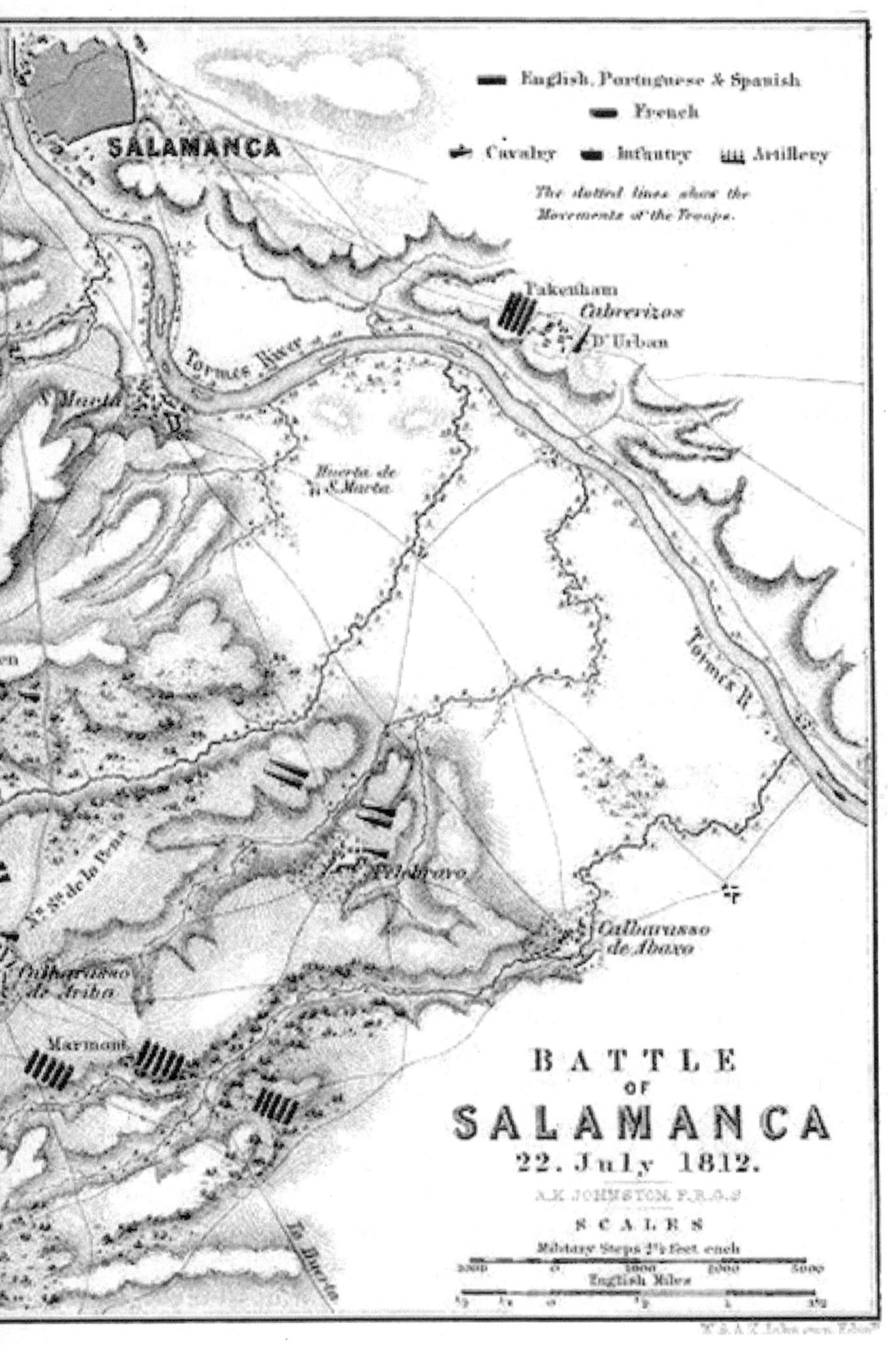

English, Portuguese & Spanish
French
Cavalry
Infantry
Artillery
The dotted lines show the Movements of the Troops.
SALAMANCA
Tormes River
Pakenham
Cabrerizos
D'Urban
S. Marta
Huerta de S. Marta
Tormes R.
Nª Sª de la Peña
Calbarasso de Abaxo
Calbarasso de Ariba
Marmont
BATTLE
OF
SALAMANCA
22. July 1812.
A.K. JOHNSTON, F.R.G.S.
SCALES
English Miles

division, was directed to advance from his place of concealment at Aldea Tejada and to take Thomieres' division in flank as it reached the heights, and at the same moment the British infantry in the centre, consisting of the fifth division under General Leith, and the fourth under General Cole, drawn up in two lines with strong reserves of British, Spaniards, and Portuguese, were to attack the enemy on the heights in front.

These movements were to be supported by the cavalry under Sir Stapleton Cotton.

The particular duty assigned to General Le Marchant was to occupy the space between the infantry in the right and the centre, and to charge as opportunities offered.

The necessity of concealing the third division from the enemy as long as possible obliged General Pakenham to take a circuitous route under the hills, which delayed him nearly half an hour. All this while the French kept up a smart cannonade upon the right of the line; but General Le Marchant having halted his men under some rising ground, where he caused them to dismount and lie on their faces, the balls passed harmlessly over them. In the midst of the fire a horse without a rider galloped across the plain from the enemy's line, and approached the brigade neighing and snorting as if in token of recognition. It was easily seized by a dragoon, who was congratulating himself on his prize, when it was discovered to be one of the horses of the fifth Dragoon Guards that had escaped in the storm, and its owner, Lieutenant Miles, happening to be on the spot, interfered and brought it back with him to the ranks, and rode it during the remainder of the day.

Lord Wellington now rode up, and, accosting General Le Marchant, told him that the success of the movement to be made by the third division would greatly depend on the assistance they received from the cavalry; and that he must therefore be prepared to take advantage of the first favourable opportunity to charge the enemy's infantry. "You must then charge," said Lord Wellington, "at all hazards." After some brief remarks on the chances of the day, Lord Wellington rode towards the centre, having desired the dragoons to remain in the same position until the time of action was come.

They had not long to wait, for in less than a quarter of an hour, it being then between four and five o'clock, the third division suddenly emerged from the hills, at some distance on the right of General Le Marchant's brigade, and struck boldly across the plain. The first glance that the general caught of them, as they issued from the defile, was the signal for him to advance. His men were on their horses in an instant, and moved forward at a walk in two lines, having the fifth and sixth divisions on their left. Captain Bull's troop of horse artillery supported their attack from a position on the heights, along which the third division had just passed.

The consternation of General Thomieres' division at the sight of General Pakenham upon their left flank, at the very moment that they believed themselves certain of success, would, with indifferent soldiers, have caused their immediate flight, as has happened in other battles; but they stood their ground undauntedly, and the cannonade they opened on General Pakenham as he advanced betrayed no irresolution or backwardness, and the fire was maintained with the same spirit along the whole of the French line.

Under this shower of bullets the third, fourth and fifth divisions had to make their way for nearly a mile before they could gain the foot of the enemy's position. The third division was particularly exposed, and the shot made fearful havoc in their advancing columns. The men, however, calmly filled up the ranks as their comrades fell, and pressed forward as quickly as their officers would permit. General Le Marchant in the meanwhile proceeded at a walk, watching anxiously for the moment when he might lead his brigade to the charge with most effect. He had previously sent Lieutenant-Colonel Dalbiac,[12] of the 4th Dragoons, and Lieutenant Light of the Staff, to reconnoitre the ground in front, and to post videttes at the difficult points, a precaution that facilitated his march and prevented confusion; and by skilfully availing himself of the inequalities of the ground, he suffered few casualties from the cannonade.

No French, cavalry came out to oppose him, General Boyer hav-

12. Later Lieutenant-General Sir Charles Dalbiac, K.C.H. and Colonel of the 3rd Dragoon Guards, and late Inspector-General of Cavalry. He served the campaigns of 1810, 1811, 1812, and 1818. His wife accompanied him, and the author cannot resist transferring from the pages of Colonel Napier a most interesting anecdote touching her adventures on this day. "The wife of Colonel Dalbiac, an English lady of a gentle disposition and possessing a very delicate frame, had braved the dangers and endured the privations of two campaigns with the patient fortitude which belongs only to her sex; and in this battle, forgetful of everything but that strong affection which had so long supported her, she rode deep amidst the enemy's fire, trembling, yet irresistibly impelled forwards by feelings more imperious than horror—more piercing than the fear of death."—Vol. vii. Mrs. Dalbiac happily survived these perils, and returned home in safety with her husband at the conclusion of the war. She is since dead, leaving one child, the Duchess of Roxburgh.

ing drawn off the greater portion of that force with a view, as was supposed, of making a sudden dash at Salamanca. A body of French infantry that showed themselves on a hill on his left, in the hope of cutting the brigade off from General Leith's division, suffered so severely from the fire of Captain Bull's troop of Horse Artillery, who threw some shells with admirable aim into the very midst of their columns, that they retired abruptly. The general was thus left at liberty to attend to the gallant efforts of General Pakenham and General Leith on his right and left, and he rode frequently up and down in front of his brigade eagerly watching their progress.

At the sight of the third division ascending the hill occupied by General Thomieres, he quickened his pace into a trot and pressed on. There was no time to spare. He saw several bodies of French infantry advancing from different directions in the rear, Marshal Marmont himself being amongst them, to the support of Thomieres, and it was only by a mighty effort that the third division, under a furious discharge of grape and canister, reached the summit of the hill. They paused to take breath, and at that moment a close volley, such as veterans only could fire, came with a fearful crash from the French columns and utterly destroyed their foremost ranks; but the survivors were not to be intimidated, and after a cheer that drowned even the din of the musketry, they returned the enemy's fire with at least equal precision and effect, and at once charged with the bayonet.

So quick was the movement, that General Le Marchant hardly saw a musket raised in the British ranks before the combatants were actually in collision. "It was like the meeting of two fierce tides, the conflict of two oceans moved by adverse winds," but the issue was doubtful only for an instant; the firm and compact order of the British, their superior personal strength, and the confidence they felt in having thus far overcome all obstacles, made their assault irresistible; and the French were forced in great confusion down the slope towards the centre and rear of their position.

All this passed with the rapidity of a vision, and every man in the brigade, inspired by the sight, wished eagerly for the moment when he should be called upon to take a part in the conflict. That moment was fast approaching. In a few minutes, having reached the crest of the hill from which the enemy had just been driven, the dragoons saw the battle, though so short a time had elapsed since its commencement, already raging with the utmost fury in the plain below them. On the left a tremendous fire was kept up between General Leith's division and the divisions of the French centre.

On the right, General Pakenham pressed hard the remains of Thomieres' division, which, broken as they were, and having lost their commander and many officers and men, still maintained an obstinate resistance, in the hope of relief from the troops that appeared hastening from the main body of the French to their support. These troops, which consisted mainly of Clausel's division, were in full march, and their advanced columns had pushed so far as almost to restore the communication between Thomieres' division and the centre. The movement, however, was still incomplete, and General Le Marchant saw at once that if he could succeed in defeating it the entire destruction of Thomieres' division must follow, and the whole of the left flank of the French. being thus laid bare, the battle would probably be decided.

In an instant his resolution was formed. The disparity of force,—the disadvantage of the ground,—for they were now on the skirts of the forest that covers a large portion of the plain of the Tormes near Salamanca,—did not intimidate him. He ranged his nine squadrons, numbering about eight hundred horse, in two lines, and giving the word to charge, led them down the slope at full gallop against the advancing masses of the enemy.

These masses, consisting of upwards of five thousand men of the best troops in the French army, presented such a formidable appearance that several British officers of distinction, who saw the brigade from the hills, pronounced the attempt too daring, and predicted its failure. Nor was this feeling confined to the spectators, for in the brigade itself there was at first a slight pause, as if the soldiers doubted whether they correctly understood the order to charge; but it was only for a moment, and then they sprang forward with the greatest vigour and alacrity; every man and horse exerting his strength to the uttermost.

The dense smoke which overspread the ground, and the clouds of dust raised by the trampling of the horses over the parched plain, concealed their approach from the enemy until they were close upon them. Taken completely by surprise, the advancing columns of the French halted abruptly, and presented a hasty front; but their formation was very imperfect, owing partly to the irregularity of their march and partly to the want of proper directions from their chiefs, Marshal Marmont and the second in command, General Bonnet, having both been just before carried off the field severely wounded. The front ranks, dazzled by the sun which shone fiercely in their eyes, fired too soon. Their volley made no impression, and the brigade, unchecked for a single moment, continued their career in perfect order and with redoubled speed. The French attempted to reload, but before they could charge their muskets, the dragoons burst in upon them with a fury that carried every thing before it. The troops first encountered, which consisted of the French 63rd Regiment, were cut off to a man. Those who resisted were hewn down indiscriminately, but the greater part threw down their arms and readily surrendered to General Pakenham's division in the flank and rear.

No sooner was the success certain than General Le Marchant, without waiting to make prisoners, led his brigade against other bodies of the enemy which had formed a second line in the rear. A more serious resistance here awaited him. The enemy were better prepared, and their fire brought down some men and horses; but he dashed gallantly through it, and penetrated their ranks with an impetuosity that quickly strewed the ground with killed and wounded, and the French were again totally discomfited.

The third, and strongest body of the French, still remained entire, and had they fallen on General Le Marchant before he could recover the shock of his previous charge, all his skill would have been required to maintain his ground. They, however, had been thrown into consternation by the sudden defeat of their front and flank; and, enveloped as they were in mixed clouds of dust and smoke, with the deafening noise of the artillery and musketry close to them, they were for the moment at a loss how to act. General Le Marchant took advantage of their hesitation, and instantly pressed onwards in as good order as the emergency would admit to his last and most hazardous conflict. The wood through which he moved becoming more thick as he advanced, had separated the dragoons from each other, and in the disorder necessarily incident to the charge, the three regiments had mixed together, and the front being at the same time constantly changing as the right was brought forward, the greater part had now crowded into a solid line without intervals.

The officers rode where they could find places, without reference to regiments, but a good front and a connected body were still maintained; and, although going at full speed, they did not fall into the least confusion. Meanwhile the French had recovered themselves, and having formed a *colonne serré* under the cover of some trees, reserved their fire with the utmost composure until the dragoons were within ten yards' distance; they then poured a volley so close and well aimed upon the concentrated mass of men and horses, that nearly a fourth of them fell. Tremendous as was the effect of this discharge, the dragoons were not arrested in their course. Diminished in numbers, but not in spirit, they still pressed on as if carried forward by an irresistible impulse, broke through the opposing bayonets, and plunged into the dense masses of the enemy.

A dreadful combat ensued, in which the bayonet and the sword were used against each other with various results. The French, cut down by the dragoons and trampled under the horses' feet, offered all the resistance that brave men could make. The loss on both sides was considerable. Captain White[13] of the Staff, and Lieutenant Selby of the 3rd Dragoons, officers both highly esteemed by General Le Marchant, were killed. The general himself had some narrow escapes. He fought like a private soldier, and as many as six men fell by his hand. It was only after a fierce struggle that the French yielded, and the general had the satisfaction of seeing them fly before him in dismay and confusion.

The rout was complete. The French masses, lately so firm and compact, soon melted away, whole companies surrendering without resistance, and all that remained of them were small bands of men united here and there, where the ground was favourable, to defend themselves against the dragoons. Not a score, however, were to be seen together: terror had seized them, and they sought safety only in flight.

The success of this brilliant charge did not end here. Thomieres' division, thus enclosed between the British cavalry and infantry, without a hope of support, saw that further resistance to General Pakenham was vain, and mingling with the crowd pursued by General Le Marchant's dragoons strove to reach the divisions on the left of the French centre. These had just been defeated by General Leith, and were already broken and retreating. The confusion spread. Pressed on the front and flank by the united efforts of General Leith's and General Pakenham's infantry, aided by General Le Marchant's dragoons, the various corps on the French left became a disorderly mass, and, involved in one common ruin, were driven with immense loss upon the centre of their position.

13. Captain White had frequently distinguished himself in the war. A monument has since been erected by his widow, in the church of High Wycombe, to his memory and that of his brother, who fell in Egypt.

General Le Marchant checked his horse to gaze upon the scene before him. His heart beat high,—nor can it be denied that it was the brightest moment of his life. The defeat of a large body of French infantry by even an equal force of British cavalry, in fair open field, would of itself have been a just subject of exultation. Far beyond this, he had signally triumphed, in less than twenty minutes, with very inferior numbers, under every disadvantage of ground, and with men and horses fatigued by nearly ten hours' unintermitted labour. Moreover, he had the proud reflection that all was due to his own brigade, no other portion of the cavalry having been in the charge. Even at this early hour it promised to be attended with results so brilliant as to decide the fate of the day, and thus lastingly associate his name with one of the most glorious achievements of the British arms.

But to resume the narrative. The violence of the onset had thrown the brigade into disorder. The dragoons, excited by the struggle, vied with each other in the pursuit, and galloped recklessly into the crowd of fugitives, sabring those who came within their reach. To restrain them at such a moment was very difficult. The general, having despatched his son for some fresh troops, continued amongst the foremost, with the view of guarding against any attempt on the part of the enemy to rally, which the nature of the ground rendered not improbable. After a few minutes he perceived a number of the enemy collecting in the wood, where they were endeavouring to make a stand. Lieutenant Gregory,[14] with part of a half squadron of the 4th Dragoons, was approaching them.

The general, with his usual contempt of danger, immediately headed this little band, and, waving his sword, with a few words of encouragement charged at full gallop. The French had formed a hollow square, they waited until the dragoons almost touched their bayonets, and then fired. Several of the dragoons fell; Lieutenant Gregory's clothes were perforated with balls, and General Le Marchant received a shot in the groin, which caused him to fall senseless from his horse, absolutely into the enemy's ranks.

The French had no sooner fired than they fled, and the dragoons, having been joined by some men of the 9th Infantry belonging to General Leith's division, raised their gallant commander from the ground, in the hope that he might yet be spared to lead them to future

14. Of this officer General Le Marchant, in common with the rest of the brigade, entertained a very high opinion. He served with the army till the end of the war, and afterwards retired to his patrimonial estate of Stevic Hall, Warwickshire.

victory; but, alas! life proved to be extinct. The bullet, passing through the sash, had lodged deeply in a vital part, and the surgeons upon examining the wound, stated that death must have been instantaneous.

The general's son, having executed the orders on which he had been despatched, now returned full of joyful exultation, revolving in his mind, with the gay fancy of youth, the honours and distinctions which he foresaw would be his father's reward for the brilliant success of the day. An officer of whom he inquired where he should find his father, had not the resolution to tell him the fatal truth. At length he overheard some soldiers say that the general had been wounded, and, lifting up his eyes, he perceived a train of dragoons bearing an officer, evidently of rank, from the field. He dashed forward almost wild with apprehension, and one glance sufficed to show him the extent of his loss. Overpowered by this unexpected calamity he threw himself upon his father's body in an agony of grief, which those who witnessed it, accustomed as they were to the miseries of war, felt they never could forget. All were deeply moved, and even many of the common soldiers were observed to shed tears as the corpse was carried along the line.

In the meanwhile Sir Stapleton Cotton, who had been too far distant to share in the charge, galloped up with a large staff, and having recalled the dragoons to their ranks would have resumed the attack; but both men and horses had suffered too much to do more service that day, and except the capture by Lord Edward Somerset of seven guns, which had been abandoned by the enemy, the brigade was not subsequently engaged.[15] It is probable that the last life lost in it was that of General Le Marchant. They did not halt, however, before they had taken fifteen hundred prisoners; and the loss of the enemy in killed and wounded was besides very severe. Indeed, the French had suffered too much to make any serious stand afterwards in this part of the field, and Sir Stapleton Cotton having joined General Pakenham with the 14th Dragoons and D'Urban's Portuguese Horse, the triumphant career of the British was not arrested even for a moment. Every attempt on the part of the enemy to rally was unsuccessful, and one

15. This fact is stated more prominently than it may seem to deserve, because in some histories of the war General Le Marchant's fall is supposed to have happened so early as to leave the credit of the charge to his successor in command, the Honourable Colonel Ponsonby. That distinguished officer behaved most gallantly in the charge, but the design and execution of that movement belong to General Le Marchant. Colonel Ponsonby commanded the brigade until the end of the war, and was afterwards second in command of the British cavalry at Waterloo, where he gloriously fell.

height being carried after another, Sir Stapleton Cotton and General Pakenham penetrated to the very centre of the French position.

Here the advance of the victors was suddenly stopped. The failure of an attack made by General Pack on the Arapiles had enabled a division in the enemy's centre to oppose a successful resistance to the fourth division, under General Cole, and that officer had been wounded and his division forced to give way. The talent of General Clausel, who had succeeded to Marshal Marmont in command, turned this advantage to more account than could have been expected; and the French Army having partially recovered themselves maintained an obstinate struggle for two hours longer. But their defeat was only delayed, and by sunset they had fled in confusion towards the Tormes, with a loss of more than five thousand men killed and wounded, leaving the British masters of the field.[16]

Seven thousand prisoners, two eagles, six standards, and eleven cannon were the immediate fruits of this victory, and but for the neglect or misunderstanding of the Spanish general at Alba de Tormes very few of the French army could have escaped. The unopposed march of Lord Wellington to Madrid, and the capture of that city, rapidly followed, and raised hopes in England of an early termination of the war. These were not realised; but the Battle of Salamanca will always be recorded as one of the most brilliant of Lord Wellington's victories. Indeed, a distinguished living historian[17] has gone so far as to say, that "it was one of the greatest blows struck *by any nation* during the Revolutionary War." It entirely changed the character of the contest in the Peninsula, and was the first step in that succession of triumphs that led to the final expulsion of the French in 1814.

General Le Marchant's body was carried off the field and placed in a stable in the rear. Two days afterwards it was interred in a grove

---

16. The object of the author in the narrative of the Battle of Salamanca given in the text, was to confine himself as closely as possible to the operations of General Le Marchant's brigade. His description of these, however, would have been unintelligible without occasional reference to the operations of other corps; but, beyond some general remarks into which he was drawn by the facts he had to relate, nothing he trusts has escaped him which can be considered as interfering with the province of an historian. The battle is ably related in the various histories of the war: Colonel Napier's narrative being, as far as the author can judge, indisputably the best.

17. Alison's *History of Europe during the French Revolution*, vol. viii. Having briefly described the charge, the author observes, "Great as his success was it was dearly purchased by the death of the brave Le Marchant, who died in the moment of victory, while carrying the standards of England triumphant through the ranks of France."

of olives, near the spot on which he fell. The brigade having advanced with the rest of the army in pursuit of the French, the military honours usual at the burial of officers of rank were necessarily omitted. A medical officer, who had been left in charge of the wounded at Salamanca, Major Onslow of the 5th Dragoon Guards with Ensign Le Marchant and a faithful domestic, who had accompanied the general from England and managed his household,[18] were all who attended. The major read the funeral service, and the corpse having been wrapped in the military cloak worn by the deceased in the battle was committed to the earth, and left to the loneliness and obscurity of a soldier's sepulchre in a foreign land.

Major-General Le Marchant was only forty-seven years of age when his career thus abruptly ended; and his vigorous constitution, fortified as it was by habits of activity and extreme temperance, had promised him a long life. He had been only one year in the Peninsula, but in that time had gained the love and admiration of those whom he commanded, and many old dragoons may still be found whom the mention of his name will kindle into enthusiasm. Various are the instances they relate of his strict discipline, and yet of his unfailing kindness; and in describing "the great charge at Salamanca," all feel a pride in dwelling on the gallantry of their leader, and supposing themselves to have been near him when he fell.

Several years after his death one of the regiments of the brigade happening to march through High Wycombe, the soldiers who had served in the Peninsula came in parties to the house where the general had formerly resided, and having obtained permission to enter it, examined everything with a veneration that showed how deeply they were attached to his memory.[19] To this day the three regiments that constituted his brigade continue to celebrate the anniversary of the battle, and the men wear laurels in their helmets on the occasion.

The intelligence of the Battle of Salamanca was received in England with enthusiasm. The officer who brought the despatch was raised at once from the rank of captain to that of lieutenant-colonel, a promotion almost without a precedent. Lord Wellington was created a marquis; and, with his brave companions in arms, received the unani-

18. This excellent person continued with the general's son during the ensuing campaigns. He is since dead; but his latter days were made comfortable by a small pension he received from the family of those whom he had so well served.

19. The general's sons, in the army, were often accosted by old soldiers, who exulted in having served under their father, and spoke with warmth of his exploits.

mous thanks of both Houses of Parliament.

The services of Major-General Le Marchant were warmly acknowledged by Earl Bathurst in the House of Lords, and Lord Castlereagh in the House of Commons, in moving the vote of thanks. The sum of 1500*l.* was voted for a monument to his memory in St. Paul's Cathedral;[20] and a pension of 1200*l. per annum* was settled on his orphan children. Now, too, the value of his long and successful efforts for the improvement of the army, and especially his own branch of it, was deeply felt, and called forth an universal expression of regret that he should have been cut off before he reaped their reward. The Duke of York actually wept when the particulars of his death were stated to him.

Great as these honours were which General Le Marchant's memory received in England, they must be considered merely as the tribute due to. the general impression of his character and services, and doubtless fell short of that expression of national gratitude which would have been elicited had the public been aware of the full particulars and importance of the brilliant exploit in which he lost his life. The accident which unfortunately befell Sir Stapleton Cotton at the close of the day,[21] had deprived Lord Wellington of the detailed information which he would otherwise have received from that officer as general in command of the operations of the cavalry in the battle, and this deficiency, as far as it related to the heavy brigade, could now no longer be supplied by its chief. Hence the great services of the brigade were only mentioned as having been performed in common with those of the rest of the cavalry.[22] Many years elapsed before any distinct statement was made public of those services; and even then it rested on the authority of an anonymous writer in a periodical work, (see note following), until the admirable history of Colonel Napier placed on lasting record the claims of General Le Marchant and his

20. This monument was afterward erected by the late Mr. Smith, to whose design the prize was awarded by the Government Committee of Taste. It is a feeble production, though, perhaps, not inferior to others of the national monuments in St. Paul's.

21. Sir Stapleton Cotton was wounded severely by one of our own sentries in returning to his quarters after nightfall.

22. "The cavalry, under Lieutenant-General Sir Stapleton Cotton, made a most gallant and successful charge against a body of the enemy's infantry, which they overthrew and cut to pieces. In this charge Major-General Le Marchant was killed at the head of his brigade, and I have to lament the loss of a most able officer."—*Lord Wellington's Despatch.*

gallant companions to the gratitude of their country.

******

Note:—*The Histories of the Peninsular War* by Dr. Southey, Sir John Jones, and Captain Hamilton, do not add to the information respecting the movements at Salamanca contained in Lord Wellington's despatch; indeed, they do little more than copy the very words of that part of the despatch. The account referred to in the text appeared in the number of the *United Service Journal*, for November 1833, under the signature of "A. Z." It is very clearly and very spiritedly written. Colonel Mitchell has adopted it in his remarks on the movements of cavalry in his work on *Tactics*; a book, by the way, most instructive and pleasant even to the unlearned. The colonel himself fully appreciates the services of the heavy brigade at Salamanca, and bestows the warmest praise on their charge.

The narrative of the charge in Colonel Napier's history is one of the finest pieces of military description that ever fell under the author's eye. Whether it attaches sufficient importance to the effect of the charge in deciding the battle is another consideration. The following is extracted from a letter to the author, written on the publication of Colonel Napier's volume by an officer, now of high rank, who bore a most honourable part in the day.

> The brigade of heavy cavalry, under your good father, has never had justice done to its service at Salamanca. Even Colonel Napier does not do it well. He goes on to detail a part of the action, of little or no consequence, before he turns to that body of cavalry. The action commenced by our artillery shelling the head of the French column that was showing itself on some rising ground, the third division, under General Pakenham, advancing at the same time, and the moment they drove back the enemy the heavy brigade charged, and completed the confusion that had begun. All this was accomplished in little more time (speaking figuratively) than I am writing it; and I have always thought it the finest combination of the use and effect of artillery, infantry, and cavalry that I ever witnessed. Now Colonel Napier's book does not show this distinctly.

******

In the Peninsula, General Le Marchant's merit was fully known and appreciated. Lord Wellington publicly and privately described him as "a most able officer;" and this opinion was shared by the whole army. Great expectations, indeed, had been formed of him, particularly by the cavalry. His daring valour, accompanied as it was by a quick apprehension and a sound judgment, suited the bold character of that warfare, in which his profound and varied knowledge of tactics gave him advantages such as were possessed by few of his contemporaries. In the science of position, so important to a commander of cavalry, he was eminently skilful He had large notions too of what might be done by cavalry,[23] and the last act of his life proved that he would have carried them fully out if his career had been lengthened.

In many respects he was endowed with the qualities that constitute a great commander. His original mind and unbending temper especially fitted him for the most prominent part of any enterprise, and he was always most successful when left most to himself. His experience also of regimental service, and his connection with the military college, enabled him to understand the dispositions both of his officers and men. He knew well how to call forth their patience under severe training and discipline, no less than their decisive energy in action. This was acknowledged even by his opponents, and the author of these sheets has been informed by French officers of distinction, that no British general of cavalry stood higher in the estimation of the French army than General Le Marchant, without whose charge they insisted that the Battle of Salamanca would have had a different result.

The author's purpose would be incomplete were he to conclude this memoir of his father's life without recording a few facts, which throw light upon the character of the man as well as of the soldier. He had a deep and practical sense of religion. His eldest son once admiring his calm composure under a very hot fire, asked him how he had attained such a command over himself, his reply:—

> I never go into battle without subjecting myself to a strict self-examination, when having, as I humbly hope, made my peace with God, I leave the result in his hands with perfect confidence that he will determine what is best for me.

---

23. Had he lived to read Colonel Mitchell's remarks on the use of cavalry, in Colonel Mitchell's *Tactics*, he would have found, I suspect, many of his own views

Even amidst the duties of an active campaign, the general found time for frequent attention to the scriptures. One of his last letters to his family, requested that another Bible might be sent to him, as the type of the copy which he had brought from England was so small as to be painful to his eyes.

A member himself of the Church of England, he was a decided friend of religious liberty, and eagerly supported Catholic emancipation. He was not less interested in the diffusion of education, and maintained, at his own expense, a school for poor children in the village of High Wycombe, at a time when public opinion on this subject was much divided. In accordance with these principles his views were generally those of the Whig school, and he gave that party his support in the elections, although he never engaged very keenly in politics. It was in contemplation to offer him the place of Under Secretary of State for War and the Colonies, had Lords Grey and Grenville come into power upon the Regency. This, however, he probably would have declined, not choosing so far to separate himself from his profession. Yet, with all his love of it, he had such a sense of the miseries and burdens of a protracted war, that no civilian could more earnestly desire the termination of the contest in which his country was engaged.

The author now feels that he has fulfilled the task which filial duty prompted him to undertake. He trusts that in this narrative of his father's life and services, a faithful portrait has been presented of his character. He abstains from entering into farther details, lest he should fall into that strain of indiscriminate eulogy which the recollection of such a parent might naturally inspire.

★★★★★★

The young and numerous family of General Le Marchant, thus bereft of their remaining parent, had to struggle with difficulties which at first appeared insurmountable; but, by the blessing of Providence, they succeeded in maintaining their station in life. Of the four sons, the eldest and the two youngest embraced the profession of their father. The former, who has been repeatedly mentioned in this memoir, became Lieutenant and Captain in the 1st Foot Guards. He served as *aide-de-camp* to Lieutenant-General the Hon. Sir W. Stewart, K.B. at Vittoria, the Pyrenees, St. Sebastian,[24] and Nive; and having thus reached nearly the end of the war, and shared in many of its most bril-

24. It may prevent a suspicion of incorrectness to state, that Captain Le Marchant was a volunteer at the storming of St Sebastian.

liant victories, he was mortally wounded in the last-mentioned battle, when in the act of rallying a regiment which had fallen into confusion. He expired at St. Jean de Luz, on the 12th of March, 1814, in the twenty-third year of his age, and was buried in the ramparts of that city. Young as he was, his personal merit had gained him many friends, in addition to those whom he inherited from his father, and his early death was deeply and generally regretted by his brother officers. To his brothers and sisters, whom he had most affectionately protected and cherished, his loss was that of a second parent.

The third son, John Gaspard, was too young to enter the army during the war. He afterwards was appointed an ensign in the 10th Foot, and having been employed some years in the colonies, rose to the rank of major in the 98th, which regiment he quitted, in 1835, to accompany the British auxiliary legion to Spain as Colonel and Adjutant-General. He served with distinction in the different operations of the corps in two campaigns, and was made Brigadier-General at the storming of the lines at St. Sebastian, and gained the first and third order of St. Carlos. On his return to England he received the honour of knighthood, and is now, (1841), Lieutenant-Colonel of the 99th Regiment.

The youngest son, Thomas, became a captain in the 7th Dragoon Guards, and *aide-de-camp* to the Governor-General of Canada.

The five daughters of General Le Marchant found an affectionate home in the house of their mother's youngest sister, [25] who, even from the time of their mother's death, had endeavoured to supply her place to all the family. This kind aunt has had the satisfaction of seeing the objects of her care all happily married; but she has likewise had to mourn the death of the general's fourth daughter, Helen, the wife of Henry Shaw Lefevre, Esq. who, in the bloom of youth and beauty, was taken from her afflicted husband and family in 1833, leaving three infant children.

25. Mrs. Mourant of Candie, in the island of Guernsey. To this lady and her excellent husband, the late Peter Mourant, Esq. The family of General Le Marchant are under obligations not to be repaid..

A Biography of Major-General Le Marchant

By John William Cole.

Happy is he o'er whose decline,
The smiles of home may soothing shine,
And light him down the steep of years;
But, oh! how grand they sink to rest,
Who close their eyes on victory's breast!

Moore's *Melodies*.

MAJOR-GENERAL LE MARCHANT.
BORN 1765.—KILLED AT SALAMANCA 1812.

This gallant officer was cut off prematurely In the first general action it was his fortune to take a share in after being appointed to a command in the Peninsular army. His death was glorious; and he sleeps in a soldier's grave not far from the spot on which he fell. He too, like Nelson, Moore, and Craufurd, was only forty-seven years of age when his career so abruptly closed. His vigorous constitution, fortified by habits of activity and systematic temperance, gave every promise of a long life, in case he should escape the casualties of the field. Had Providence so ordained, he would have returned home at the close of the war, wearing as many honorary distinctions as the most renowned of his contemporaries; for he was eminently gifted with courage, perseverance, and clear judgment, the three innate elements which carry warriors above the crowd, and win for them an exclusive page in the records of history.

John Gaspard Le Marchant, born in the island of Guernsey, was one of the few remaining descendants of a Norman family believed to have settled there as far back as the reign of King John. His lineal ancestor, Peter Le Marchant, appears to have been the foremost man of the place, under Edward the First, as he was not only bailiff, or chief civil magistrate, but lieutenant-governor, or king's representative. The subject of our memoir received his second Christian name of Gaspard, after the celebrated Admiral de Coligni, a collateral ancestor of his mother, Mary, the eldest daughter of Count Hirzel de St. Gratien. His father, John Le Marchant, had served in the seventh dragoons, in which regiment he purchased a cornetcy under the Marquis of Granby, in the army of Prince Ferdinand of Brunswick, during the three last campaigns of the Seven Years' war, and retired on half pay at the declaration of peace in 1763. Young Gaspard was placed at an early age at Dr. Morgan's school in Bath (a seminary of high reputation), where he passed several years, and left with the character of having been, with the exception of the late Sir Sidney Smith, the greatest dunce that had ever been there.

When speaking of the subject in after years, General Le Marchant frankly admitted that the fault lay more in the pupil than the school. Suddenly, on his return home, he became studious, and acquired habits of industry and application which he ever afterwards retained. As he evinced an early inclination for a military life, his father indulged him with a probationary trial in a regiment of the York militia, which happened to be commanded by a friend of the family. At the age of eighteen he was appointed to an ensigncy in the Royals, and joined the regiment in Dublin in 1783. His prospects on entering his profession were anything but brilliant He had scarcely any influential connections, and possessed a foreign name, with an insignificant fortune. But nature had endowed the young soldier with a tall, manly, and muscular form, a resolute spirit, and a constant mind. By personal merit he obtained admission into the best society, and formed some acquaintances which proved of value in his future career.

In 1784, he embarked with his battalion for Gibraltar, where he remained for nearly three years, until attacked by yellow fever, from which he with difficulty recovered, and on his convalescence was sent, on the sick list, to England. On his return to Gibraltar, finding himself still a junior ensign without any immediate prospect of promotion, he purchased a cornetcy in the Inniskilling Dragoons, and shortly after joined that regiment in England. While doing duty there, he was appointed by Lord Heathfield to command the guard of honour employed to escort King George the Third from Dorchester to Weymouth.

This accident introduced him to the notice of His Majesty, and, backed by the recommendation of Sir George Yonge, then Secretary at War, obtained for him, a short time afterwards, a lieutenantcy in the Queen's Bays. While at Gibraltar he had employed much of his leisure time in making sketches of the fortress and the Barbary coast. These drawings were shown at court by Sir George Yonge, and admired. They procured for the young officer invitations to the royal circle, through which he won the personal esteem and approbation of the king, which were never afterwards withdrawn from him.

In less than three years after his entrance into the Bays, he purchased his troop, and during this interval became united in marriage to the eldest daughter of John Carey, Esq., a young lady of Guernsey, of great beauty, to whom he had been for a considerable time engaged and affectionately attached. His domestic happiness was soon interrupted; for a few months after the birth of his eldest son, in 1793, he received orders to join the allied army on the continent. The British forces at that time were badly organised, unaccustomed to continental warfare, directed by a young and inexperienced commander, and opposed to an enemy numerically superior, flushed with victory and enthusiasm, and led by a succession of unfettered veterans of established reputation and proved ability. On our side many instances of individual daring were exhibited; but we could show no brilliant generalship to equalise the balance.

The operations undertaken in 1793, 1794, and 1795, were lamentable failures; but it would be out of place to dwell here on the many causes which produced that unhappy result. They have been amply discussed elsewhere; and impartial truth ascribes them principally to the incompetence of our own ministers and the duplicity of our allies. Let it be remembered only, and always, that these allies were Austrians and Prussians, who treacherously negotiated terms with the enemy while they were maintaining their armies with British subsidies. They did this again in 1806, and once more again in 1809; and judging by past experience, may be expected to prove their sincerity after the same fashion in 1856, if we are weak enough to afford them added repetitions of the same opportunity. Politicians who rely on the stability of co-operation from these powers, in our struggle with Russia, may, with as much demonstrated reasoning, expect support from a broken reed.

Yet there are legislators, in office and out of office, with average understandings and the experience of history, who still believe in the honesty of Austria, and expect, sooner or later, the open support of Prussia. In our dealings with questionable implements, if we must deal with them at all, we should, to a certain extent, do as they invariably do by us, not act with duplicity, but use them without confidence. And yet to such sources the late government looked, in the emergency they had themselves created, to fill the gaps in our ranks for which they are chiefly answerable. We have better and safer foundations of hope, in a firm reliance on Providence, in the innate courage of our incomparable soldiers, in the attachment of the people to the throne, and in the constancy of our late hereditary antagonist, who is now our truest and ablest friend.

There are ambitious states amongst the Teutonic Confederacy, who hate England in their hearts, are ever ready to prey upon her vital strength, ever on the look-out, with an open grasp, to pocket her money, jealous of her supremacy, and at any moment prepared to sing *Io pæans* over her anxiously anticipated downfall. It would be well for peace and civilization if some of them were swept from the map of Europe, and a young, vigorous, steady, independent barrier kingdom created from those who are bound to us in ties of consanguinity, to occupy the places at present so unprofitably filled. It may probably come to this at last; for the leading powers of the world will not always continue blind to transparent facts, or forego political advantages for objects which may be weak in themselves, and of no intrinsic moment, but sometimes become pernicious from undue consideration. The days are passed away forever when nations warred for a family compact, or to support a particular dynasty.[1]

Captain Le Marchant first saw actual warfare in an attack made by the Austrians under Count Hohenzollern on the French camp at Cassel, on the 30th of June, 1793. For his conduct in this affair, he received particular mention in a special order from the Austrian commander, which ran thus:—

> I beg the officer commanding the British cavalry in the absence of Lord Herbert, to express my thanks in my name to Captain Le Marchant, and to all his brigade, for the precision with which he executed my instructions at the engagement at Cassel this morning, and to assure all the corps that I esteem myself both happy and honoured to have had him to command troops that showed as much spirit as intrepidity.

1. The "War of Succession," and that for the first restoration of the Bourbons in France.

Such a flattering distinction has rarely been conferred on so young an officer in a subordinate capacity, and in his first field. On the occasion of this intended *coup de main*, the troops employed were ordered to begin their march before sunrise. Captain Le Marchant visited his men during the night, to see whether their accoutrements were in proper condition for the expected day's work. He was surprised to find them all turned over on their faces. On inquiring the reason, he was informed that they had just dressed their queues for the morrow, and they were afraid of lying in any other position, lest it should become necessary to dress them again. Such was the appliance of what was then considered practical discipline in the British army; and to such childish or doting absurdities were the energies of the highest officers in the service ludicrously and grievously misapplied.

The skirmish at Cassel drew from Captain Le Marchant the following observations, in a letter to his wife:—

> I am just returned from a scene that, on cool reflection, makes my soul shrink within me; but it is one of the horrors of war. What gave me most pain was to see that the Austrians gave no quarter. Poor devils on their knees, merely begging for mercy, were cut down. My own people, thank God, were as merciful as possible; and, I think, destroyed none in the pursuit, except such as would not give themselves up. Dives's (his junior captain) party had taken five men alive, but leaving them for an instant in pursuit of others, some Austrians came up and butchered them. I made a complaint to Hohenzollern, who supposed his men might have seen some of their comrades receive similar treatment from the enemy during the engagement. He seemed to be very sorry for it. My people behaved remarkably well in face of the enemy; that is, for young troops. They have an implicit confidence in me, so that I hope in time we shall be esteemed by our friends the Austrians, who are, at present, as superior to us as we are to the train-bands in the city.

The Prince of Hohenzollern, in addition to his public testimony of approbation of the conduct of Captain le Marchant, named him particularly in a report transmitted to the Duke of York; and in the August following he was appointed major of the brigade commanded by the Honourable General Harcourt. As he was personally unacquainted with the general, he owed the advancement entirely to his reputation. The day after he assumed this office, he witnessed the engagement at

Lincelles, in which the three battalions of Foot Guards eminently distinguished themselves, and obtained a name on their standards which is still emblazoned there in company with the more recent trophies of Egypt, the Peninsula, Waterloo, and the Crimea. There were sharp contests during the campaign of 1793; but there was a want of combination and unity of plan on the part of the allied commanders, which gave the enemy advantages that the fair chances of war would not otherwise have afforded them. Few laurels were gained, but many hardships were endured. Captain Le Marchant says, in his journal, dated in the month of September, and intended for private perusal:

> At Dixmude I slept undressed between sheets for the first time these two months. Would you believe it? I did not sleep sound. Perhaps I did not enjoy myself the less in musing on my novel situation. In fact, during these same two months, I have not even taken off my clothes or boots, except to change them. Often fatigued to deaths so much so as to fall asleep on my horse. A little bit of dry bread that has been lying in the bottom of my great coat, was as carefully divided between the general and his staff, as would have been the richest dainty between epicures at home. It would appear unaccountable to you how persons, accompanied by the number of servants and horses that we all are, can be in want of the comforts, much less of the necessaries of life. The fact is this: attacks are generally made by the enemy at moments least expected, when we hurry on our horses, and think of nothing but our immediate responsibility as officers; we take our posts, and the army changes its position half a dozen times before our servants can find us out again. All they can do is to stick to some column, and to trust to chance for a rencontre.

But in the midst of all these active vicissitudes, there was occasionally monotony and leisure, which Captain Le Marchant turned to account, by making drawings of all such articles in the military equipages of our allies as appeared to him to differ from and be better than our own. He also studied with great care the superior mode in which the Austrian cavalry were trained to the use of the sabre, and employed himself in making military plans of the different positions of the army, which gained for him both notice and credit.

While thus engaged, he received intelligence that his father was dangerously ill, and anxiously desired to see him before he died.

Through the interest of General Harcourt, he obtained a short leave of absence, but arrived at home only in time to meet the funeral procession departing from the door.

In the first week of February, 1794, he rejoined the army, which was then in quarters at Ghent. Here he encountered the notorious General Mack, who long continued to impose upon the world the idea that he was an able commander, until his subsequent misconduct at Ulm exhibited him in his real character. Lord Nelson saw through him at Naples in 1798; but his opinion was attributed to English prejudice. Captain Le Marchant thus describes his personal attributes:—

> Mack is a man of forty, extremely like the Abbé Mac Carty; he has some complaint in the head that keeps him in constant pain. In consequence, he wears a black caul over his skull, sewed round the bottom with thick black hair, which gives him a very grotesque appearance. He lies all day on his bed, writing with a pencil his instructions for the movements of the army. When an action takes place, he is lifted from his bed to his horse. It is singular that, with these habits, he is a passionate admirer of the sex. He is accompanied everywhere by a female attendant. I have made a sketch of his face, which is thought to be very like him.

Three important affairs took place between the allies and the French, on the 17th, 21st, and 22nd of April, at all of which Captain Le Marchant was present, and in less than five weeks participated in seven general actions. But, notwithstanding some brilliant successes, his clear penetration saw and foretold that the final result of the campaign would be disastrous,—an opinion quite at variance with the sanguine expectations of older officers of much superior rank. The sequel soon showed that he judged correctly. When the allies were preparing to go into winter quarters in 1794, Captain Le Marchant, on the recommendation of General Harcourt, was promoted to a majority, by purchase, in the 16th Light Dragoons, and at the same time, received orders to join that regiment at Weymouth, where it was then quartered in attendance on His Majesty. He had been absent about a year and a half,—a short time, into which many events had been crowded, offering impressive lessons in the art of war, from the repeated battles and complicated movements of such large armies within a very limited circle of operations. The conflicting hosts on both sides have been computed at four hundred thousand men.

Major Le Marchant's residence at Weymouth, after the hardships and privations of an active campaign, illustrated in a striking manner the extremes of military life. He scarcely expected, after an interval of seven years, to be recollected by the king; but His Majesty received him in the most gracious manner, and honoured him by repeated marks of kindness both in public and private,—a distinction which led to his intimacy with the most influential persons of the day.

While quartered at Weymouth, he commenced his first efforts to introduce the *sword exercise*. The original idea of this suggested itself to his mind in Flanders, from observing the many instances of discomfiture which our dragoons experienced in single combat with the enemy; nor was it in such personal duels alone that the English troopers exhibited their awkwardness with the sword. Major Le Marchant was informed by the surgeons that many of the wounds which the men received in the field could have been inflicted by no other weapons than their own. One of his own acquaintances, a captain of dragoons, wounded himself in the foot seriously during the confusion of a *mêlée*. The horses were perhaps the principal victims, as they were often gashed about the head and neck by their riders.

He therefore determined to instruct himself by consulting all individuals amongst the different armies who were supposed to be the ablest swordsmen, according to the system practised by each. The immense body of cavalry in the field, and the diversity of the nations of which it was composed, materially aided his researches. Through this process, combined with many new principles of his own, he formed a system of attack and defence, which he embodied in a code of instructions, and commenced its practical exercise in his own person. He was not long in acquiring a considerable degree of skill and graceful execution. His next step was to instruct two privates of his own regiment, who made rapid proficiency. A detachment of twenty selected men and a few officers was formed with equal success. The co-operation of other corps was then invited; but the overture was rejected, partly from prejudice, but more from laziness.

The inventor of the new system was prepared for this, and appealed to higher authority. The method under which he proposed to train the whole British cavalry in the use of the sword was submitted to the Duke of York. The result of the personal inquiries of his Royal Highness, and the report of a committee of general officers, decided the question in its favour. The proposed code became established amongst the permanent regulations of the service; and Major

Le Marchant received orders to begin his course of instruction with all possible despatch. The subsequent events of the war afforded many triumphant tests of the merit of the invention. On repeated occasions, in the Peninsula and elsewhere, our dragoons evinced as marked a superiority in single combat with the enemy as they had experienced defeats during the early campaigns in the Netherlands. The system survived the founder, and was adopted without alteration for several years. Towards the close of the war, another and an improved form of practice was introduced, with an important change in the shape of the sword, to render it more handy for the thrust. This occurred in the natural course of things, as no system is likely to be perfect on its first introduction; but the merit of an invention is not diminished because it has been subsequently surpassed. The first pioneer who opens a passage through the rock has quite as hard a task to perform as the succeeding labourers who smooth and macadamise the road.

Major Le Marchant's *Treatise on the Sword Exercise* was printed, by authority of the adjutant-general, in the year 1797, and many thousand copies were sold for the benefit of the service, as he declined all pecuniary remuneration. His labours received a far more gratifying recompense in his promotion, without purchase, to a lieutenant-colonelcy in Hompesch's Horse, from whence he was speedily transferred to the 29th Dragoons, and finally to the 7th Hussars. These successive appointments he owed solely to the estimation in which his abilities were held by the king. In consequence of the absence of Lord Paget, his senior officer, he commanded the 7th for a considerable time, and set himself vigorously to work to produce regimental reforms, much needed, but unpalatable to both officers and men, from their severity and the personal exertions by which they were attended. This course rendered him for a time unpopular; but the permanent advantages long outlived the unfavourable impression. The intimacy which sprang up between Lord Paget and his junior lieutenant-colonel, from their serving together in the same regiment, terminated only with the life of the latter.

Shortly before joining the 7th, Colonel Le Marchant prepared and submitted to the commander-in-chief, "a plan for preventing peculation in the foraging of the cavalry," which was approved by his Royal Highness, and carried into effect. Up to that period the existing system had degenerated into a most fruitful source of fraud. The advantage lay with the quarter-master, rather than with the captain of the troop. The colonel next composed a work called *The Duty of Officers of Cavalry on the Outpost*, the substance of which he had collected whilst serving with the advanced guards of the Prussian cavalry in Flanders. This treatise was also approved, and directed to be printed under authority from the Horse Guards, but by some intervening accident it never went to the press, and no trace of it can be found amongst the papers of the author. Another work, being an enlarged revision of his code of instructions, under the title of *An elucidation of several parts of his Majesty's regulations for the formation and movements of Cavalry*, was published in 1797, and has since passed through five very large impressions. To this he added one more, under the head of *Instructions for the movements and discipline of Provisional Cavalry*, a popular and useful manual, which his accustomed disinterestedness rendered as little profitable to himself as his previous publications.

Colonel Le Marchant had now established his reputation as one of the ablest regimental officers in the army; but his active and ambitious spirit was little disposed to rest satisfied with that ordinary distinction. He had long satisfied himself that much of the deficiency in our military character and practice, arose from the total absence of professional education on the part of the officers. This could only be remedied by the establishment of some uniform system of instruction, embracing the principles and practice of war in all its branches, and which should be accessible to officers of every grade and arm. England, then engaged in a most arduous struggle, was the only leading nation of Europe without a military school or college. The seminary at Woolwich admitted only cadets for the artillery. The subject of our memoir having maturely revolved the question in his mind, and feeling convinced that it might be carried into effect, drew up an essay, under the title of *A plan for establishing Regimental Schools for Officers throughout the service;* but he soon became convinced that the scope therein proposed was too narrow for the purpose, and abandoned his first conception.

Ruminating continually on his favourite speculation, as he was travelling alone in the autumn of 1798, he became firmly persuaded that nothing short of a national establishment, on a scale far more extensive than he originally meditated, would be found to yield any solid or adequate advantage to the state. At once he committed his ideas to paper, and was often heard to say afterwards, that, as he wrote, he acquired the most perfect confidence in the success of his . undertaking. His work being sufficiently matured, he submitted it to the Duke of York in January, 1799. His Royal Highness, after an attentive perusal, at once expressed his approbation of the design, but added his fears that the difficulties were too great to be overcome. The Duke of Richmond had some years before proposed a national military institution, and ministers had received the suggestion favourably. But when the subject came to be more minutely discussed, so many objections were stated by public men, as well to the principle as to the expense of the measure, that his Grace proceeded no farther in it. His Royal Highness then observed:

> I have no wish to discourage you, yet I can hardly recommend you to sacrifice your time and talents to a project which seems so very unlikely to succeed. Nothing can be done as long as people think on the subject as they do now, and I despair of removing their prejudices, for prejudices they are, unless you can absolutely demonstrate them to be groundless. This cannot be done in a moment, and it will require stronger arguments than those you have laid before me. If you will revise your plan, and accompany it with all the details necessary for satisfying the public, it shall have my warm support.

Here was as much encouragement as the sanguine projector could have hoped or desired at the outset. Accordingly he left the duke with an assurance that he would soon render the measure worthy of the public support: and he kept his word. In three months from that time be presented his Royal Highness with an elaborate statement of his views, comprising all the financial estimates, which formed the most important calculation in elucidating the expense of the proposed plan. The income and expenditure of the establishment in all its branches were enumerated with mercantile minuteness, and the result certainly showed the possibility of conducting it at little or no charge to the government.[2]

The Duke of York, convinced by the able arguments of Colonel Le Marchant (who, as soon as the leading objections were placed tangibly before him, grappled with and overthrew them), entered into his plans with entire acquiescence. It so happened that General Jarry, a French tactician, and an officer of the highest eminence, who had served under Frederick the Great throughout the whole of the Seven Years' War, and afterwards with Dumouriez, was at that time an exile in this

2. The college then projected has now, (at time of first publication), been carried on for more than fifty years; and no institution in the kingdom, of corresponding magnitude, has produced so much benefit with so slight a pressure on the revenue of the country.

country, and ready to turn his talents to the best account.

On the invitation of His Royal Highness, the veteran willingly undertook to instruct our officers in the art of war, with Lieutenant-Colonel Le Marchant as his associate in the task. A temporary establishment on a limited scale was then formed at High Wycombe in Bucks, which opened on the 4th of May, 1799, under the direction of the above-named officers, without the aid of professors. Thus began what has since risen into the senior and junior departments of the Royal Military College at Sandhurst. The lectures then delivered by General Jarry were greatly admired by the select few who could understand them; but being confined to the higher branches of the military art, and delivered in a foreign language, they were quite lost on the great majority of officers, who knew little of the science of their profession beyond the mere routine of regimental duty. It soon became obvious that a preparatory course of instruction was indispensable, and the government was reduced to the necessity of appointing the requisite professors, or of breaking up the establishment in its infancy.

Colonel Le Marchant knew and felt from the first that his plan must stand or fall by public opinion; he had, therefore, taken care to distribute, on the opening of the institution, a concise sketch of his design amongst those persons whose interest or advice was likely to afford him any assistance. The effect of this limited circulation increased his confidence and more than answered his expectations. Letters poured in upon him from all quarters, expressing the highest approbation of his plan; one in particular of a most gratifying nature from the Duke of Richmond. That high-minded nobleman praised his design in the strongest terms, and wished him the success that his abilities and perseverance deserved.

The Duke of York being now secure of the support of some of the most distinguished political characters in the country, came forward actively as the avowed patron of the institution, and authorised Colonel Le Marchant to select the necessary professors,—a trust he most conscientiously discharged. His first appointment was that of Mr. Isaac Dalby to the mathematical chair, and the situation could not have been filled by an abler or a better man. His two immediate colleagues were Mr. Thomas Leybourn and Mr. W. Wallace[3], who were carefully and judiciously selected after much deliberation. Isaac Dalby then prepared a *Course*, in two volumes, for the exclusive use of the new establishment, and which, having gone through several editions,

3. Afterwards professor of mathematics in the Edinburgh University.

is still the text-book at Sandhurst. He was a natural genius, self-taught, and originally of humble origin. It has been said that he had ridden as a post-boy in his early youth. His manners were homely, almost uncouth, but his disposition was kind, and his character unsophisticated; moreover, he had mastered his science with the power of a giant, and conveyed instruction in clear, impressive language, abounding with apposite illustrations, and concise withal. (See note following).

******

Note:—The writer had the good fortune to be a special favourite of the great professor, with whom he often came in contact during his periodical visits to examine the cadets of the junior department, then at Great Marlow. They were awful moments, when, with chalk in hand, he designed a complicated problem on the blackboard, and muttered in a gruff tone, "Let me see what you can make of that!" If you succeeded without boggling, he patted you on the head with a gracious, "You may go." As he entered the grounds on those momentous occasions, many would gather round him with obsequious bows and earnest inquiries after his health; but as he saw through the overstrained courting, he replied half jocularly, "Ah! I suppose you are coming up presently. Take care I don't spin you like tops." By a strange arrangement of the authorities, Mr. Dalby was also appointed examiner in history, of which, although a professed mathematician, he knew nothing beyond very general notions. He usually began with a common-place question in chronology; such for instance as, "When was the Battle of Hastings fought?" which, as a matter of course, you were unable to answer; and as you hesitated, he helped you out by saying, "Never mind a hundred years or so, give me a good round guess." Peace be to the ashes of Isaac Dalby! who, with all his eccentricities of manner and appearance, was generally loved and reverenced by young and old.

******

Colonel Le Marchant, having settled the mathematical branch, was proceeding to select the professors of fortification and military drawing, when the Queen's Dragoon Guards, the regiment to which he had been transferred from the seventh, and then commanded, was ordered to prepare for immediate embarkation on foreign service. Here was an unexpected check when he had overcome many difficulties; but, without solicitation, the authorities permitted him to name an officer to hold his post, in connection with the college, during his absence. He accordingly fixed upon an intimate friend, the late Major Brock of the 16th Light Dragoons, and then joined his regiment, which was one of the finest in the service, with the most sanguine expectations of distinguishing himself in the field. He wrote to his wife:—

> I am determined to rise to the head of my profession, and nothing but death shall stop me.

But the expedition of which he was to form a part, being abandoned after many preparations had been completed, he was released in the course of a few months from his regimental command, and allowed to return to High Wycombe, where he found everything at a stand-still, and exactly as he had left it, government having made no appointments after his departure. The fate of the institution seemed as doubtful as ever. The ministers were unwilling to add a shilling to the overloaded estimates under which the country was groaning, and the Duke of York felt a natural reluctance to add to their embarrassments by proposing the slightest increase in the expenditure of the army. Still Colonel Le Marchant persevered in his efforts, and offered to lend his services gratuitously until the institution should be fully established, and then to retire without any other recompense than the honour of having thus contributed to so important a measure.

Finally he won over the Hon. Mr. John Villiers, Mr. Huskisson, and through them, Mr. Pitt, to adopt his views warmly and effectually. The latter proposed that the Duke of York should appoint a committee of general and staff-officers, under directions from His Majesty, to decide on all the details connected with the permanent existence and extension of the present establishment. The committee was appointed in due course, and with some modification, adopted and recommended the plans so elaborately explained by Colonel Le Marchant. In their "report," they advised that the institution should be established under the Royal warranty and that a sum of 146,000*l* should be laid out in building a proper edifice for its reception. The report, dated the 2nd of December, 1801, was accompanied by a letter from the Duke of York, the president of the committee, to the Secretary of War, which concluded with these words:—

> The committee have further desired me to express in very strong terms the sense they entertain of the ability and uninterrupted assiduity which Lieutenant-Colonel Le Marchant has displayed

> in preparing and arranging the very intricate and voluminous details necessary to bring this important object to the state in which it is now presented to His Majesty's ministers; and from a consideration of the unavoidable expenses to which he has been exposed, during the long period he has been engaged in this undertaking, they recom mend that he shall receive, not less as a token of approbation than as a just remuneration for the same, the sum of 500*l*.

Lord Hobart (secretary of state) immediately forwarded the king's warrant for 500*l*., with expressions of his high sense of Lieutenant-Colonel Le Marchant's merit. A board was then appointed to manage the affairs of the institution, which for the present was not enlarged, but from thenceforth received the title of the Royal Military College. The expedition to Egypt under Sir Ralph Abercrombie had afforded a favourable opportunity of employing on the staff some of the officers who were most forward in their studies. The manner in which they acquitted themselves vindicated the judgment with which they had been selected, and stamped the utility of the new establishment. The historian of that short but brilliant campaign. Sir Robert Wilson, bears ample testimony to the merit of those students, and his praise is confirmed by an enlightened French writer of the present day, Dupin, in his work entitled *The Military Force of Great Britain.*

Soon after the first warrant received the royal assent, Lieutenant-General the Hon. William Harcourt was appointed the governor; at the special recommendation of the committee, General Jarry the inspector-general of instruction[4], and Colonel Le Marchant the lieutenant-governor and superintendent-general of the Royal Military College. On the 4th of May the latter received the final triumph of his long and persevering exertions. On that day His Majesty issued a second warrant:

> For the formation and government of the Junior Department of the Royal Military College, for the instruction of those who, from early life, were intended for the military profession, and who might thereby be grounded in science previously to their

4. General Jarry died in 1807, aged 75, and was succeeded by Sir Howard Douglas. It was at one time intended that the office should be filled by General Dumouriez, and negotiations were entered into with that view; but the government declined to give him the rank in our service which his overweening pretensions led him to demand as an accompanying stipulation.

attaining the age that enables them, consistently with the regulations, to hold commissions in the army;[5] and to afford a provision also for the orphan sons of those meritorious officers who had fallen or been disabled in the service of their country, as well as for the sons of those officers, who from pecuniary difficulties might not otherwise be able to give them a proper education.

The new college being thus firmly established and elevated. Colonel Le Marchant resigned the command of the Queen's Dragoon Guards, and devoted himself entirely to the duties of his new and most responsible office. The subsequent years of his residence at High Wycombe formed the brightest period of his life. More fortunate than most public benefactors, he had received an early and substantial re ward. He had been appointed, without any solicitation on his part, to the most distinguished as well as the most lucrative post in the service that was compatible with his rank; and to crown all, his wife and children were the witnesses and partners of his elevation. It cannot be disputed that to Colonel Le Marchant is due the full, undivided merit of giving to England a permanent school of instruction for her army.

Promotion, honours, and titles achieved on the battlefield, are undoubtedly the most brilliant and captivating of the soldier's trophies, as well as the most popular evidences of his courage and executive ability; but here is a remarkable example to show that other avenues to distinction fall within the wide scope of his duties, and may be followed with success by an active and accomplished mind. The prompt conception which executes a daring manoeuvre in the decisive moment, and the happy courage which braves and escapes the accompanying danger, are dazzling endowments; but they are intrinsically inferior to, and more commonly exhibited, than the high intellectual energy which plans, matures, and establishes, in the face of many obstacles and prejudices, such an extensive innovation as a National Military College.

---

5. This was fixed at sixteen, and as thirteen was the age for entering the college, three years was the allotted time for completing the regular course of study, and passing the examination before the supreme board, which entitled the successful candidate to a certificate and a commission. The writer had the singular good fortune to accomplish this within sixteen months, so that he became a gazetted officer, without purchase, at the age of fourteen and a half, and received the additional indulgence of continuing his studies for eighteen months more before he was ordered to join his regiment. During this time his pay and promotion went on regularly.

The appointment of a governor was little more than a nominal dignity. The active duties rested with the lieutenant-governor, whose immediate province, the personal charge and supervision of the senior department, by no means interfered with his constant visits to the junior branch of the institution, which occurred regularly twice a week. The resident *commandant*, Colonel Butler, transmitted to the lieutenant-governor a weekly report detailing every particular connected with the studies, discipline, and general state of his charge. Colonel Le Marchant exercised his extensive authority with strict impartiality, and although naturally of an irascible temper, never suffered himself to be betrayed by constitutional warmth into an act even bordering on injustice. If he was sometimes severe, he was always upright, inflexible in principle, kind where indulgence was appropriate, and sedulous to discover merit. It would have been difficult indeed to have selected another individual so admirably adapted to the post he filled.

Many young men of humble fortunes were materially forwarded by his support. Few persons possessed the art of reproving, with such effect. The serious expression of his features, combined with the dignity of his manner, and the deep tones of his voice, struck his youthful audience, when he addressed them, with an awe which many of them were unable to forget when grown to manhood, and engaged in the stirring scenes of military life.

The compiler of these memoirs happened to be sent to Marlow, under the immediate patronage of the late Sir Herbert Taylor, within four years of the opening of the junior department. A relation of high rank in the artillery accompanied him, and took the opportunity of introducing the shy and trembling stripling to the notice of the lieutenant-governor, with whom he was intimately acquainted, and who sat with other magnates at the board while the neophyte was undergoing his preliminary examination. Ever after this, Colonel Le Marchant kept an eye upon the young cadet, and constantly addressed a few words of friendly encouragement to him, when he visited the halls of study, and received favourable reports of his progress from the different professors.

Once he justly incurred his displeasure for a heavy breach of discipline. He was on sentry at the main guard, and had placed an open book of light reading on the arm-rack, to solace his monotonous walk by the occasional perusal of a page. Suddenly the lieutenant-governor came round the angle of the guard-room, accompanied by two or three of the officers, and detected the culprit in the very act.

He recovered himself as well as he could, presented arms in trepidation, and stood motionless, with visions of the black hole and bread and water swimming before his eyes. "A sentry reading on his post," pronounced the well-known sonorous voice; and on this text a severe homily was delivered, which the delinquent long remembered, and inwardly blessed the lenity that suffered him to escape with so slight a punishment.

Colonel Le Marchant was particularly careful in administering the finances of the college, and with this view was ever on the watch to prevent waste or peculation in any of its departments. By this assiduity, serious abuses were brought to light and checked with a strong hand. He had also a strong aversion to carry on business of any importance by conversation, when it could be done in writing, which he conceived to be the best check on bad men and the best security to good ones. He was accustomed to say that this habit had on one occasion saved him from utter ruin. His *official* letters, purely relating to college matters, during the nine years that he held his command, fill five massive folios.

Many practical men of business, on the other hand, hold that in most cases half an hour's conversation does more than a volume of correspondence. As in most other arguments, there is much to be said on both sides; but the question of *time* would seem to be the first consideration. Notwithstanding the multifarious duties attached to his post) Colonel Le Marchant found leisure hours, during which he principally occupied himself in drawing) in which he was originally self-taught, but had recently improved by taking lessons from Payne and Glover. The beautiful environs of High Wycombe, and occasional visits to his native island of Guernsey, afforded picturesque subjects for the pencil, of which he availed himself with mingled delight and assiduity. He rose early, slept little, and was by constitution both temperate and abstemious.

Under the excitement of society, he spoke with fluency and spirit on subjects with which he was well acquainted; but as his knowledge of books was limited, he never ventured beyond his depth. By nature he was habitually taciturn, and, though tenderly attached to his wife and children, he seldom joined in their conversation. His pen was constantly in his hand, and he composed many treatises on subjects connected with the military profession. Amongst the most important were, *A Plan for recruiting the Army*, which the adjutant-general strongly recommended the government to carry into effect; *A Plan for the gen-*

eral Enrolment and effectual Discipline of the Population of the country capable of bearing Arms, the substance of which was introduced into an act passed at the close of the session of 1803; *An Outline of the general Staff of the Army*, in a volume of two hundred and eighty pages; and at the suggestion of Mr. Windham (then secretary of state for war and the colonies), an elaborate treatise entitled *Outline of a general Organization of the Military Establishment of Great Britain.*

On the 7th of April, 1804, the lieutenant-governor was honoured with a conversation by George the Third, on the terrace at Windsor, in which His Majesty expressed himself in the most complimentary terms:—

> I consider the military college an object of the deepest national importance. The Duke of Cambridge has just given me a most favourable account of it, and I hear from scientific men that your studies are conducted by very able masters, and according to an excellent system. I entirely approve of the measures you have pursued in the late disturbances[6], and I think the example must lead to the improvement of the cadets. There was no expecting them to be docile at first, but their management will become, every day, less difficult; and you will all the while be raising a race of officers who will make our army the finest in Europe. The country is greatly indebted to you.

After the Battle of Corunna, in January 1809, the immediate attention of England was directed to the preservation of Portugal; it was therefore determined to reorganise the Portuguese Army on the British system, and under British officers. Colonel Le Marchant was named by the ambassador, the secretary of state, and the general in command on the spot, as the most eligible person to assume this arduous duty. He received the notice of this intended appointment with the most unfeigned satisfaction. It was a great advance on the road to high professional distinction, for which, in the midst of his many avocations, he incessantly panted. But the commander-in-chief refused his consent, on the ground, as His Royal Highness informed Lord Castlereagh, "that Colonel Le Marchant could not be spared from the college." It remains only to add that the colonel submitted to his Royal Highnesses decision without a murmur, being sensible, as he

6. There had recently been a sort of rebellion or mutiny at the Junior Department, which was speedily suppressed by a judicious blending of decisive with lenient measures.

said, that the college was his chief care, and its success the great object of his life.

He now conceived his connection with the institution to be indissoluble, and perhaps he was not sorry for it. The conviction operated a material change in his views and feelings. Ambitious, as he had hitherto been, of military honours, he felt an attachment almost paternal for the college, and its growing: success was continually adding to his reputation. Many of the most rising officers in the Peninsular army, both staff and regimental, had issued from its walls. In the early summer of 1811, Colonel Le Marchant was raised, in the ordinary routine of promotion, to the rank of major-general, and about the same time he went to Sandhurst to inspect the progress of the long-projected new buildings, which were at last commenced on the magnificent scale originally contemplated.

All that he saw increased his satisfaction, and he returned to Wycombe, happy in the certainty that all difficulties under which the college had been labouring were removed, and that he was destined to pass the remainder of his days where he could witness and participate in the accomplishment of the schemes that had occupied him for so many years.

The work was scarcely over, before he received a letter from the adjutant-general, acquainting him "that their Royal Highnesses the Prince Regent and the Duke of York were of opinion that his situation at the college was incompatible with his rank in the army, and he must therefore expect to be immediately removed."

The communication came upon him with the effect likely to be produced upon a man of strong feelings, who was totally unprepared for such an announcement. His wife was in a very advanced state of pregnancy; and although the pay and appointments of lieutenant-governor of the college were nominally considerable, they had hitherto proved inadequate to the incidental expenses (much increased by the non-residence of the governor), and his private fortune had suffered in consequence.

All these expenses would have ceased on the removal of the college to Sandhurst, and an honourable opportunity would have been afforded to him of recruiting his finances. Though what may be termed a very successful soldier, he was many thousand pounds poorer than when be entered the army. His letter, in reply to the adjutant-general, is so manly and characteristic that we may be excused for quoting it.

High Wycombe, 9th June, 1811.

My dear Sir,—Allow me to thank you for the early intimation that you have had the goodness to give me of my intended removal from the Military College. I would have answered your letter immediately and without hesitation, to the same effect as I am now about to do, but unfortunately there was yesterday no post.

I cannot disguise from you that this change in my situation will make a very sensible difference in my income, which must unavoidably be heavily felt by a numerous and young family. I had certainly (though without sufficient consideration) looked forward to my continuance at the college, as the more natural course that my military life would have taken, under the particular circumstances of my having given rise to an establishment which is admitted to have been of essential service to the army, and of my having devoted my best military years to its advancement and improvement, during which time I have unavoidably lost every opportunity of distinguishing myself, in common with those of my own standing, by active service in the field.

But as the appointment of lieutenant-governor is deemed incompatible with my present rank in the army, I hope that I need not say to you that these thoughts shall never occupy me for a moment; and I shall thank you to assure His Royal Highness the commander-in-chief, that I never can have any other object in view as to my professional employment, than that of showing myself worthy of that situation (whatever it may be) in which his Royal Highness may be pleased to think my humble services may be most useful and acceptable.

Of course, I do not know whether it is to you alone that I am indebted for this early communication of what is intended; if so, pray allow me to repeat my best thanks; but if you have done it with the permission of his Royal Highness, I beg that you will express in the strongest terms my humble acknowledgment of this mark of his condescension and kindness.

Within little more than three weeks from the transmission of this letter, the general received official notice that an additional brigade of cavalry was ordered for immediate service in Portugal, and that he was selected for the command. He accepted the proffered distinction with alacrity, and two days afterwards issued the following order at the college:—

> Royal Military College, 6th July, 1811.
>
> His Royal Highness the Prince Regent having been graciously pleased to appoint Major-General Le Marchant to the command of a brigade of cavalry, under immediate orders of embarkation to serve in Portugal, he desires that, until further orders, all reports may be made to Colonel Butler, as senior officer at the college.
>
> The lieutenant-governor cannot resign his command of an institution which he had the good fortune to be instrumental in forming, and to the advancement of which he has devoted so many years, without expressing his ardent wishes for the welfare of its members; and his sincere hope and conviction that it will completely fulfil the just expectations of the army and public from so important an establishment.

The retirement of the general produced the strongest expressions of regret; and it may encourage others in a strict and honourable discharge of their duty, to learn that one so scrupulously just and fearlessly impartial as he had always proved, carried away with him, not only the respect, but, in general, the attachment of those under his command. He was immediately waited upon by a deputation of the officers, requesting him to name a day on which a public dinner might be given in testimony of their sentiments; but the urgent nature of his orders precluded his receiving so gratifying a tribute to his merit, and the dinner was not given. In little more than a week he was obliged to take leave of his family, and proceed to London, on his way to Plymouth, where he was to find the frigate appointed to convey him to Lisbon.

He visited some of his friends in town preparatory to his departure, and, amongst others, the late Marquess of Anglesey, whom he requested to furnish him with any hints that a more recent experience of active service might suggest. "The best advice that I can give to a cavalry general," said His Lordship, "is to inspire his men as early as possible with the most perfect confidence in his personal gallantry. Let him but lead. they are sure to follow, and I believe hardly anything will stop them."[7]

---

7. This appears to have been Murat's secret, and Napoleon understood its effect; for he once observed at St. Helena, "I wish we had had Murat at Waterloo; one of his daring charges might have retrieved the day." (Continued next page).

General Le Marchant sailed from Plymouth in the middle of August. His brigade had already embarked in the transports convoyed by the frigate. On the morning of the 24th, they entered the Tagus, and the general landed at Belem on the afternoon of the same day. For sixteen years he had not left England, and had never penetrated into the continent beyond Flanders and France. All was equally new and interesting to him. His sketch-book was busily employed, and his residence at Lisbon passed profitably and agreeably. He remained there with additional satisfaction, as it afforded him the means of receiving more frequent tidings of his wife. He had left her in a state that caused great anxiety, but constant letters assured him that all was going on well. The last was most encouraging.

Two days after its receipt, in the midst of his gratitude and hope, the news arrived that the object of his affections, the mother of his children, was no more. She had gone to bed in perfect health, but the pangs of labour had come on during the night, and after giving birth to a fine boy, she had expired. The blow, so sudden and unlocked for, completely crushed his spirit for a time, and he never after recovered its perfect elasticity. A long union had cemented the early attachment between him and the object of his choice. She became the partner of his fortunes from his youth up, and not only participated in, but aided all his plans for advancement. The most perfect community of thought existed between them, and whether it were joy or sorrow, hope or fear, it came upon them both alike. By the same packet which communicated to General Le Marchant his heavy domestic bereavement, the Duke of York, anticipating that he might wish to return to his family, had written to Lord Wellington to request leave of absence for him. The act was kind and spontaneous, but the general declined availing himself of it.

His relations in Guernsey undertook the charge of his children, eight in number, and he resolved to remain at his post. His brigade consisted of three splendid regiments, the 4th and 5th Dragoon Guards, and the 3rd (King's Own) Dragoons; mustering two thousand sabres and horses of a superior quality. With very few exceptions, they were young soldiers, who had never yet faced an enemy; but the Portuguese, who had not seen any English heavy cavalry before, were struck with admiration at their imposing appearance, and predicted

Murat, with very little tactical science, performed some wonderful exploits by sheer courage, and his soldiers conceiving themselves to be invincible under his guidance, pursued, perhaps, the best means of being so.

their signal triumph when brought into conflict with the enemy. For many family and private reasons, it would have been extremely agreeable as well as convenient to General Le Marchant to have taken his eldest son, then an ensign in the First Foot Guards, as his *aide-de-camp*, on his first appointment; but he refrained from doing this for some time, on strictly conscientious motives, until he felt that the young man had qualified himself by more experience, and a more competent knowledge of the leading continental languages.

In the middle of September, 1811, General Le Marchant, under orders from Lord Wellington, marched from Lisbon with his brigade to watch the movements of Regnier at Alcantara. He fixed his headquarters with the 4th Dragoons at Fundao, a small town in the mountains, and posted the 3rd and 5th at Castello Branco, Thomar, and the neighbouring villages. His duties required activity and a sharp look out, but the early part of the winter passed over without any offensive movements on the part of the enemy. The supineness of the French enabled him to visit Frenada to pay his respects to Lord Wellington, to whom he was no stranger by reputation, and who gave him a cordial welcome. He was still further gratified by renewing intercourse with many of his oldest and dearest friends, at that time attached to his lordship's immediate command. One of these officers has thus recorded, in a letter, the impression left upon him by the unexpected meeting:—

> I found the general as active and energetic as when I had first known him fourteen years before. I was happy also to perceive that his temper had greatly improved; and, indeed, he seemed to have spared no pains to get it under his control. He once said to me, 'I have been all my life squabbling and quarrelling, and unable to get out of troubled waters. I am determined henceforward that no one shall have any just ground of complaint against me.' I thought this was being too hard upon himself, and could not help telling him that it was not so much from defect of temper that he had fallen into these difficulties, as from expecting all men to be as eager and able to do their duty as himself, and treating them, in case he happened to be disappointed, as if they were the very reverse of what he had supposed them.
>
> If he would but adopt a more humble standard, he would form a more accurate estimate. I afterwards observed that my advice had not been thrown away; for no general could show more

judicious indulgence than he did to his officers and men, or in return be more beloved by them.

Towards the close of 1811, Lord Wellington conceived the design of attacking Ciudad Rodrigo. The project had been suspected by some of his staff for some weeks, but nothing certain transpired until he communicated the necessary orders at the appropriate time. The investment of the doomed fortress commenced on the 8th of January, 1812, and General Le Marchant was ordered to bring up the heavy brigade from Castello Branco to cover the operations of the besieging army. He marched on the 13th, and on the 17th arrived within a league of the place. His headquarters were established at Aldea da Ponte, a straggling town on the Portuguese side of the Agueda, which with the surrounding neighbourhood had been so exhausted that it was found extremely difficult to procure either forage or food. The siege was pressed rapidly, and from the unprecedented vigour of Lord Wellington's operations, terminated much sooner than could have been expected.

The French had been accustomed to say, that although the English might win battles, they would never take a town. The assertion was now about to be dissipated by a plain proof to the contrary, destined to be corroborated by others of even a more signal character, before the long competition for ultimate victory was brought to a conclusion. The storming and capture of Ciudad Rodrigo took place on the 19th of January. As there was no probability of the cavalry being engaged, Lord Wellington directed General Le Marchant to remain with him during the assault. Accordingly he continued by his side until the struggle was over, and accompanied him when he entered the city to take formal possession. He witnessed with pain the excesses committed by the troops upon the unfortunate inhabitants, and with many other superior officers used the most strenuous efforts to suppress them.

The French governor, General Barrio, was for a while placed under his charge; but his manners were uncouth, and he appeared so little accustomed to the courtesies of society, that there was considerable rejoicing when orders were issued for his removal to Lisbon. General Le Marchant wrote a detailed account of the storming of Ciudad Rodrigo, for the information of one of the highest military authorities in England, which was greatly praised at the time, but unfortunately cannot now be found. This noble feat of arms was performed by the third and light divisions, under their two distinguished commanders, Picton and Craufurd; the latter of whom fell, and was buried close to the breach, up to which he led his darted followers with his usual undaunted courage. In the memoir of that brave officer, we have quoted the celebrated parallel between him and Picton from the masterly pen of Sir W. Napier. We here introduce another by the writer from whom we have compiled the present biography, differing in some points from the earlier one—more minute, perhaps, (as some may think), more just, and equally deserving to be read and remembered.

> Picton and Craufurd were officers alike distinguished by gallantry and talent, but most opposite in disposition and deportment, and, it may not now be uninteresting to add, in person. Picton, when wrapped in his military cloak, might have been mistaken for a bronze statue of Cato, and was equally staid, deliberate, and austere; whilst Craufurd, of a diminutive and not imposing figure, was characterised by vivacity almost mercurial both in thought and act; his eager spirit and fertile brain ever hurrying him into enterprises of difficulty and danger, which he loved the more because they sometimes left him at liberty to follow his own view of the crisis of the moment. Others shunned responsibility—he courted it. He had served on the staff of the Austrian armies during the revolutionary war, and was well versed in their tactics, as he had shown by his translation of one of their best military histories; but this knowledge was of very questionable benefit to him, for it occasionally led him to try experiments which were hardly consistent with the comparative insignificance of his corps.
>
> In short, he was too much disposed to aim at objects which were the province of the commander rather than of a subordinate general. Picton had no such ambition, but he was slow to execute orders of which he disapproved, and the quickness of his perception was not equal to the soundness of his judgment. Craufurd had the faults incidental to a hasty temper—Picton those belonging to a morose one. Each was possessed of indefatigable industry, and perfect familiarity with all the duties of his profession; and last, though not least, both were men of the highest integrity and honour. Next to Lord Wellington, none stood higher in the estimation of the army. Both these officers were the friends of General Le Marchant. He had known

Craufurd long and intimately; and there existed between himself and Picton, a degree of affection, which the latter did not often show but could most strongly feel. He was a man much more generally admired than beloved, though he possessed in an eminent degree, qualities calculated to inspire attachment. In this respect, as well as in his military talents,—and, in some degree, his person,—a resemblance might be traced between his friend and himself.

The constant intercourse which General Le Marchant had so fortunately enjoyed with Lord Wellington at Frenada and Ciudad Rodrigo, inspired the great commander with such confidence in his subordinate, that he left him almost the independent control of his brigade without interference from other authorities. Too exalted for jealousy himself, he required only to be well served, and possessed the peculiar tact of all superior minds in discovering the ability and activity of those under him. These qualities he ever turned to the best account by giving their possessors the most unfettered facilities for their exercise. A new field was at this time opened to General Le Marchant by his being appointed president of the Board of Claims; a busy and complicated office, which required great knowledge of business, with more than common sagacity and discernment. The encroachment on his time often abridged the few hours that after a hard day's march remained for repose; but his decisions, however, were so carefully made, that they materially contributed to the high estimation which he gained in the army.

Lord Wellington having carried Ciudad Rodrigo with a rapidity which utterly disconcerted the French generals, determined to follow up his success by a similar attempt against the more formidable stronghold of Badajos, which had twice foiled his utmost endeavours. He disregarded the season, and seized the favourable contingency which circumstances presented. In co-operation with this design. General Le Marchant's brigade of heavy cavalry moved from Castello Branco on the 21st of February, and crossing the Alemtejo, he halted on the 6th of March at Villa Vicosa. Here they were detained several days by the incompleteness of the preparations for the projected siege. Every officer in every department worked with untiring zeal to advance the object of their chief. The subject of our memoir in particular exerted himself; and those who saw him labouring early and late, with a mind always collected, vigorous, and apparently at ease, little guessed the depth of anguish which lay concealed under this calm exterior. The real state of his feelings betrayed itself in his private correspondence. In a letter to an intimate friend, written about this time, he says:

> As for myself, my days have been woefully embittered by misfortune, and discouraged by disappointment. I have now little to look forward to. Whenever I allow myself to think of my family in their present dispersed and dependent state, I am made truly wretched. Still, whatever may be my lot, I feel that I shall have done my duty to my country and to them, and if I have not been more successful, it will not be owing to any want of exertion on my part to merit a more fortunate issue.

Badajos was invested on the 16th of March, and fell on the 6th of April. During the operations, the cavalry were posted in advance with the covering army under Sir Thomas Graham, and two or three unimportant skirmishes took place which led to nothing. Soult advanced with a strong corps to relieve the endangered city, but retired precipitately when informed, to his utter amazement, that he was too late, and it was already taken. On the evening of the 10th of April, the cavalry of his rear-guard were somewhat carelessly posted between Villa Garcia and Usagre; and Sir Stapleton Cotton conceived hopes that it might be possible to cut them off. The forces collected for this enterprise numbered about nineteen hundred men, consisting of the heavy brigade under General Le Marchant, and the light brigade of General Anson, then commanded by Lieutenant-Colonel the Hon. Frederick Ponsonby, who had distinguished himself at Talavera and Barossa, and was destined to achieve still higher fame in after days, by his romantic escapes at Waterloo. The French cavalry amounted to nearly two thousand three hundred, all experienced soldiers; and Lallemand, one of the brigadiers, was a favourite pupil of Napoleon, and had already established a brilliant reputation. Peyremmont was also a first-rate soldier, but given to boasting, and entertaining an utter contempt for the English cavalry and their leaders, which he expressed on all occasions in unmeasured terms.

The troops marched on the night of the 10th, Sir Stapleton Cotton accompanying Ponsonby's brigade. It was intended that he should attack the enemy in front, while Le Marchant assailed their rear, and intercepted the retreat on Llerena by the Benvenida road. The success of the surprise entirely depended on simultaneous action. General Le Marchant approached the ground he had been directed to occupy, without being discovered by any of the French out-piquets, but found that Ponsonby, by some mistake, had arrived before the appointed time and commenced the action too soon. The surprise had failed. The enemy were thus enabled to escape the snare, and retired; but soon halted and drew up in order of battle, concentrating their squadrons for a decisive charge, when they discovered the weakness of the attacking force; for Le Marchant's brigade were concealed from their view.

They then advanced boldly against the weak body under Sir Stapleton Cotton, who stood patiently to await the onset, although opposed to such odds, that their total overthrow appeared certain and immediate. Lallemand at this crisis suddenly descried a small body of British cavalry emerge from an olive-grove in his rear, and push boldly towards him across the plain. They evidently did not exceed three or four hundred men, and no others were in sight, but they moved with such confidence, compactness, and precision, that he suspected a support could not be far distant.

These troops were four squadrons of the 5th Dragoon Guards, which General Le Marchant had moved quickly on through a defile, while the rest of the brigade hastened by the longer circuit of the road, to sustain him. Everything depended on time, and with this select body he resolved to make a daring effort to gain the day. Lallemand hurried to Peyremmont, and delivered his opinion of the danger; but his suggestions were ill received by his superior. He insisted that the officer commanding the British detachment must be a blockhead, and was throwing himself upon certain destruction. To Lallemand's more correct eye, the disposition of the British denoted any thing rather than want of skill, and he could not help observing that if their commander were not a blockhead, he must be no ordinary soldier. Peyremmont smiled contemptuously at a supposition which he treated as absurd, and turned away.

The question was soon decided, for while the French were in the confusion inseparable from a sudden change of position to encounter an unexpected enemy, Le Marchant dashed upon their flank with desperate impetuosity at the head of his brave followers, who, in close array, unbroken by their extraordinary speed, went as one unbroken mass into the ranks of the enemy, from whom they encountered a very ineffectual resistance. A sanguinary conflict ensued, in which several single combats took place, and many wounds were given and received by the victors. A moment or two after, Ponsonby charged against the front, and the two other regiments of the heavy brigade arriving in support, the French gave way in all directions: the rout was complete, and the plain was soon covered with fugitives. The pursuit continued for more than four miles, and was pushed up to the suburbs of Llerena.

In this creditable affair, as skilfully combined as it was gallantly fought, the English had only fifty-six troopers killed and wounded, forty-five of these being of the 5th Dragoon Guards. The French deserters (and the account was corroborated by other evidence) stated their loss at little less than five hundred men in killed, wounded, and missing, of whom one lieutenant-colonel, two captains, and one hundred and twenty-eight privates were made prisoners.

The cavalry action at Usagre, being fought in the vicinity of both armies, attracted unusual attention, and established General Le Marchant's character as a quick, daring, executive officer. Lord Wellington, in his despatch, speaks of the engagement as "highly creditable to Sir Stapleton Cotton, General Le Marchant, and the officers and troops under their command"; thus coupling the subordinate general with his chief—an unusual distinction, which plainly showed the sense that his Lordship attached to his services on that occasion. The merit which he claimed for himself was very moderate; for in a letter to a friend, he merely observes:

> The affair, though of no great consequence, brought myself and my brigade acquainted on essential points, and I have reason to believe that we are mutually well pleased with each other.

The day after the combat, the general was joined by his eldest son, who had obtained permission to quit Cadiz (where he was quartered with his battalion), that he might serve in future under his father's eye on the staff of Lord Wellington's army. His arrival was the source of great delight to his father, who had ever preferred him above his brothers, and indulged towards him a mingled feeling of pride and affection.[7] Time passed on, and the events of the campaign led to the great movements and complicated manoeuvres between the mighty hosts of Wellington and Marmont, which worked up to the crowning

7. This accomplished and promising young officer fell at the early age of twenty-three, being mortally wounded at the Battle of the Nive. He expired at St. Jean de Luz, on the 12th of March, 1814, and was buried on the ramparts of that city. The writer bears willing testimony to his talents and amiable qualities, for he knew him intimately when they were both cadets at the Military College, and afterwards when they served together for a short time in Sicily.

glory of Salamanca. General Le Marchant, in the midst of incessant and harassing duties, still found intervals during which to indulge in his favourite recreation of sketching, and to write many letters to his family and friends.

During the whole of May, the headquarters of his brigade continued at Crato, about three leagues from Portalegre. This month passed so quietly that it would have been difficult for a casual writer to believe that vast combinations of war were gathering together in the neighbourhood, and two large armies gradually moving, as through a labyrinth, to meet in a common centre. The surprise and destruction of the bridge of Almaraz, on the 19th of May, by General Hill, insulated the force of Marmont from the army of the centre, and thus opened to Lord Wellington the prospect of fighting a general action on more equal terms than the vast numerical superiority of the enemy usually admitted.

On the 1st of June, General Le Marchant, having received orders to join Lord Wellington, left Crato, and proceeding through Castello Branco, Alcaniz, and Casea, reached the headquarters of the British army at Gallegos, on the 9th. Forty thousand men were here encamped ready for action, and confident of victory under the chief who had never been defeated. On the 12th, the heavy brigade (5th Dragoon Guards, 3rd and 4th Dragoons) bivouacked on the Agueda, not far from Ciudad Rodrigo, and was inspected by Lord Wellington, who bestowed the warmest commendations on their service-like appearance and steady discipline. For the latter quality they found favour even in the eyes of Sir Thomas Picton, who, with all the stubborn prejudices of an old infantry officer, was slow to accord any praise to the cavalry branch of the service which could reasonably be withheld. After relating, on one occasion, how he found an unfortunate subaltern of Light Dragoons with his piquet all fast asleep on their post close to the French, he added:

> I always feel easy when Le Marchant's men are between me and the enemy; they do their duty, and can be trusted, and I heartily wish the rest were like them.

This systematic superiority was produced by personal example. The general absolutely identified himself with his brigade, in which he appeared like a parent amongst his children. The hardest day's march could not prevent his walking through the cantonment or bivouac to see whether the comforts of the men had been properly cared for; and to the surprise of those who had known him in early life, if there ever was a complaint raised against him in these campaigns, it was that of over-indulgence to the men, who in return almost idolised him.

On the 13th of June, the heavy brigade crossed the Agueda, and on the 19th, marched through Salamanca. Marmont had evacuated the city, leaving strong garrisons in the forts, which he trusted would hold out until he could return to relieve them. Lord Wellington followed him, but had little disposition to risk a general battle until the forts were taken.

On the 20th, Marmont, who had not fallen back further than two leagues from Salamanca, collected four divisions and advanced towards the British position, appearing to invite an engagement. Lord Wellington's army was strongly posted on the heights of St. Christoval. General Le Marchant's brigade was stationed in the centre. During the three or four following days, a battle appeared inevitable. At first the allies were superior in number, and a victory might be safely anticipated. But Lord Wellington knew his own plans better than those about him, and no temptation could induce him to depart from them. On the 27th, the forts fell, and during the night which followed. Marmont retreated towards the Duero, by the roads of Tordesillas and Toro.[8] Some military critics of pretension, have blamed the English general for not striking a blow on this occasion when the chances were so palpably in his favour; others of equal repute have shown by strong argument that he decided wisely.

At that moment, Marmont had everything to gain by a battle; Wellington had every thing to lose. The French general crossed the Duero and the two armies remained eagerly watching each other on opposite sides of the river for nearly a fortnight, without undertaking any hostile movements. At length, activity was resumed on both sides; the ground that had been already traversed was crossed and re-crossed again in complicated manoeuvres, and a trial of skill took place between the two contending chiefs, as nicely balanced and as carefully calculated as a game of chess between two equal players. During this, there occurred many skirmishes both of cavalry and infantry, with

8. Major-General Bowes, a rising officer, who had never been engaged without distinguishing himself, lost his life in the first attempt to carry the forts by escalade. He was wounded early, but hearing that the troops were giving way, he returned to head them a second time, and fell. There was no occasion for his leading so small a force, which duty belonged more properly to a lieutenant-colonel or major; but British generals are ever prone to sacrifice themselves by unnecessary daring.

mutual interchanges of daring gallantry, but without any decisive result.

On the 21st of July, the English found themselves in their old position of St. Christoval in front of Salamanca, and the French behind Calvariza de Ariba. As the infantry kept the high ground, the cavalry scoured the plain, and it was beautiful to behold the latter performing the various evolutions of their arms, sometimes in large bodies, sometimes in small, constantly on the point of engaging, yet seldom coming into serious collision. The skill with which General Le Marchant handled his brigade during these movements was much remarked, as was his noble and imposing mien, enhanced in no slight degree by his admirable horsemanship. The Spaniards and Portuguese, who greatly value personal advantages, watched him with admiration as he rode along the field with his men; and indeed there were none amongst his followers who excelled him in the ordinary qualifications of a soldier.

As Sallust has recorded of Pompey, he was perfect in all martial exercises; and in spite of his grave demeanour, he could not always keep himself under restraint sufficiently, to withstand the temptation of displaying his personal prowess. Once in particular, when in Estremadura, seeing a party of German horse give way before an equal force of the enemy, he hastily collected a few of his skirmishers, at the head of whom he fell furiously on the victors, cut down two of the foremost with his own hand, and speedily routed and dispersed the whole body, after which he returned to his former position with his usual composure, as if nothing had happened. He was, however, far from approving of such exhibitions being made by officers of superior rank; and so little did he contemplate the probability of these occurring in his own case, that during the whole campaign he was not possessed even of a pair of pistols, and upon being recommended to provide himself with them, merely answered that a general officer had always abundance of protection, and he almost considered his sword an unnecessary appendage.

The heavy brigade halted for some hours during the afternoon of the 21st at Cabenza, a village on the banks of the Tormes, within half a league of Salamanca; from the mill of which place General Le Marchant took the last sketch in which his pencil was ever employed. The relic possesses a melancholy interest, and was carefully preserved in his portfolio. Whether, while thus employed, any thought of his impending fate entered his mind can never be ascertained, but his letters to various friends at home, furnish ample evidence of the impression continually hanging over him that he should fall in battle. His own family were tremblingly alive to such apprehensions, but from them he carefully concealed his own forebodings. He repeatedly urged that the risk must be slight, when not one cavalry general had been killed during the whole contest in the Peninsula, and why should he be the first?

During the night of the 21st, a storm of unusual violence came suddenly on, in the progress of which a thunderbolt fell amongst the 7th Dragoon Guards who were bivouacking in the open field. Fortunately none of the soldiers were struck by it, but many of the troop horses, breaking loose from their piquet-ropes in terror, ran wildly about, trampling upon and wounding their dismounted riders, who lay sleeping beside them, and finally darted off at full speed across the plain towards the enemy's outposts. The confusion, which was at first supposed to have been caused by the enemy's cavalry charging in the darkness, was soon suppressed when the real cause became known; but, notwithstanding the exertions of both officers and men, from the general downwards, the loss of the 5th Dragoon Guards eventually proved to be twenty-eight horses. These had escaped into the French lines, and although no great number, they must have been very acceptable there. Marmont had recently been driven from absolute necessity to seize all the horses in his camp, not belonging to mounted officers, for the use of the cavalry,—a measure that made him very unpopular.

At seven o'clock on the morning of the 22nd of July, the heavy brigade, headed by their general, marched to take the post allotted to them in the rear of the infantry, towards the right-centre of the army. An hour or two after they were called to escort Lord Wellington in a reconnoitre of the enemy's position, which he carefully examined in close proximity until a discharge of artillery warned him to retire. The day waned on, and the expected conflict seemed once more about to be postponed, when suddenly, Marmont determined on the rash attempt of turning Lord Wellington's right with the division of Thomieres, which led to his destruction. It was then half-past three in the afternoon, some of the English infantry had been allowed to cook their dinners, and General Le Marchant had sent the 3rd Dragoons into the village of Aldea Tejada to rest and feed their horses.

In a moment, all was activity and high expectation in Lord Wellington's ranks, and the battle began in fearful earnest. It is unnecessary here to recapitulate the general details which have been given elsewhere in these pages. We shall therefore confine ourselves to the movements of General Le Marchant's brigade, and a description of the decisive charge by which they operated so materially on the fortune of the day.

The orders of the British commander-in-chief were simple and precise. General Pakenham with the third division was directed to advance from his place of concealment at Aldea Tejada (where he had been most skilfully posted out of sight of the enemy), and to take Thomieres' division in flank as it reached the heights. At the same moment, the infantry in the centre, consisting of the fifth division under General Leith, and the fourth under General Cole, drawn up in two lines, with strong reserves of British, Spaniards, and Portuguese, were to assail the enemy on the high ground in front. These movements were to be supported by the cavalry under Sir Stapleton Cotton. The particular duty assigned to General Le Marchant was to occupy the space between the infantry in the right and centre, and to charge as opportunities might offer.

During the advance of General Pakenham's division, and while they were still concealed, the French opened a smart cannonade upon the right of the English line. General Le Marchant having halted his men under some rising ground, caused them to dismount and lie on their faces, while the balls passed harmlessly over them. In the midst of the fire, a horse without a rider galloped across the plain from the enemy's ranks, and approached the brigade, neighing and snorting as if in token of recognition. It was easily seized by a dragoon, who was congratulating himself on his prize, when it was discovered to be one of the horses of the 5th dragoon guards that had escaped in the storm, and its owner, Lieutenant Miles, happening to be on the spot, interfered and brought it back with him to the ranks, and rode it during the remainder of the day.

Lord Wellington now came up, and accosting General Le Marchant, told him that the success of the movement, then in progress of execution by the third division, would greatly depend upon the assistance they received from the cavalry; and that he must therefore be prepared to take advantage of the first favourable opportunity to engage the enemy's infantry. "You must then charge," said Lord Wellington, "at all hazards."

After some brief remarks on the chances of the day; Lord Wellington rode towards the centre, having desired the dragoons to remain in their present position, until the time of action was come. They had not long to wait, for in less than a quarter of an hour, and towards five o'clock, Pakenham emerging from the hills, fell furiously upon Thomieres at the instant when that general, deeming his own movement successful and unopposed, expected to see the allies in full retreat towards the road to Ciudad Rodrigo, closely followed by Marmont from the Arapiles. Thomieres was confounded by the unexpected counter stroke. He and his division felt that they were lost, but they stood their ground undauntedly, and fought with the stem resolution of veterans, surprised but not intimidated. Pakenham's attack, well supported by artillery and cavalry, proved irresistible.

With the rapidity of a vision Thomieres was checked and broken, he himself was killed, and his corps were thrown into irremediable confusion. But Clausel hastened to repair the disaster, and the advanced columns had pushed so far as almost to restore his communication between the left and centre of the French Army. The movement was still incomplete, and General Le Marchant saw at once that if he could succeed in defeating it, the entire destruction of Thomieres' division must follow, and the whole of the left flank of the French being thus kid bare, the battle would probably be decided. In an instant his resolution was formed.

The disparity of force, the disadvantage of the ground—for they were now on the skirts of the forest that covers a large portion of the plain of the Tormes near Salamanca—did not intimidate him. With happy decision, he saw and seized the right moment, which constitutes the leading secret of all generalship. Ranging his nine squadrons, of about eight hundred horse, in two lines, and giving the word to charge, he led them down the slope at full gallop against the advancing masses of the enemy.

These masses, consisting of upwards of five thousand of the best men in the French army, presented such a formidable appearance, that several British officers of distinction, who saw the advance of the brigade from the hills, pronounced the attempt too daring, and predicted its failure. But at that distance they could not discern that the troops of Clausel, as well as those remaining of Thomieres, were not in the compact order which the crisis demanded: some were in double lines, some in columns, some in squares; the sun shone full in their eyes, whirlwinds of dust and the smoke of artillery came towards them in stifling clouds, driven onward by a strong breeze which arose at the instant of attack; they could scarcely distinguish the assailants, and their fire was given with uncertain aim and trifling effect.

The volley made no impression, and the brigade, unchecked for a single moment, continued their career in perfect order and with redoubled speed. The blood of the men was up, and their horses were in perfect condition. The French attempted to reload, but before they could charge their muskets, the dragoons burst in upon them with a weight and impetuosity that nothing could withstand. The troops first encountered, which consisted of the French 63rd regiment, were cut off to a man. Those who resisted were hewn down indiscriminately; but the greater part cast away their arms, stooping and demanding quarter, and readily surrendered to Pakenham's division, then on the flank and in the rear.

No sooner was the success certain, than General Le Marchant, without waiting to make prisoners, which he left to the infantry, led his brigade against other bodies of the enemy, which had formed a second line in support of the first. A more serious resistance here awaited him. The enemy were better prepared, and their fire brought down many men and horses; but he dashed boldly through it, and penetrated their ranks with an impetuosity that quickly strewed the ground with killed and wounded, and the French were again totally discomfited. The third and strongest body of the enemy still remained entire, and had they fallen on General Le Marchant before he could recover the shock of his previous charge, all his skill would have been required to maintain his ground. But a defeated foe does not always take advantage of a momentary opening, and the leader who pauses to calculate every chance against him will never achieve a great exploit.

The French were thrown into consternation by the sudden overthrow of their front and flank, and enveloped as they were in mixed clouds of dust and smoke, with the crashing thunder of artillery and musketry closing on them, the reserve lost their opportunity and stood in wavering doubt as to what they were to do. General Le Marchant took advantage of their hesitation, and instantly pressed onwards in as good order as the emergency would admit, to his last and most hazardous conflict. The three regiments had become mixed together, the officers rode where they could find places, but a good front and a connected body without intervals was still maintained, and although going at full speed, they did not fall into the least confusion.

The French, in the meantime, recovered themselves, and having formed a *colonne serreé*, partly covered by some trees, reserved their fire with the utmost composure until the dragoons were within ten yards distance; they then poured a volley so close and well aimed upon the concentrated mass of men and horses, that nearly a fourth of them fell. Tremendous as was the effect of this discharge, the dragoons were not arrested in their course. Diminished in numbers, but exhaustless in spirit, they still pressed on as if carried forward by an irresistible impulse, broke through the opposing bayonets, and plunged into the dense masses of the enemy. A dreadful combat ensued in which the bayonet and sabre were used against each other with various results. The French, cut down by the troopers, and trampled under the horses' feet, offered all the resistance that brave men could make.

The loss on both sides was considerable. Captain White of the staff, and Lieutenant Selby of the 3rd Dragoons, officers both highly esteemed by General Le Marchant, were killed. The general himself had some narrow escapes. He fought like a private soldier, and more than one of the enemy fell by his hand. It was only after a fierce struggle that the French yielded, and he had the satisfaction of seeing them fly before him in helpless confusion.

General Le Marchant checked his horse to gaze upon the scene before him. His heart beat high,—nor can it be denied that it was the brightest, as it proved unhappily nearly the latest of his life. The defeat of a large body of French infantry by even an equal force of British cavalry would of itself have been a just subject of exultation. Far beyond this, he had signally triumphed in less than twenty minutes, with very inferior numbers, under every disadvantage of ground, and with men and horses who had been for ten hours actively moving in the field. Moreover, he had the proud reflection that all was due to his own brigade, no other portion of the cavalry having been in the charge. Even at that early hour it promised to be attended with results so brilliant as to decide the fate of the day, and thus lastingly associate his name with one of the most glorious achievements of the British arms.[9]

The violence of the onset had thrown the brigade into disorder. The dragoons, excited by the struggle, vied with each other in the pursuit, and galloped recklessly into the crowd of fugitives, sabring

9. More than one French officer of distinction has asserted that, but for the charges of the heavy brigade under Le Marchant, the Battle of Salamanca would have had a different result. Alison, in his description (*Hist, of Europe*, voL viii.), says, "Great as the success was, it was dearly purchased by the death of the brave Le Marchant, who died in the moment of victory, while carrying the standards of England triumphant through the ranks of France.". There is a little inflation in the concluding sentence, which, nevertheless, does not interfere with the justice of the intended eulogy.

those who came within their reach. To restrain them at such a moment was almost beyond the control of the officers. The general having despatched his son (and *aide-de-camp*) for some fresh troops, continued amongst the foremost, with the view of guarding against any attempt on the part of the enemy to rally, which the nature of the ground rendered far from improbable. After a few minutes, he perceived a considerable body collecting in the wood, where they endeavoured to make a stand.

Lieutenant Gregory, with part of a half squadron of the 4th Dragoons, was approaching them. The general, with his usual contempt for danger, immediately headed this little band, and waving his sword, with a few words of encouragement, charged at full gallop. The French had formed a hollow square; they waited until the British cavalry almost plunged on their bayonets, and then fired. Several of the dragoons fell. Lieutenant Gregory's clothes were perforated with balls, and General Le Marchant received a shot in the groin, which caused him to fall senseless from his horse, absolutely within the enemy's ranks. The French had no sooner fired than they fled, and the dragoons, having been joined by some men of the 9th Foot, belonging to General Leith's division, raised their gallant commander from the ground, in the hope that he might yet be spared to lead them to future victory. Life was totally extinct. The bullet, passing through the sash, had lodged deeply in a vital part, and the surgeons upon examining the wound stated that death must have been instantaneous.

In the meantime Sir Stapleton Cotton galloped up with a large staff, and having recalled the dragoons to their ranks, would have resumed the attack; but both men and horses had suffered too much to do more service that day, and with the exception of the capture by Lord Edward Somerset, of seven pieces of artillery, abandoned by the enemy in their retreat, the brigade was not subsequently engaged. They did not halt, however, until they had taken fifteen hundred prisoners, and killed and wounded vast numbers of their opponents. It seems probable that the last of their own slain was General Le Marchant. The facts we have here detailed are specifically dwelt upon, because some historians of the war have stated that General Le Marchant fell at the onset instead of at the close of the movements which he alone conceived and executed.

Much of the credit which was his due has thus been given to his successor, the Honourable Colonel William Ponsonby, who, in the action, commanded the 5th Dragoon Guards, and behaved most gallantly. He was afterwards second in command of the British cavalry at Waterloo, where he gloriously fell.

General Le Marmont's body was carried off the field and placed in a stable in the rear. Two days afterwards it was interred in a grove of olives, adjoining the spot where he received his death-wound. The brigade having advanced with the rest of the army in pursuit of the French, the military honours usual at the burial of officers of rank were necessarily omitted. A medical officer who had been left in charge of the wounded at Salamanca, Major Onslow, of the 5th Dragoon Guards, with Ensign Le Marchant, and a faithful domestic, who had accompanied the general from England and managed his household, were all who attended. The major read the funeral service, and the corpse, having been wrapped in the military cloak worn by the deceased in the battle, was committed to the earth, and left to the loneliness and obscurity of a soldier's sepulchre in a foreign land.

The full particulars of the brilliant exploit in which General Le Marchant lost his life were slowly and imperfectly disclosed to the public The accident which unfortunately befell Sir Stapleton Cotton at the close of the day[10] had prevented his sending in a detailed report, of the operations of the cavalry throughout the fight, and the deficiency, as far as related to the heavy brigade, could no longer be supplied by its chief. Lord Wellington, in his despatch, stated generally that:

> The cavalry under Lieutenant-General Sir Stapleton Cotton, made a most gallant and successful charge against a body of the enemy's infantry, which they overthrew and cut to pieces. In this charge Major-General Le Marchant was killed at the head of his brigade, and I have to lament the loss of a most able officer.

The histories of Dr. Southey, Colonel Jones, and Captain Hamilton do little more than repeat the very words of that part of the despatch. Many years elapsed before any more distinct statement appeared, and then it rested on the authority of an anonymous writer, under the signature of A, Z., in the *United Service Journal* for November, 1833. Colonel Mitchell adopted this account in his remarks on the movements of cavalry in his work on Tacitus, and finally it was reserved for Sir W. Napier to place on lasting record the claims of General Le Marchant and his gallant comrades to the gratitude of their country.

10. He was wounded severely by one of our own sentries in returning; to his quarters after nightfall.

The narrative of this charge in the *History of the War in the Peninsula* is a noble specimen of military description, which stirs the soul of the reader "like the sound of a trumpet," as Sir Philip Sydney said of the old martial ballad of Chevy Chase; but still it may be questioned whether it attaches sufficient importance to the effect of the charge in deciding the battle. The following passage is extracted from a letter to one of General Le Marchant's sons, written on the first publication of Sir W. Napier's fifth volume, by an officer, then of high rank, who bore a most honourable part in the day:—

> The brigade of heavy cavalry under your good father has never had justice done to its service at Salamanca. Even Colonel Napier does not do it well. He goes on to detail a part of the action of little or no consequence, before he turns to that body of cavalry. The action commenced by our artillery shelling the head of the French column that was showing itself on some rising ground, the third division under General Pakenham advancing at the same time, and the moment they drove back the enemy, the heavy brigade charged and completed the confusion that had begun. All this was accomplished in little more time (speaking figuratively) than I take to write it; and I have always thought it the finest combination of the use and effect of artillery, infantry, and cavalry that I ever witnessed. Now, Colonel Napier's book does not show this with sufficient distinctness.

The services of Major-General Le Marchant were warmly acknowledged by Earl Bathurst in the house of Lords and Lord Castlereagh in the Commons, in moving the vote of thanks. His old and attached friend the Duke of York, actually wept when the particulars of his death were related to him. A pension of 1200*l.*. *per annum* was settled upon his orphan children, and fifteen hundred guineas were voted for a monument to his memory in St. Paul's Cathedral. The monument is tabular, and was executed by Rossi from a design of the late Mr. Smith, to whom the prize was awarded by the government committee of taste. The infant represents Spain placing trophies of victory on the tomb of the hero, while Britannia inspires a young cadet with emulation. It is but a feeble production, though not inferior to many of its companions.[11]

11. The inscription runs thus:—"Erected at the public expense to the memory of Major-General Gaspard Le Marchant, who gloriously fell at the Battle of Salamanca, July 22nd, 1812."

Of the deceased general's four sons, the eldest, as we have seen, was killed in early youth, at the passage of the Nive in 1813; the second became Sir Denis Le Marchant, Bart; the third. Sir John Gaspard, a full colonel in the army, and governor of Nova Scotia; the fourth, Thomas, (at the time of first publication), has reached the rank of an unattached lieutenant-colonel. Their five sisters were brought up with the affection of a mother by their maternal aunt, and all married happily; but the fourth, Helen, the wife of Henry Shaw Lefevre, Esq., died prematurely, in the bloom of youth and beauty.

We approach the term of our memoir; but it cannot be inappropriate to add that General Le Marchant had a deep and practical sense of religion as a member of the Church of England. His eldest son, once admiring his calm composure under a heavy fire, asked him how he had obtained such a command over himself. His reply was:

> I never go into battle without subjecting myself to a strict self-examination; when, having, as I humbly hope, made my peace with God, I leave the result in his hands with perfect confidence that he will determine what is best for me.

Even amidst the duties of an active campaign the general found time for frequent attention to the Scriptures. One of his last letters to his family requested that another Bible might be sent to him, as the type of the copy which he had brought from England was so small as to be painful to his eyes.

In the foregoing pages we have endeavoured to present a faithful transcript of the life and actions of an upright honourable man, a zealous servant of the public and his country, and a first-rate cavalry officer. The character combines, in blended harmony, the Christian, the soldier, and the gentleman; the noblest elements which nature and education can unite in one individual, to adorn society and spread abroad the lustre of example.

ALSO FROM LEONAUR

AVAILABLE IN SOFTCOVER OR HARDCOVER WITH DUST JACKET

THE FALL OF THE MOGHUL EMPIRE OF HINDUSTAN *by H. G. Keene*—By the beginning of the nineteenth century, as British and Indian armies under Lake and Wellesley dominated the scene, a little over half a century of conflict brought the Moghul Empire to its knees.

LADY SALE'S AFGHANISTAN *by Florentia Sale*—An Indomitable Victorian Lady's Account of the Retreat from Kabul During the First Afghan War.

THE CAMPAIGN OF MAGENTA AND SOLFERINO 1859 *by Harold Carmichael Wylly*—The Decisive Conflict for the Unification of Italy.

FRENCH'S CAVALRY CAMPAIGN *by J. G. Maydon*—A Special Correspondent's View of British Army Mounted Troops During the Boer War.

CAVALRY AT WATERLOO *by Sir Evelyn Wood*—British Mounted Troops During the Campaign of 1815.

THE SUBALTERN *by George Robert Gleig*—The Experiences of an Officer of the 85th Light Infantry During the Peninsular War.

NAPOLEON AT BAY, 1814 *by F. Loraine Petre*—The Campaigns to the Fall of the First Empire.

NAPOLEON AND THE CAMPAIGN OF 1806 *by Colonel Vachée*—The Napoleonic Method of Organisation and Command to the Battles of Jena & Auerstädt.

THE COMPLETE ADVENTURES IN THE CONNAUGHT RANGERS *by William Grattan*—The 88th Regiment during the Napoleonic Wars by a Serving Officer.

BUGLER AND OFFICER OF THE RIFLES *by William Green & Harry Smith*—With the 95th (Rifles) during the Peninsular & Waterloo Campaigns of the Napoleonic Wars.

NAPOLEONIC WAR STORIES *by Sir Arthur Quiller-Couch*—Tales of soldiers, spies, battles & sieges from the Peninsular & Waterloo campaingns.

CAPTAIN OF THE 95TH (RIFLES) *by Jonathan Leach*—An officer of Wellington's sharpshooters during the Peninsular, South of France and Waterloo campaigns of the Napoleonic wars.

RIFLEMAN COSTELLO *by Edward Costello*—The adventures of a soldier of the 95th (Rifles) in the Peninsular & Waterloo Campaigns of the Napoleonic wars.

www.ingramcontent.com/pod-product-compliance
Lightning Source LLC
LaVergne TN
LVHW091640100826
845152LV00006B/104/J

* 9 7 8 1 7 8 2 8 2 2 9 7 4 *